Storms and Shipwrecks of New England

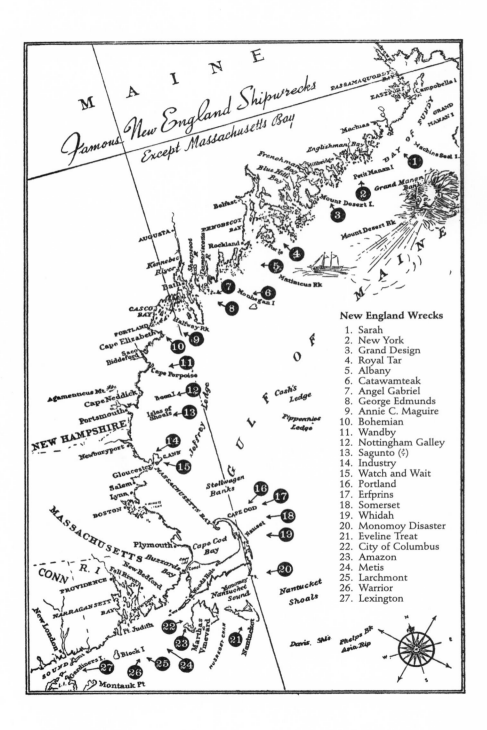

Famous New England Shipwrecks
Except Massachusetts Bay

New England Wrecks

1. Sarah
2. New York
3. Grand Design
4. Royal Tar
5. Albany
6. Catawamteak
7. Angel Gabriel
8. George Edmunds
9. Annie C. Maguire
10. Bohemian
11. Wandby
12. Nottingham Galley
13. Sagunto (?)
14. Industry
15. Watch and Wait
16. Portland
17. Erfprins
18. Somerset
19. Whidah
20. Monomoy Disaster
21. Eveline Treat
22. City of Columbus
23. Amazon
24. Metis
25. Larchmont
26. Warrior
27. Lexington

Storms and Shipwrecks

of New England

EDWARD ROWE SNOW

Updated by Jeremy D'Entremont

———————— ∾ ————————

Issued to commemorate the
centennial of the birth of Edward Rowe Snow

———————— ∾ ————————

Commonwealth Editions
Beverly, Massachusetts

This Snow Centennial Edition originally published in hardcover, 2003,
by Commonwealth Editions (ISBN 1-889833-57-6).

ISBN-13: 978-1-933212-21-0
ISBN-10: 1-933212-21-7

Publishing history:
Previously published by Yankee Publishing Company, Boston:
first edition, 1943; second edition, 1944; third edition, 1946

Cover and interior design by Judy Barolak.

Printed in Canada.

Published by Commonwealth Editions,
an imprint of Memoirs Unlimited, Inc.,
266 Cabot Street, Beverly, Massachusetts 01915.

Visit our Web site: www.commonwealtheditions.com.

Contents

CONTENTS

Foreword

The early commercial maritime operations in and around New England were the foundation for myriad legends and romantic narratives about the sea. Reports of fact and more often fiction were the bywords that moved writers to spin yarns about the sea and the men who sailed on it. It was said that most of the survivors of shipwrecks were seamen. These men were less than truthful when questioned about the loss of the ship, fearing the blame was on them for the loss of the vessel.

In this classic volume of storms and shipwrecks in New England, Edward Rowe Snow takes us back to those days when little was known about the real cause of marine accidents other than that reported in the media and from "Official Government Reports." Mr. Snow, in his introduction, invites us to sit down in front of "a roaring blaze crackling and sparkling in the fire-place at your side" and get lost in his stories of stormy adventure with none of the risks suffered by those who lived in the tales so eloquently presented by New England's classic storyteller.

The recorded wrecks and rescues in New England began in 1626, when the small vessel *Sparrowhawk* was cast ashore by a storm on what is now Nauset Beach in Orleans on Cape Cod. The equipment of navigation in those times left much to be desired by today's standards. The mariner had a compass, a lead-line for soundings, a barometer, and some questionable charts. When the barometer began to drop and the weather turned dark, the sailors had to shorten sail to prepare for rough seas ahead. Since that time, thousands of vessels have been wrecked along the shores of New England.

The primary cause of shipwrecks is stormy weather. Ships sink or are capsized while others strand on the rocks or beaches up and down the New England coast. Then there are collisions: ships hitting bridges or hitting derelicts at sea or even ramming whales. There were also boiler explosions and fires aboard ships. During the war years, ships were torpedoed, and some hit mines and were lost. A large percentage of accidents, however, are due to human error, which includes illness, injury, exhaustion, drunkenness, mutiny, and at times sabotage. The most famous wreck on record was Britain's White Star Liner *Titanic*. While on her maiden voyage, she hit an iceberg on the North Atlantic in the fog-shrouded waters south of Newfoundland.

In the late eighteenth century a group of men formed the Massachusetts Humane Society in Boston to help the shipwrecked sailor cast ashore. Several sheds were erected along the coastline of the Bay State with food, firewood, and first-aid kits. The surviving mariner had to make his way from the beach to one of these buildings, sometimes late at night, and hope that the rescue supplies had not been pilfered by vandals. In 1871 the federal government improved this service by erecting stations along both coasts and the Great Lakes to improve the lot of shipwreck survivors, and the United States Life-saving Service was born. This greatly ameliorated the problem, and lives and property were saved in great numbers.

Probably the greatest storm to hit the coast of New England was the so-called Portland Gale, named after the steamer *Portland*, lost with all on board—some 170 to 200 people—during the worst of a November hurricane. The details of this event constitute a complete chapter toward the end of this book. This storm wrecked more ships than any other in the history of New England. It was estimated that more than 150 vessels were lost during this gale.

As a young man, I was always interested in tales of the sea. Growing up on Cape Cod in the 1930s, I saw four-masted schooners passing the outer Cape beaches and daydreamed one day of sailing along on a windjammer with all sails set and the bone in her teeth. However, my dreams of sailing ended abruptly in 1943, when the first edition of this book was published. At that time, I was a seaman in the U.S. Navy on my way to the South Pacific to help maintain the freedom of our country in World War II.

Edward Rowe Snow was truly a master yarn spinner. His many books about the sea are still popular today. He has written about light-houses, shipwrecks, storms, ghosts, sea creatures-real and imaginary, treasures, mysteries of the deep, pirates, and folklore. His many books have served to earn him the title of the Dean of New England Maritime Storytellers.

William P. Quinn
Orleans, Cape Cod, Massachusetts
2003

Introduction to the 1946 Edition

When wintry gales are stirring up the mighty Atlantic until the surf thunders with awe-inspiring fury upon the New England shores, when white, biting flakes of a violent blizzard hit in from the northeast in ever increasing tempo to make you realize that a great storm is in the making, or when driving sleet rattles against the windows with such ferocity that the strongest mansion shudders and creaks from the efforts of the tempest, I offer you this volume.

After settling back in your easy chair, with a roaring blaze crackling and sparkling in the fire-place at your side, you can feel that nature reigns supreme, and that man is indeed a puny being in contrast. With your thoughts in proper perspective, then is the time to peruse the pages of this book.

The volume contains the story of the constant struggle between man and the elements, nature against what civilization has built to oppose her. And here in New England is a proving ground of all efforts to conquer the storms and gales as they sweep in from the sea, for northeastern United States gets far more than its share. So crowded are the archives of New England history with tales of not hundreds, but thousands of shipwrecks that I know some of you will look in vain for a wreck which you in particular recall. It was physically impossible to include every storm or wreck of interest, but all the important disasters form a part of this volume.

There is an average of three outstanding storms a year. About every five years, according to my research which includes from 1630 to 1942, there is what might be called a "snorter," while each quarter century has its terrific gale. Once a century a storm of gigantic proportions sweeps across the New England area, leaving death and desolation in its wake.

The book follows either a chronological or geographical pattern with two exceptions, the *Somerset* and the Portland Gale. In addition to the major storms and wrecks, which are arranged chronologically, there are others which are grouped together by geographical or state classifications.

Slightly under 9200 wrecks and over 650 storms were examined as to their importance, only a relatively few had the outstanding characteristics to allow inclusion. In spite of the research work I realize that many shipwrecks have eluded my notice, but if they are important enough to be included in a future edition, you must let me know about them.

As the volume nears completion, Byron's lines about the ocean come to mind:

> *Ten thousand fleets sweep over thee in vain;*
> *Man marks the earth with ruin—his control*
> *Stops with the shore.*

Edward Rowe Snow
1946

Introduction to the Snow Centennial Edition

Storms and Shipwrecks of New England is in many ways the definitive Edward Rowe Snow book. Snow's dozens of books and countless shorter publications in later years updated and expanded on many of these stories, but here in this volume originally published in 1943 (on the title page called *Great Storms and Famous Shipwrecks of the New England Coast*) is his most comprehensive collection, covering more than three centuries of our region's most memorable disasters. This new edition is based on the 1946 edition of the book, which had additional chapters on the devastating gales of 1944 and 1945.

Edward Rowe Snow was descended from sea captains reaching back to the *Mayflower* and toured the world as a young seaman. As a boy he witnessed two terrible maritime disasters near his Winthrop, Massachusetts, home (see the sections in this book on the *Davis Palmer* and the *Moxie*). According to his wife, Anna-Myrle, he saved at least twenty lives over the years as a lifeguard and in boating incidents. Snow was not a casual dabbler in maritime drama. He had an insider's respect for the "vengeful sea," to borrow the title of one of his later volumes.

We can experience vicarious thrills and chills as we soak in Snow's vivid storytelling from the warm, dry comfort of our couches. But besides being gripped by terror and tragedy, it's hard to not be deeply moved by the awe-inspiring examples of courage, heroism, and survival that fill these pages. This is perhaps most striking in the instances when the men of the U.S. Life-Saving Service went to the aid of vessels against sometimes impossible odds—simply because it was their duty.

Edward Rowe Snow was a fan of mysteries and devoted much time and effort to solving some of the sea's greatest riddles, especially those surrounding the final resting places of the steamer *Portland* in 1898 and the famous 1717 pirate shipwreck, the *Whydah*. In fact, Snow was wreck hunting long before men like Clive Cussler and Barry Clifford used advanced technology to haul treasure and history up from the ocean's depths.

It's a shame that Edward Rowe Snow wasn't alive to see the *Whydah* and the *Portland* definitively located in recent years. He would have welcomed the news, and in the case of the *Portland* he would no doubt have tried to rework the known facts to account for the location, which is many miles from where he believed the wreck to be. But discoveries of sunken vessels never fill in all the blanks. Scrupulous detective work is always needed when trying to make sense of chaos, and Snow, whose favorite TV show was *Perry Mason*, was up to the task. In the case of the *Portland*, he may have missed the mark with the final location, but his quest for the hidden story did much to preserve the wreck in the public mind through the decades.

The text presented here is almost entirely as it was written by Snow, with my notes at the end of the chapters bringing the stories up to the present day or sometimes adding a nugget of information. There have been some minor corrections to punctuation and spelling, and occasional factual corrections—mostly in cases where Snow repeated errors that had been passed down from other authors. This is especially obvious in the first chapter on the wreck of the British warship *Somerset*, a story that was retold in questionable fashion so many times that legend had blurred with fact.

We've eliminated the notes included by Snow at the end of the first edition and instead included many of the substantive notes within the text, either in parentheses or as footnotes. We've collected his bibliographic material into a reference list at the end of the book. We've also omitted lists of shipwrecks Snow had included, in part because many of the listings lacked a year or location, and because many of the wrecks covered in the book were not on the lists. This also left more room for more photos. Most of the photos from the 1946 edition have been included, along with additional historic photos and some modern ones. Another feature of this edition is a new comprehensive index.

Besides the many authors cited and the various persons and organizations mentioned in my notes, I want to single out those most responsible for launching this new edition. Webster Bull of Commonwealth Editions has an understanding of the timelessness of Edward Rowe Snow's writings and their importance to the region that has kept the project on course, and managing editor Penny Stratton has done a magician's job of keeping the book's structure clear. Bob Jannoni has been a catalyst and vital supporter of the effort to return Snow to print. And Dolly Snow Bicknell—daughter of the man himself—has provided moral support and good humor that means more than I can say.

So get that fireplace crackling, brew a cup of hot cocoa, and immerse yourself in some primal human drama.

Jeremy D'Entremont

CHAPTER 1

The Story of the Somerset

During the height of the American Revolution, a powerful enemy warship was caught in that graveyard of shipping, the Peaked Hill Bars, and wrecked on the white sands of Cape Cod. The complete account of what happened to the ship, its supplies, and crew forms an intriguing part of American history. Paul Revere, as well as Lord Byron's uncle and Henry Wadsworth Longfellow are connected one way or another with the tale, which includes the ship's capture by an enterprising Province-town blacksmith and a 120-mile hike of the prisoners from Cape Cod to Boston. Although many Cape Cod narrators mention the shipwreck, the entire account of the *Somerset* has never been told as a separate story.

The huge British sixty-four-gun man-of-war *Somerset* was launched at Chatham, England, on July 18, 1746, as a guard ship of the British fleet. Not until after the Boston Tea Party were conditions in North America considered serious enough for the Earl of Dartmouth to take action. Writing from England on October 17, 1774, to Governor Gage in Boston, Dartmouth told the governor that he had ordered three guard ships to proceed to Boston with British marines, under command of the noted Major Pitcairn. The names of the vessels were the *Asia*, the *Boyne*, and the *Somerset*.

The warship* *Somerset* sailed by Boston Light December 19, 1774, and

---

*Although Snow referred to the *Somerset* as a frigate, it was actually a warship carrying sixty-four guns. We have corrected the text throughout..—*Ed.*

headed for the inner harbor. Commanded by Captain George Ourry, with more than 500 sailors and marines aboard and her guns plainly visible to the onlookers ashore, the great battleship presented itself as a formidable opponent to scions of liberty. Four years later she was defeated by a greater antagonist—the sea.

The following spring the *Somerset* dropped anchor between Boston and Charlestown. In the evening of April 18, 1775, an alert watcher from the ship could have detected two signal lamps flashing their warning messages from the Old North Church. On the Boston shore three men climbed into a skiff and started across the harbor. Their leader was Paul Revere, on his way to warn the patriots that the British were planning to march to Lexington and Concord. Revere was apprehensive lest the guard on the *Somerset* should halt them as they rowed by, but he escaped by five minutes the restraining order which reached the *Somerset* from shore. Years later Revere wrote of the incident as follows:

> *Two friends rowed me across Charles River, a little to the eastward where the Somerset man-of-war lay. It was then young flood, the ship was winding, & the moon was Rising.*

In his well-known poem about Paul Revere's ride, the poet Henry Wadsworth Longfellow also mentions the British warship *Somerset*:

> *Then he said, "Good night!" and with muffled oar*
> *Silently rowed to the Charlestown shore,*
> *Just as the moon rose over the bay,*
> *Where swinging wide at her moorings lay*
> *The* Somerset, *British man-of-war,*
> *A phantom ship, with each mast and spar*
> *Across the moon like a prison bar,*
> *And a huge black hulk, that was magnified*
> *By its own reflection in the tide.*

Paul Revere went on to arouse the Middlesex farmers until he was captured between Lexington and Concord. The *Somerset* lay in Boston Harbor until May 28, when during the battle of Chelsea Creek the *Somerset* kept up a continuous fire on the Americans defending the Chelsea shore. (The battle at Chesea Creek has been inexcusably neglected by historians.)

The *Somerset* also played an important role at Bunker Hill. During the peaceful hours in the early morning of June 17, 1775, the sentry on the deck heard the rattle of picks and shovels coming from the nearby Charlestown shore. With the arrival of dawn Captain Ourry noticed there were breastworks thrown up on Breed's Hill and weighed anchor at once, maneuvering for a position to command Charlestown Neck.

The *Somerset*'s captain watched the two unsuccessful attempts upon Breed's Hill by the British soldiers. His men assisted Clinton's reinforcements by rowing them over in the *Somerset*'s longboats in time for the third and successful assault on what the British called Bunker Hill. Thus the *Somerset* and Captain Ourry had a vital part in the eventual British victory in the Battle of Bunker Hill.

After the battle, the *Somerset* remained near Boston for some months, later receiving orders to report back to England. By the spring of 1777 the warship was again off the New England coast, capturing and sinking many American privateers and supply ships.

On Friday, May 30, 1777, the frigate *Boston* was cruising near the Banks when she sighted an English convoy. She immediately gave chase, but fled the scene on falling in with a large English man-of-war, which Captain Hector McNeill of the *Boston* wrote down in his journal as the "Sumner Set of 64 guns."

After keeping free of the *Somerset* for several days, the *Boston* completely eluded the British warship one stormy night, forcing Captain Ourry to abandon his plans for the capture of the American frigate.

During these raids up and down the New England coast, Captain Ourry found that Provincetown Harbor was admirably suited to his purposes, and he and his vessel were frequent visitors at the tip of the Cape. Helpless to offer resistance, the men of the Cape gradually grew to hate the tall spars and majestic sails of the British man-of-war as they spied the *Somerset* beating her way into the Cape's best harbor.

With the ladies it seems that a different story can be told. The girls of Provincetown were just as pretty and attractive then as they are now, and it was not long before many feminine hearts were made to beat faster when the *Somerset* came back into the harbor from a voyage. With several hundred of the sturdiest British marines and sailors aboard, perhaps it was only natural that the ladies of Provincetown responded to the admiration of the British navy.

With the men of Provincetown it was another matter, naturally. The marines and sailors were sent ashore on countless occasions to gather whatever supplies of eggs, butter, and meat they could obtain, and tradition suggests the only pay the people ever received was a sermon the ship's chaplain preached in Provincetown. During this period Captain Ourry, probably a pleasant Englishman, was pictured as a blackhearted pirate, whom the mothers of the Cape conveniently adopted as a symbol of what would happen to bad little boys and girls if they did not behave, threatening the youngsters with the appearance of the black-whiskered Captain Ourry.

There is no reason to doubt that the British officers and men made considerable progress with the young Cape Cod girls, the war evidently causing little difference in the ardor of the courtship. For tangible evidence, E. A. Grozier, late editor of the *Boston Post*, is the authority for the statement that the surgeon on a British ship, Dr. William Thayer, and Miss Lucy Rich of North Truro were married, with Dr. Thayer later leaving the British navy and becoming an American citizen. Descendants of this happy union are still living on Cape Cod.

But the days of the *Somerset* were numbered. One morning in the fall of 1778, reports came that the French fleet was near, headed for Boston, so all English sail quickly left the Provincetown Harbor in pursuit. There were around 550 men aboard the *Somerset* at this time.

When the fleet was at sea, on November 1, an easterly storm began to lash the entire coast with unusual fury. The *Somerset*, far out in the Bay, tried to make Provincetown Harbor, but the gale increased. Captain Ourry found himself caught in the dangerous triangle of the Highlands, Chatham, and Pollock Rip Shoals. Soon the dreaded stretches of the Peaked Hill Bars could be seen. Captain Ourry maneuvered the *Somerset* to escape, but the breaking waves of the great reef soon had the mighty ship in their grasp. The treacherous currents swung her around until she was in the trough of the sea, the ship plunged her keel into the sands of the outer bar, and the sailing days of the *Somerset* were over.

Back in Provincetown the inhabitants had gathered on High Pole Hill. Jubilant or depressed as the case may have been, the men and women of the Cape realized that the *Somerset* was doomed. What a cry of satisfaction must have gone up from all except a few of the crowd on the hill when the *Somerset* struck the bar!

One of the men on the sand dune that day organized a small band of husky citizens to capture the crippled vessel should she come ashore. He was William Spenser, a young blacksmith, who took his force across the dunes to the beach, there establishing a watch over the shipwreck. The tide was coming in and Spenser believed the ship would be delivered to him at high water.

Out on the doomed *Somerset*, exciting events were taking place as spar after spar crashed down on the deck. Many men were soon lost overboard in the great billows which swept over the *Somerset*. Captain Ourry now ordered the abandonment of the ship. The first longboat was manned and launched. With about fifty men aboard, the journey of the longboat through the breakers began. But the surfman's terror, a breaking wave with a giant crest, came riding toward the longboat, crashed into it, and engulfed the sailors. All were lost.

The tide was now coming in rapidly. Captain Ourry ordered every gun thrown through the ports, with all available merchandise put over the side to lighten the ship. Just before the tide reached its height, a giant wave swept in, lifting the *Somerset* off the bar. Another and another followed, carrying the battleship toward shore. Blacksmith William Spenser and his men were waiting, however, and when the *Somerset* grated on the beach, he rushed down with his men and placed an armed guard around the ship. Two hours later the tide had receded enough to allow Spenser to go aboard with a small detail. He demanded the surrender of Captain Ourry.

Captain Ourry had already realized the impossible situation he was in. Perhaps to Spenser's surprise, he unbuckled his sword, surrendering it along with the *Somerset* to the Provincetown blacksmith. Spenser now organized the men of Cape Cod for the task of handling the British prisoners. Of the marines and sailors on the *Somerset*, 480 had landed safely on the beach; probably from fifty to seventy perished in the surf. The beach was crowded with people, anxious to turn the tables on the Britishers who had visited them under slightly different circumstances a few days before. At low water the populace began to salvage articles of every description from the sea. An unbelievable amount of material actually was saved from the ocean, making the wreck of the *Somerset* one of the most valuable enterprises in Cape history.

Before long utter confusion reigned at the scene of the wreck. Men appeared on the beach from almost every hamlet and village within twenty-five miles, plunging at once into discussions and arguments as to the disposition of the rich spoils from the ship. But as Captain Ourry had surrendered to William Spenser, the Provincetown blacksmith decided to go up the coast to Plymouth and libel the vessel. Brigadier

Joseph Otis, at home with his dying father, describes the events at the wreck as "very Riotous doings" and feared that "Wicked work" had been carried out. His letter to the Council in Boston follows:

> *Barnstable November 4 1778*
> *Kind Sir*
> *I have just received express from the Commanding Officer of the Millitia Truro, informing Me that the Somersett a British Ship is Wreckt about four miles East of the Race, and bilged, that they had gott out yesterday about 60 men the Capts of the Ship and marriners included. The Sea is running high they lost one boatload of them. how many was alive aboard the wreck they could not tell.*
> *There was some American Prisoners aboard who say they parted in the storm with 15 Sail of the line bound for Boston. Have ordered an officer from here to go down and assist the officers below in conducting the prisoners along. Who shall march without delay for Boston. But what to do for bread for them I know not as there is none to be had where they are and their own being all wett. Any Orders from the Hon. Councill. if my conduct is not approved of. Please to tell me by word and they shall be Pursued.*
> *I send this by express whose bill I hope will be paid which he will give in.*
> *I am yr Honours Humble*
> *Servt Joseph Otis.*

An immediate reply was sent to Brigadier Otis from the Council in Boston. The Massachusetts Board of War approved the actions of the brigadier, and only in the matter of feeding the prisoners were the members unable to find a solution. Their only comment regarding food borders on the classic:

> *If you have not bread for the prisoners*
> *let them live without as many better*
> *men have done before them.*

Before the message arrived much had happened. Brigadier Otis had sent Major Hamblin and Colonel Hallett to take charge of the goods at the wreck, but ran into the organized band of blacksmith Spenser, who prevented the officers from "Interfering with what was saved."

Spenser had told Colonel Doane of Wellfleet to take charge in his absence while he went to Plymouth to libel the *Somerset*. This action greatly upset Brigadier Otis, who wrote the Council that "I have meet with nothing more Chimerical," adding that Spenser was quite haughty in his demeanor. "I look on him a poor being and his abettors" were Otis's words.

The tremendous task of moving the 480 prisoners began. The officers were allowed to sail to Boston, but the 450 men had to traverse the great wastes of the Cape land on foot. This enormous, ragged horde, with little food and in winter time, began their 120-mile journey from the tip of Cape Cod to Boston. Several of the sailors, bruised and bleeding from their encounter with the storm, were forced to march along with the rest.

The 450 prisoners, together with their captors, started their strange journey. One of the unwritten sagas of Revolutionary history was the march of the 500 across the sands of Cape Cod during the winter of 1778. Naturally, they had to be fed. From the beginning of their walk until they passed through the limits of Eastham, they cost the inhabitants a total of over $2,000. (Eastham's food cost ran to £392; Harwich, £78; Yarmouth, £19; Sandwich, £40.)

After the outskirts of Sandwich had been passed, the residents of Cape Cod decided their part of the march was over. Many of them left and returned to their homes. The 450 British marines and sailors now broke up into smaller bands, some of them without guards. Apparently able to choose their own destination, some of the *Somerset*'s sailors never reached Boston at all, appearing in Abington, Bridgewater, and other nearby towns.

When the authorities heard what was happening, sheriffs were dispatched to round up as many of the prisoners as could be found. Most of the trouble developed after Plymouth had been left behind, so traffic sentinels for the prisoners were set up along the way to guide the men. By this time every Cape Cod man seems to have departed for home, with no other guards to take their place. Gradually the prisoners were found and collected into groups by the sheriffs, but it is not clear who led the bands into Boston town. We do know that special guards had to be placed near Boston Neck to round up the men when they arrived. Evidence points to the date of November 13 as the time when the majority finished their 120-mile journey. Probably half a hundred escaped before Boston was reached. The men were placed aboard the old French snow *Penet*. This decrepit old hulk was admittedly unsea-worthy, and proved a poor vessel for the quartering of prisoners. (The guard ship *Rising Empire* was first chosen, but as the *Penet* was older and less seaworthy, it was made the prison ship.)

One pitiful case was that of the purser, Edward Cyron. An old and tired man, he had been injured in the shipwreck. Forced to march on with the others, he collapsed on the road, where he lay several days before the guard found him. Finally he reached Boston, and was con-fined with others aboard the *Penet*. On December 5 he petitioned for his release, signing his request in the feeble, quivering signature of an old man. By arrangement with Admiral Byron, uncle of the poet, Edward Cyron finally was released and sent to Rhode Island.

Five vessels were needed to transport the entire cargo of the *Somerset* to Boston. Captain Hedge of the sloop *Sally* brought sixteen cannon, mostly eighteen pounders, while the sloop *Cumberland* under Captain Rider landed eighteen cannon at Boston. Captain Ingraham's vessel made two trips between the Cape and Boston loaded with cannon each trip. On April 7, 1779, Colonel Paul Revere announced that he had been able to mount several of the *Somerset*'s guns on platforms at Castle Island, and would soon have all of the twenty-one cannon which had been landed there in place.

Returning to the officers who had been sailed across to Boston, we find that it was suggested they be placed ashore on Noddle's Island, where Henry H. Williams then lived. Williams reminded the billeting officers that his houses had been burned shortly before the battle of Chelsea Creek, the same engagement in which the *Somerset* had shelled the Chelsea shore. Samuel Sewall's old farmhouse on Hog Island, now Orient Heights, was finally agreed upon as the logical quarters for the officers of the British navy. After a few weeks spent in Sewall's old res-idence, Captain Ourry of the *Somerset* presented a petition to the gen-tlemen of the Massachusetts Council requesting his inclusion in an exchange of officers. The letter follows:

> *State of Massachusetts Bay*
> *Council Chambers*
> *Jan. 28, 1779*
> *Ordered that this Commissary of Prisoners of War for this State be*
> *and hereby is directed to convey without loss of time from this State to*
> *Providence in the State of Rhode Island Captain Ourry and the other*

Officers late Belonging to the Sommersett *and there cause them to be sent to Newport on Rhode Island first taking Captain Ourry's Parole that he will cause Colonel Joseph Ward now Prisoner at New York & Capt Burke now on Parole here to be liberated and discharged from Parole for his the said Ourry & one Lieutenant arriving there or to return himself and the other officers late belonging to the* Somersett *to be given in exchange for Officers of ours of equal rank. . . . And first causing the said Ourry & other Officers at Hog Island to settle their accounts which they have contracted since their captivity. Attest—John Avery Deputy.*

In a few days the exchange was agreed upon, and Captain Ourry left Hog Island for Providence, taking with him one of his lieutenants. A short time later a mate and thirteen sailors escaped from the prison snow *Penet*, presenting themselves to the captain of one of the American naval ships then in the harbor. After considerable discussion they were all admitted into the service of this country, and, as far as is known, never returned to England. The remaining officers and men were gradually exchanged in cartels landing them at Providence and Newport. Other events crowded into the Revolutionary picture, with the story of the *Somerset* fading into the background.

Timbers of the British frigate Somerset, *wrecked in 1778, in an 1886 photo. In his 1946 edition of this book, Snow wrote, "Her bones are pictured as they showed through the Cape Cod sands in 1886." (Photo by John Rosenthal)*

More than 100 years after the wreck, the bones of the British man-of-war pushed their huge bulk up through the sands of Cape Cod. Shortly after she was exposed, in the winter of 1885–1886, E. A. Grozier of the *Boston Post* visited the wreck on the beach. He found the *Somerset* in Dead Man's Hollow, often referred to as Aunt Sukie's Hollow. In the early months of 1941, the late Levi Kelly, veteran lifesaver, visited the scene where in 1886 he had last noticed the warship. In the presence of First Class Boatswain's Mate Manuel Henrique, the ancient lifesaver estimated that the massive hulk of the *Somerset* was about fifty to seventy-five yards east of the present location of the Halfway House of the Race Point Coast Guard beach patrol.

When she was exposed in the year 1886, several fine photographs of her ancient timbers were made by Provincetown cameramen. The writer has talked with four different men who believe that they know where the *Somerset* lies buried at the present time. Not one of them agrees on the location. It is no wonder, however, that confusion may exist as to the location of the British man-of-war. The sands of the Cape can shift a tremendous amount in one tide, and it is almost unbelievable what a windstorm can do on a winter's night above the high tide mark. With these two forces at work together over a period of years, entire contours disappear and new identifications have to be made. Possibly an easterly gale in the next few years will again uncover this patriarch among Cape Cod shipwrecks, or she may lie undiscovered indefinitely. Perhaps it would be wisest in any case to let the bones of the mighty *Somerset* rest in the white sands which have shared her secret for so many years, for what more fitting end to the saga of the *Somerset* than that it should lie buried forever in its sandy grave on the great beach of Cape Cod?

Edward Rowe Snow had one opportunity in his lifetime to see the timbers of the *Somerset* protruding through the sands of Cape Cod. He was among those who visited the beach near Provincetown to see the rare attraction in the summer of 1973.

Although Snow and many other writers have referred to the *Somerset* as a frigate, according to Marjorie Hubbell Gibson's book, *H.M.S. Somerset 1746–1778: The Life and Times of an Eighteenth Century British Man-O-War and Her Impact on North America*, the vessel was not a frigate but a "British third rate line of battle warship carrying 64 guns." A frigate would have been much smaller, with only thirty-two guns.

Gibson's book disputes other oft-repeated *Somerset* stories as well. There is no evidence that the ship's chaplain ever preached in Provincetown. In fact, strangely, the log of the *Somerset* contains no mention of visits to Provincetown Harbor, despite the persistent and romantic legends to the contrary. Either the log was incomplete, or later writers (before Snow) had colorful imaginations. The *Somerset* did not leave Provincetown Harbor in pursuit of the French fleet; it actually had just arrived from New York to engage the French fleet in Boston Harbor when it was wrecked on the Peaked Hill Bars.

The story about the romance of the ship's surgeon and a local lass has also been called into question. It seems the *Somerset's* surgeon was actually Henry Watson, not William Thayer. Thayer was a Truro doctor who salvaged some of the materials from the *Somerset*, a fact that might have contributed to the birth of a legend. Thayer was married to Susannah (not Lucy) Rich. But legends die hard, and this one has been repeated by many authors.

And according to Marjorie Hubbell Gibson, the casualty figures that were often cited were inaccurate. Captain Ourry reported that twenty-one men drowned. The precise number of survivors is not known.

"Cathead" from the Somerset *(courtesy of the Cape Cod Pilgrim Memorial Association, Provincetown)*

CHAPTER 2

The 1635 Tempest

A majority of the readers will remember the great hurricane of 1938, but relatively few are aware that history tells of one of equal if not superior force which swept along the New England coast over three centuries ago, during the month of August 1635. There are not many sources to which we can refer in covering this epic storm of the days of the Pilgrims and Puritans, but those who did record their experiences in that terrific gale were exact in their statements and concise in their accounts.

Anthony Thacher, John Winthrop, William Bradford, and Richard Mather have all left references to the tempest in their writings, but there were countless others whose stories of that terrible August hurricane will never be known.

Thacher's Island itself is named because of the shipwreck of Anthony Thacher during that wild gale along the New England shores. It was on this island off Rockport, Massachusetts, that the tiny pinnace, *Watch and Wait*, was hurled during the first great storm for which we have records. Shortly after the wreck, Thacher wrote to his brother, Peter, telling the complete story of this early shipping disaster. The pinnace, which ran regularly up and down the coast, was owned by Isaac Allerton, and stopped at many settlements between Piscataqua and Boston. (Point Allerton, Hull, is named for Isaac Allerton.) This was the vessel on which Thacher planned to take passage.

Reverend John Avery and Anthony Thacher were cousins, and had sworn "a league of perpetual friendship," which included an agreement never to foresake each other. Avery, formerly a preacher of Wiltshire, England, came to Newbury in 1634. The residents of Marblehead were anxious that he assume leadership of their church, so Avery made plans to move there with his family and Anthony Thacher's household.

The pinnace *Watch and Wait* on its trip down the coast stopped at Ipswich, August 11, 1635, to pick up the eleven members of the Avery family, the seven members of the Thacher clan, and a William Eliot, "sometimes of New Sarum." Four mariners manned the boat. After proper religious observances, the pinnace was soon on the high seas bound for Marblehead. Nothing of importance occurred until the night of August 14, when a gale hit the vessel, ripping apart the sails. The crew refused to go aloft in the darkness of that August night, as the wind and waves had created an angry sea, so the captain dropped anchor until morning.

Before the sun came up, the tempest had increased until it blew a veritable gale. Thacher says that even the Indians could not recall a fiercer blow than the storm which caught the pinnace off Cape Ann. Possibly it was the worst hurricane in all New England history. The anchors on the *Watch and Wait* began to drag, then snapped completely. The horrified crew and passengers were helpless to act. Anthony Thacher tells us in his own words what followed:

Engraving of the crew of the Watch and Wait *cutting away the anchor as they are wrecked (uncredited illustration from Edward Rowe Snow's* True Tales of Terrible Shipwrecks)

> *My cousin and I perceived our danger, solemnly recommended our-*
> *selves to God, the Lord both of earth and seas, expecting with every*
> *wave to be swallowed up and drenched in the deeps. And as my*
> *cousin, his wife, and my tender babes, sat comforting and cheering one*
> *the other in the Lord against ghastly death, which every moment*
> *stared us in the face, and sat triumphing upon each one's forehead,*
> *we were by the violence of the waves and fury of the winds (by the*
> *Lord's permission) lifted up upon a rock between two high rocks, yet*
> *all was one rock, but it raged with the stroke which came into the pin-*
> *nace, so as we were presently up to our middle in water as we sat.*
> *The waves came furiously and violently over us, and against us; but*
> *by reason of the rock's proportion could not lift us off, but beat her all*
> *to pieces. Now look with me upon our distress, and consider of my*
> *misery, who beheld the ship broken, the water in her, and violently*
> *overwhelming us, my goods and provisions swimming in the seas, my*
> *friends almost drowned, and mine own poor children so untimely (if I*
> *may so term it without offense), before my eyes drowned, and ready*
> *to be swallowed up, and dashed to pieces against the rocks by the*
> *merciless waves, and myself ready to accompany them.*

The captain resigned himself to the elements. The foremast went by the boards, the mainmast snapped into three pieces, and the pinnace began to break up. When the waves smashed into the cabin, the children started to cry frantically, while the older people knelt in prayer. One of the sailors was washed overboard and then into the cabin, striking against Thacher. Aroused by the impact, Thacher looked out of the cabin to see trees on a nearby island. The captain, determined to find out what the land was, went out on deck, but never was seen again. The sailor who had hit Thacher went out, jumped into the water, and started to swim to land. He, too, was never seen again.

Commending themselves to the Lord, the two families awaited the end of their sufferings. The children wept silently now, as all seemed resigned to their fate, whatever it might be. Suddenly a gigantic wave, much higher than any other, struck the weakened craft, sweeping Thacher, his daughter Mary, his cousin Avery, and Avery's eldest son away. Anthony Thacher continues:

> *All the rest that were in the bark were drowned by the merciless*
> *seas. We four by that wave were swept clean away from off the rock*

also into the sea; the Lord, in one instant of time, disposing of fifteen souls of us according to his good pleasure and will. . . . God in his mercy caused me to fall by the stroke of the wave, flat on my face, for my face was toward the sea, insomuch that as I was sliding off the rock into the sea the Lord directed my toes into a joint in the rock's side, as also the tops of some of my fingers with my right hand, by means whereof, the waves leaving me, I remained so, having on the rock only my head above the water. . . . I stood bolt upright as if I had stood upon my feet, but I felt no bottom, nor had any footing for to stand upon, but the waters.

Thacher grabbed at a fragment of the ship's mast, but missed it, and was washed along by the waves until he was beached on the island. (He is believed to have reached land near what is now the fog signal.) His wife, caught in some of the wreckage, was also hurled up on the shore, and they discovered each other, alone of all the passengers and crew still alive. They thought of their five children, now gone from them, and Thacher blamed himself for taking them on the voyage.* But Thacher tells us that they soon made plans for the future, whatever it might bring:

I found a knapsack cast on the shore, in which I had a steel, flint, and powderhorn. Going further I found a drowned goat, then I found a hat, and my son William's coat, both of which I put on. My wife found one of her petticoats, which she put on. I found also two cheeses, and some butter, driven ashore. . . . So taking a piece of my wife's neckcloth which I dried in the sun, I struck fire, and so dried and warmed our wet bodies; and then skinned the goat, and having found a small brass pot, we boiled some of her. Our drink was brackish water; bread we had none.

There we remained until the Monday following; when, about three of the clock in the afternoon, in a boat that came that way, we went off that desolate island, which I named after my name, Thacher's Woe, and the rock, Avery his Fall, to the end that their fall and loss, and mine own, might be had in perpetual remembrance. In the isle lieth the body of my cousin's eldest daughter, whom I found dead on the shore.

---

*They had four, not five children; all were Anthony Thacher's by a previous marriage. —*Ed.*

The next day Thacher and his wife reached Marblehead. Later their plans took them to Yarmouth, on Cape Cod, where their three children, born after the disaster, continued the family traditions. As a memorial to their ancestors, the Thacher family has preserved a fragment of the cloth saved from that wreck by Thacher.

John Greenleaf Whittier describes the shipwreck off the coast of Cape Ann in his "Swan Song of Parson Avery":

> *There was wailing in the shallop, woman's wail and man's despair,*
> *A crash of breaking timbers on the rocks so sharp and bare,*
> *And, through it all, the murmur of Father Avery's prayer.*
> *There a comrade heard him praying, in the pause of wave and wind,*
> *"'All my own have gone before me, and I linger just behind;*
> *Not for life I ask, but only, for the rest thy ransomed find!'"*
> *The ear of God was open to his servant's last request;*
> *As the strong wave swept him downward,*
> *the sweet hymn upward pressed,*
> *And the soul of Father Avery went singing to his rest.*

Elsewhere along the coast there were other terrible disasters and occurrences. The tide rose to a height of twenty feet in the neighborhood of Buzzard's Bay and Providence. William Bradford, in his story of the Plimoth Plantation, tells of the great cyclone:

> *This year the 14. or 15. of August (being Saturday) was such a mighty storm of wind and raine as none living in these parts, either English or Indians, ever saw. Being like (for the time it continued) to those Hurricanes and Tuffoons that writers make mention in the Indies. It began in the morning, a little before day, and grue not by degrees, but came with a violence in the beginning, to the great amasmente of many.*
>
> *It continued not (in the extremities) above 5. or 6. hours, but the violence began to abate. The signes and marks of it will remaine this 100. years in these parts wher it was sorest.*

The storm also showed its violence off the coast of Maine. Reverend Richard Mather and his family, later important in Boston and New England history, were aboard the ship *James*. They were off the Isles of Shoals when the gale hit the Bristol ship. The master ran the vessel into a strait between the islands, trusting that he had reached a protecting harbor, but the *James* was soon in trouble. Three anchors were lowered and lost, whereupon the *James* sailed away from the questionable advantage of the Isles of Shoals, running before the wind until near the mainland. Soon the captain found himself on a lee shore off Piscataqua, with no hope of rescue. When the ship was less than a cable's length from the rocks, the wind swung around to the northwest, and the *James* was saved. All around the vessel could be seen the wreckage from other less fortunate ships which had foundered. The Mather family, together with about one hundred others from Lancashire, England, reached Boston the next day, but they had narrowly escaped death in that August hurricane of 1635.

The *Angel Gabriel*, also from Bristol, England, left the old world in company with the *James* on June 22, 1635. Passengers claimed to notice many indications of approaching disaster as the days passed, so that when the storm actually hit, it confirmed the worst fears of the super-stitious ones aboard. Monhegan Island was landmarked and passed, with the great ship approaching the iron shores of Pemaquid Point, Maine. The anchors failed to hold when the ship reached a point directly off the shore, and the *Angel Gabriel* crashed high on the rocks

Pemaquid Point Lighthouse, where, as Snow wrote, "the Angel Gabriel *hit in 1635 and the* Edmunds *struck in 1903" (photo by Jeremy D'Entremont)*

where now stands Pemaquid Point Light. Johnston tells us that there were only five drowned in the disaster, but that all the possessions of the one hundred passengers were lost.

A story that has reached us concerning the wreck of the *Angel Gabriel* is about a Mr. Bailey. When the ship sailed, Bailey said farewell to his wife, planning to send for her as soon as he was established in New England. After he was wrecked on Pemaquid Point, he wrote a long letter back home telling of the fury of the great storm. The letter was so vivid and realistic in its portrayal of the terrible shipwreck that when his wife read the communication, she was afraid to make the journey across the Atlantic as had been planned. He, in turn, had been so impressed with the shipwreck's terrors that he did not dare to brave the Atlantic again, staying on in America without returning to her. And so the years went by, she in England, he in America, each hoping and praying that the other would make the journey across the water. Neither ever did, however, and they never saw each other again.

Sidney Perley tells us of an old man, living in Ipswich, who sailed often with his dog, which he had taught to steer the boat. When the storm threatened, it was believed the old man would not sail, but he started down the river just the same, the dog at the wheel. Having been warned of the hurricane, he remarked he would sail out even though the devil awaited him on the high seas. Neither the old man nor his steering dog was ever seen again.

Governor John Winthrop of Massachusetts, writing in his journal of August 16, tells that a southwest wind had been blowing the previous week, changing at midnight to a northeast gale, which blew with much violence and was accompanied by heavy rain. Many hundreds of trees all around Boston were blown down, some houses were destroyed, and several ships parted their cables in the harbor. The tempest continued fiercely all that night until dawn. John Winthrop tells us that it then changed to northwest:

> *About eight of the clock the wind came about to N. W. very strong, and it being then about high water, by nine the tide was fallen about 3 feet. Then it began to flow again about one hour, and rose about two or three feet, which was conceived to be, that the sea was grown so high abroad with the N. E. wind, that, meeting with the ebb, it forced it back again.*

Thus the northeast wind gave Boston two tides in twelve hours, which has never happened again. Governor Winthrop says that the tempest was felt as far away as Cape Sable (at the southern extremity of Nova Scotia) but was more violent to the south of Boston.

Meteorologists now categorize the 1635 tempest as one of five intense (category 3 or greater) hurricanes that have made landfall in New England in recorded history.

According to Sidney Perley's *Historic Storms of New England*, first published in 1891 and cited here by Snow, for many years the spot now known as Avery's Rock was thought to be the place where the *Watch and Wait* was wrecked, but "later investigations have brought about the conclusion that Crackwood's Ledge is the place." The ledge is about a hundred yards off Thacher Island.

The General Court of Massachusetts awarded Anthony Thacher the island where he was wrecked to recompense him for his losses. The island remained in the Thacher family for eighty years. It eventually was bought back by the Massachusetts colonial government at a cost of £500 for the purpose of establishing a lighthouse station, and today it is home to the only operating twin

Thacher Island and its twin lighthouses today (photo by Jeremy D'Entremont)

lighthouses in the United States. The Cape Ann Light Station on Thacher Island was named a National Historic Landmark in 2001.

Some of the contemporary accounts of the wreck of the *Angel Gabriel* describe it breaking apart while at anchor from the force of the storm, rather than being driven against the rocks. Efforts to find the remains of the *Angel Gabriel* have proven fruitless. For two decades, nautical archaeologist Warren C. Riess, associate professor of history at the University of Maine, has been at the forefront of the efforts to locate the vessel, and in 2001 he published a book called *Angel Gabriel: The Elusive English Galleon.*

Although the efforts have been unsuccessful, Riess's research has revealed what an important part the vessel played in English and early American colonial history. He says there is strong evidence that the *Angel Gabriel*, under the name *Jason*, was part of Sir Walter Raleigh's fleet in 1617.

CHAPTER 3

Cannibalism in Maine

The observant traveler who makes his way along the southern coast of Maine near York Beach notices far off the shore a lighthouse rising high into the sky. This tall, slender beacon seems to come sheer out of the ocean but a keen eye can clearly see a narrow ledge at the base. On this ledge, which the surf submerges in the severe winter storms, one of the most harrowing tragedies of New England maritime history was located more than two hundred years ago.

On the 25th of September, 1710, Captain John Deane sailed from London on his ship the *Nottingham Galley*. After loading stores in Ireland, he began the long journey to America. Prevailing weather so hindered his progress that for over eighty days he did not sight land. Then thick weather shut in. Another two weeks went by before the ship reached a point near Boon Island, where the lighthouse stands today. Without warning, the *Nottingham Galley* crashed against the ragged ledges and quickly went to pieces.

Although the night was dark, all the crew landed safely. When morning came they saw that they were far from the mainland. In spite of their unhappy situation, Captain Deane tells us in his original narrative (which he recommends "to the serious perusal of all, but especially seafaring men") that they were joyful to be alive and thanked Providence for their deliverance.

Several miles to the southeast they could see vessels entering and leaving Portsmouth Harbor, but there was no response to the shipwrecked

Boon Island Light (photo by Edward Rowe Snow)

men's frantic signals. A tent made from a torn remnant of the sail was their only shelter. Through it the bitter winds of late December whistled and blew, swirling the snow across the icy ledges. Fire they had none, nor were they able to kindle one in all the time they were forced to spend on the ledge.

Food was scarce—three cheeses and some beef bones that had washed ashore—and this little supply was soon gone. The mariners made plans to leave the desolate rock since the only chance of being rescued was the slight possibility of a sailing vessel's coming within hailing distance. So the hungry men built a crude boat only to have the pounding surf break it before it had hardly been launched. A short time later three sailing vessels passed the island on their way down the coast but there was no response to the sailors' frantic attempts to attract attention.

In spite of the handicap of frostbitten feet, a Swedish sailor directed the building of a small raft. On it they stepped a mast and hoisted a sail made of two canvas hammocks. The Swede and another sailor launched the craft into the breakers, which immediately overturned the raft. The two sailors barely escaped with their lives. Again the determined Scandinavian set out, this time with another sailor, the first man having been weakened by immersion. Off toward the mainland the raft floated, with the two men waving their farewells to the hopeful crew. But misfortune struck, for later in the week the body of the sailor was found frozen on the mainland; the Swede was never again seen.

Let Captain Deane continue the story:

> About the latter end of December the Carpenter, a fat Man, naturally of a dull, heavy, phlegmatick Constitution, and aged about 47, always very ill from his first coming on Shore . . . soon grew speechless, tho' retaining his Senses. . . . Dying that night, his Body remain'd in the Tent till the Morning, when the Master, as usual, going out in Quest of Provisions, order'd the People to remove the Corps to some Distance.

The marooned men's hunger became intense. Starving, they discussed means of preserving their existence. Inevitably, the body of the dead carpenter engaged their attention. At last a vote was taken and a majority was for eating the dead body. Did the captain tell the truth when he wrote that he, at first, would have no part in it and only yielded when he found himself overruled? In any event the carpenter's remains were at once cut up.

> *A few thin Slices, wash'd in Salt-water, were brought into the Tent, and given to every one, with a good Quantity of Rockweed to supply the Place of Bread. The first Piece the Master eat, was Part of the Gristles that compose the Breast, having the Flesh scrap'd clean off, for his Stomach, as yet, abominated the loathsome Diet, tho' his importunate Appetite had, more than once, led him to survey with a longing Eye the Extremities of his fore Fingers. . . . The Mate, and two other Opposers refus'd to partake of the Flesh that Night, but were the first next Morning to beg an equal Share in the common Allowance.*

But better times were in store for the men at Boon Island. The unfortunate men who had braved the seas on the raft had not died in vain, for they were the means of the eventual rescue of their comrades at Boon Island. Some men from Portsmouth, their curiosity excited by the finding of the dead sailor and the raft on the shore, sailed in a shallop to explore the rocks of Boon Island. When they arrived, they found the survivors and took them to the mainland.

So runs the captain's story. But although the account of Captain Deane has seldom been challenged by modern writers there exists another version of the tale. Written by the mate, the boatswain, and one of the crew, the book was printed in London in 1711 and differs in many respects from the captain's narrative.

The authors charge that early in the voyage Captain Deane beat several of the crew so severely as to cripple them. From then on matters went from bad to worse. The captain had intended to betray the vessel to the French, but never could get close enough to a French ship to give himself up. When Cape Sable was sighted, the captain seemed purposely to delay the voyage. Noting the proximity of land, the mate appealed to the captain to haul off, whereupon the captain answered "that he wou'd not take his Advise though the Ship should go to the Bottom, threatened to shoot the Mate with a Pistol." That night, the 11th of December 1710, the *Nottingham Galley* struck on Boon Island. The wreck, declared the captain's accusers, was deliberately planned in order to get the ship's high insurance money. Other items in the captain's account were challenged by his subordinates, but regardless of motives, the two narratives agree in the essential facts.

Boon Island and its lighthouse today (photo by Jeremy D'Entremont)

In his 1956 historic novel *Boon Island*, Kenneth Roberts (who lived in Kennebunkport, Maine) painted a rather heroic portrait of Captain John Deane. The *Nottingham Galley* affair aside, Deane had an impressive naval career. Perhaps to rebuild his reputation a few years after the Boon Island wreck, Deane joined the Russian naval service and became a successful frigate commander. During a long war with Sweden, Deane was credited with capturing more than twenty enemy ships. He later worked against the Russians as a British spy.

In 1995 nine cannons and other artifacts from the *Nottingham Galley* were brought up from about twenty-five feet of water near Boon Island. Nautical archaeologist Warren Riess headed the recovery operation. After five years of conservation treatment at the University of Maine, the nine cannons are now in the collection of the Maine State Museum in Augusta.

The Boon Island Lighthouse is now licensed to the American Lighthouse Foundation of Wells, Maine. The Kittery Historical and Naval Museum has the old second-order Fresnel lens from the lighthouse on display.

Danica Crosby, Dr. Warren Riess, and Aaron Taylor with artifacts from the Nottingham Galley *(photo by Linda Healy, Darling Marine Center, University of Maine)*

CHAPTER 4

The Pirate Ship Whidah

One of the outstanding marine calamities in New England during the eighteenth century was the wreck of the pirate ship *Whidah* at Cape Cod in April 1717. This disaster terminated the career of the infamous Captain Samuel Bellamy, as notorious a pirate as ever sailed the Spanish Main. A rich treasure was lost when the ship crashed off the shores of the Cape, and the white sands of the beach still conceal the pirate's booty from Bellamy's wrecked flagship.

Captain Bellamy, who hailed from the west of England, journeyed in 1716 to the West Indies to raise a sunken vessel. As the venture proved a failure, he hoisted the Jolly Roger and sailed away in search of ships to plunder and treasures to steal. After cruising and looting for several months, the pirate captured the *Saint Michael*, out of Bristol, and brought her into the harbor at Blanco. Four men from the seized vessel were forced by Bellamy to sign papers with the pirate band. One of them, Thomas Davis, figured prominently in the shipwreck, which occurred the following year.

In February 1717 the London galley *Whidah* was sailing through the Windward Passage between Puerto Rico and Cuba.* Having just finished a successful slaving voyage, the *Whidah* carried a rich cargo, which included gold, ivory, and silver. Captain Lawrence Prince commanded

---

*The Windward Passage is actually between Cuba and Haiti.—*Ed.*

the crew of fifty men, and his subsequent behavior indicated that he was an extremely timid man.

Cruising through the same waters, pirate Bellamy sighted the heavily laden *Whidah* far ahead of him and gave chase. Three long days and nights he followed the ship, and at the end of the third day sailed close enough to fire a shot at the galley. To the amazement of Bellamy, this single shot ended the chase, for the *Whidah* hauled down her flag in surrender. Somewhat taken back by the speed of Captain Prince's capitulation, Captain Bellamy rewarded the Englishman for giving up so easily by presenting him with the *Sultana* of the Bellamy fleet. Captain Lawrence Prince was then allowed to sail for England with ten members of his original crew. It is possible that some of Bellamy's good nature was caused by the discovery aboard the *Whidah* of £20,000 in gold and silver treasure.

Captain Bellamy was still in good spirits a few weeks later when he ran in with a sloop in charge of Captain Beer of Newport. After capturing the sloop and removing the cargo, Bellamy wished to let Beer sail away with his ship, but the other pirates objected so strenuously that Bellamy finally gave in. Part of the conversation between the two men has been preserved by Johnson in his *History of the Pirates.*

"I am sorry they won't let you have your sloop again," said Bellamy. "Damn the sloop, we must sink her, and she might be of use to you. Though damn you, you are a sneaking puppy." Bellamy then suggested that Captain Beer would be a welcome addition to the pirate band, but the Newport man declined the doubtful compliment.

"You are a devilish conscience rascal, damn ye," answered Bellamy. "I am a free prince, and I have as much authority to make war on the whole world as he who has a hundred sail of ships. . . . This my conscience tells me." But at the end of his speech, Bellamy agreed to set Captain Beer ashore at Block Island, and before the end of the month Beer reached his home in Newport.

A few days after the above incident, the *Whidah* fell in with the pinky *Mary Anne*, loaded with wine. Captain Andrew Crumpstey, master of the pinky, was placed aboard the *Whidah*, with a pirate crew taking charge of the *Mary Anne*. Four vessels now made up the Bellamy fleet, and orders were hoisted to set sail on a northwest by north course. On the afternoon of April 26, 1717, a heavy fog shut in, followed by a severe thunderstorm about 10:00 that evening.

By this time most of the pirates aboard the wine pinky *Mary Anne* had drunk to excess, and as a result their navigation suffered. The fleet was off Cape Cod, although the sailors aboard the *Mary Anne* probably did not realize it. It was not until the vessel was wallowing in the trough of the sea just outside the breakers on the beach that the pirates realized their position. Before they could claw off, the *Mary Anne* grounded amidst the breakers off what is now Orleans, Massachusetts. The masts were quickly cut down and the pinky drove high on the beach. When morning came, the pirates found themselves near Slutts-Bush at the back of Stage Harbor [believed to be Pochet Island in East Orleans—*Ed.*]. In the distance, safely anchored beyond the surf, were two other vessels of the fleet, but the *Whidah* was nowhere in sight.

Ten miles to the northward, Captain Bellamy was having his own troubles. Losing sight of the remainder of his fleet, he continued to shape his course to the northward, but finding breakers ahead, he anchored. The anchors failed to hold, and the *Whidah* crashed against a sandbar off the shore with terrific force, capsizing almost at once. Soon the 146 persons were struggling in the raging surf. One by one they gave up the fight and sank to their death. Of the pirate crew, only two were tossed by the ocean's waves above the edge of the receding tide, Thomas Davis and John Julian, a Cape Cod Indian.* This tragedy, which cost the lives of 144 men, was Cape Cod's first great shipwreck. (Only two other Cape Cod wrecks have had greater loss of life, the *Portland* and the *Erfprins*.)

Although the *Boston News-Letter* of April 29, 1717, gives Captain Crumpstey credit for purposely steering the *Whidah* aground when the pirates were intoxicated, there is no testimony to substantiate the newspaper report. Davis, the only white survivor of the *Whidah*, makes no mention of this theory in his sworn testimony, so that the reader is left to form his own conclusions.

The two survivors walked to the residence of Samuel Harding, two miles away, where they asked the Cape Cod man to go over to the vessel with them. By noon more than a score of persons were removing supplies from the wreck. Meanwhile, Justice Doane, the local magistrate, arrived and arrested the two survivors of the pirate ship. Seven others from the *Mary Anne* had already been apprehended at the Eastham Tavern, and the nine men were taken to the Boston jail, where they languished in irons until the following October.

---

*Julian was actually a Muscheta (or "Mosquito") Indian from the coast of Central America.—*Ed.*

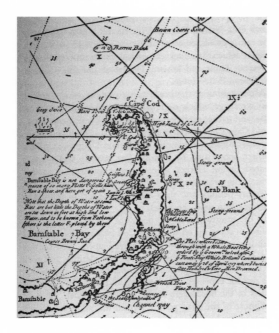

Map of Whydah *location (from Snow's* True Tales of Buried Treasure*)*

When Governor Samuel Shute heard of the treasure ship ashore at Cape Cod, he decided to take definite action in the matter. Issuing a proclamation taking possession of everything of value from the wreck, the governor sent his most trusted mariner, Captain Cyprian Southack, to the scene of the disaster.

Captain Southack seems to have been a most colorful individual. Before 1700 he had already made a map of the Boston shoreline, and by 1734 his chart of Massachusetts Bay was completed. His sketch of Boston Light of that period is still preserved. Master of the *Province Galley* for at least twenty years, Southack without question knew more about our treacherous coastline than any other mariner of his generation. In spite of his many interests, it is safe to say that he never forgot his experiences at the scene of the pirate shipwreck on Cape Cod.

Leaving Boston May 1 on the sloop *Nathaniel*, he sailed into what is now Provincetown Harbor the following afternoon. At this time a narrow though shallow channel called Jeremy's Dream by some, and Jeremiah's Gutter by others, cut Cape Cod in two between Orleans and Eastham, and Captain Southack came through this natural canal in his whaleboat.

The people were not willing to give up their spoils from the wreck of the *Whidah*. Caleb Hopkins of Freetown and Samuel Harding, to whose house Davis went the morning of his escape, were especially eager to keep their goods. Arriving at Eastham, Southack posted notices to the effect that the governor had authorized him to go into any house or cellar and open any chests or trunks to look for plunder belonging to the pirate ship.

Captain Southack now decided to salvage the treasure from the *Whidah*. He could see the anchor of the vessel at low water out on the bar, but the sea was too rough for a trip in the whale boat. Southack waited for a week before the sea quieted enough for a visit to the scene of the wreck. Rowing out to the remains of the vessel, the master of the *Province Galley* was unable to find any treasure. Discouraged by his failure, Southack loaded what goods he could find aboard a sloop sailing for Boston. This sloop in turn was captured by pirates.

The following October the pirates from the Bellamy fleet were tried in Boston, and seven condemned to death. Thomas South and Thomas Davis were freed, while evidently the Cape Cod Indian, Julian, had died in jail. The other six pirates were sentenced to be executed at Charlestown Ferry, November 15, 1717. A large and fascinated crowd witnessed the hanging of the six buccaneers, whose bodies were later cut down and thrown into open boats to be taken out to one of the harbor islands. (Both Nix's Mate Island and Bird Island were used for this purpose.)

What had happened to the treasure? There have been many conflicting stories told of the wreck and subsequent events. Henry David Thoreau was informed by John Newcomb, the Wellfleet oysterman, that he had seen the iron caboose of the *Whidah* during an extremely low run of tides. Around 1863, according to Perley, the wreck was exposed again, but the treasure still eluded the searchers. Thoreau and his companion, William DeCosta, found some of the coins on the bar near the wreck during the middle of the last century.

The usual legend is told of the pirate who returned to the scene of the disaster. Year after year he hovered nearby, refusing companionship and operating alone at night on the beach. His last days were spent near the wreck, and when he died a belt with considerable gold was found on his body. There are those who say that this returned pirate had located the treasure, but the writer is among those who think the tale should be doubted.

Whether or not Thoreau and his companion found coins from the *Whydah* (now the generally accepted spelling based on the recovered bell from the ship) is questionable. There were other eighteenth-century wrecks in the area, and one of the coins Thoreau found was dated thirty years after the sinking of the *Whydah*. It also can't be known with any certainty that the "iron caboose" Newcomb saw was the *Whydah*'s.

Searching for the lost treasure of the *Whydah* became a favorite pursuit for Snow in the years following publication of *Storms and Shipwrecks of New England*. He wrote in his 1951 book *True Tales of Buried Treasure* that he had "spent the equivalent of a small treasure hoard at the scene of the pirate ship's wreck." Snow built a diving platform at what he believed to be the wreck site, but all diver Jack Poole was able to recover was an encrustation containing a few pieces of eight. The operation was halted when a storm smashed the diving platform to pieces.

Snow came to believe that it would be a "very lucky treasure hunter who ever does more than pay expenses while attempting to find the elusive gold and silver still aboard the *Whidah*." Today, those words can be seen on a sign

Artist John Barky's rendition of the Whydah *(courtesy of the Whydah Joint Venture, Inc.)*

Bell from the Whydah
*(courtesy of the Whydah
Joint Venture, Inc.)*

hanging in the offices of Expedition Whydah, the group that has successfully recovered much from the pirate ship.

Back in 1951, Snow could not foresee the tremendous technological advances in the underwater salvage field. A tenacious underwater explorer and Cape Cod native named Barry Clifford has now spent nearly two decades bringing up an estimated 200,000 individual items from the wreck site, including a bell inscribed "The Whydah Galley 1716." Among the recovered objects are thousands of pieces of eight, cannons and smaller weapons, and articles of clothing. In recent years Clifford and his team have located what they believe to be the hull of the vessel, raising hopes that much more treasure remains to be found.

According to pirate historian and *Whydah* Museum director Ken Kinkor, "The site has proved to be much larger and more widespread than originally thought by either Edward Rowe Snow or Barry Clifford. As Snow learned to his chagrin, it is also an extremely difficult site to work given that it is very close to an exposed coast with treacherous and unpredictable seas." It can't be known, says Kinkor, whether the coins recovered by Snow and Poole were from the

Whydah. "His description of the wreck," explains Kinkor, "is not at all consistent with what we have found in the central area of the debris field. Given that there is no record of the precise coordinates of Snow's platform, it is impossible to make a concrete judgment as to whether he was on an isolated section of *Whydah* hull or an entirely different wreck site. The fact that he even attempted such salvage, however, is a tremendous testimonial to the man's optimism and spirit."

A selection of the artifacts recovered by Clifford and his team are now displayed in a museum on MacMillan Wharf in Provincetown. The wreck and recovery of the *Whydah* treasure has been the subject of several books, including Clifford's own *Expedition Whydah.*

Although Clifford has met with criticism from some archaeologists, he has never sold any of the pirate ship artifacts for profit. His work has received praise from many quarters, including *National Geographic* and the *Discovery Channel,* both of which have helped sponsor his underwater exploration activities in other areas of the world.

Underwater explorer Barry Clifford with treasures from the Whydah *(photo by Margot Nicol Hathaway, courtesy of the Whydah Joint Venture, Inc.)*

CHAPTER 5

The Gale of 1723

Almost a century elapsed after the 1635 storm swept the New England coast when the great February hurricane of 1723 descended on the inhabitants. If we are able to believe the chroniclers of the period, it was the highest tide ever seen in Boston, rising to a height of sixteen feet. Although Governor William Bradford of Plymouth reported a twenty-foot tide in 1635, it was not in Boston but around the shores of Cape Cod.

The prolific and versatile writer Cotton Mather was so impressed by the power of the elements during that Sunday gale that he thought the event of enough significance to write a lengthy paper on it for the Royal Society of London. It is probably the first storm so honored in the entire history of America.

The effects of the gale were seen first when the tide came in Saturday night, February 23, much higher than usual. At noon the next day it rose two feet higher than anyone then living could recall. The people had managed to arrive at church that morning without extraordinary difficulty, but when the services ended found they were marooned in the meetinghouses by the ocean.

Cape Cod bore the brunt of the gale. At Chatham the marshes overflowed and a fine harbor was destroyed, with the sea sweeping up over the banks to inundate hundreds of haystacks, which had been securely standing on their staddles. The water rose four feet higher than usual on the bay side of the Cape, while it went ten to twelve feet above normal on the back side. In Plymouth the tide was four feet higher than the previous record.

Along the New Hampshire shores the waves broke across the tops of natural banks for miles near Hampton, flooding the surrounding marshes and meadows deeper than it had ever been known before. The results of the gale of 1723 were seen for many years in this vicinity. Piscataqua was flooded, the wharves being several feet under water. Supplies stored on the piers suffered heavily.

At Gloucester, Massachusetts, the storm swept many craft ashore, but there was no outstanding loss of life. The waves pushed the sand up into the cut at Gloucester, blocking it completely for marine traffic. Farther down the coast, at Marblehead and Salem, the high water flowed inland for miles and there were many narrow escapes from the ravages of the sea. It is said that in several instances people took shelter in trees to escape the high tide.

In Falmouth, now known as Portland, Maine, damage to wharves and warehouses located along the harbor front was probably more severe than in any other storm of the town's history. The merchants did not recover financially for almost a lifetime from the great storm of 1723.

Comparatively few vessels were in trouble in the storm, which occurred well along in the winter time when sea travel was light. Many outlying islands and districts were heavily damaged, however. Boston Light, then in its seventh year, was feared to have suffered greatly, but after minor repairs, was adjudged by its keeper John Hayes to be in satisfactory condition. (John Hayes was keeper at historic Boston Light from 1718 until 1733.)

Perley tells us that Dorchester, Massachusetts, suffered a severe flood in this storm, one which was not equaled until the Minot's Light Storm of 1851. In Boston the residence of Mr. Hunt on Union Street was reached by the grasp of the sea, which did terrific damage in that town. (This location was known for many years as Hunt's Corner.)

The Reverend Cotton Mather's account was given considerable attention when it arrived in England, so we quote most of the minister's letter describing the "Tide and Storm of Uncommon Circumstances." The communication is addressed to Dr. John Woodward of the Royal Society in London:

> *The reading of a storm is not so bad as the feeling of it; I shall*
> *therefore think it no trespass on civility to entertain you with a short*

*relation of a storm and tide, wherein these parts of the world saw
what no man alive remembers to have seen before, and suffered
incomputable damages. It was on February 24th, 1723, when our
American philo-sophers observed an uncommon concurrence of all
those causes which a high tide was to be expected from. The moon
was then at the change, and both sun and moon together on the
meridian. The moon was in her perigee, and the sun was near to his
having past it, but a little before. Both the sun and moon were near
the Equinoctial, and so fell within the annual and the diurnal motion
of the terraqueous globe. There was a great fall of snow and rain,
the temper of the air was cool and moist, and such as contributed
unto a mighty descent of vapours. A cloudy atmosphere might also
help something to swell and raise the waters. Finally the wind was
high, and blew hard and long, first from the southward, and it threw
the southern sea in a vast quantity to the northern shores: Then veering eastwardly, it brought the eastern seas almost upon them. And
then still veering to the northward, it brought them all with even
more accumulations upon us. They raised the tide unto a height
which had never been seen in the memory of man among us. The
tide was very high in the night, but on the day following, it being the
Lord's day, at noon, it rose two feet higher than ever had been
known unto the country, and the city of Boston particularly suffered
from its incredible mischiefs and losses. It rose two or three feet
above the famous long wharf, and flowed over the other wharves
and streets to so surprising an height, that we could sail in boats
from the Southern Battery [Rowes Wharf] to the rise in ground on
King Street [Merchants Row], and from thence to the rise of the
ground according to the north meeting house. It filled all the cellars,
and filled the floors of the lower rooms in the houses and warehouses
in town. The damage was inexpressible in the country. On the
inside of Cape Cod the tide rose four feet, and without, it rose ten or
a dozen feet higher than ever was known.*

If, as Cotton Mather says, the tide was two feet higher than ever
known, then the 1723 storm caused a greater flood from the ocean than
even the 1635 tempest. Conclusive evidence is naturally impossible, but
it is safe to place the 1723 gale in the "Big Four" of New England storms,
along with the 1635, 1815, and 1938 hurricanes.

As mentioned by Snow, the "cut" from the Annisquam River to Gloucester Harbor, originally opened in the 1640s, was filled with sand by this storm. It remained closed for another century, until 1823. Today the Blynman Bridge at the "cut" is the busiest drawbridge in Massachusetts.

Benjamin Franklin, a teenager at the time, reported on the "Great Tide of 1723" in his *New England Courant* newspaper. He mentioned the outlandish theory put forth in the *Boston News-Letter* that Boston's many wharves had displaced so much water that they contributed to the "Rise of Water." Franklin had a field day with this, writing that "some begin to blame the Dutch for damming out the sea, and sending the Tide over the Atlantic upon us; Some more reasonably conclude, that a large Fleet of Ships have been sunk in the Storm off our Coast . . . which occasion'd the rising of the tide."

CHAPTER 6

The Grand Design

On July 28, 1741, the ship *Grand Design*, commanded by Captain Rowen, sailed from Ireland with about 200 passengers, bound for America. On board were many persons of wealth and distinction, who had brought along their servants and attendants. They were going to Pennsylvania, where many of them had relatives, and were to begin life again in the new world.

The *Grand Design* sailed for ten weeks before sighting land. Mighty storms she encountered, her masts going by the board, until finally the cliffs of Mount Desert loomed ahead. Captain Rowen's first landfall was the Cranberry Islands near Mount Desert. As he approached land, a southeast gale caught the ship and pushed her by the Thumper, where she slid in near Baker's Island and Dead Man's Point.

Captain Rowen now tried to maneuver the *Grand Design* into the lee of Great Gott Island, but when the vessel smashed against the Nubbles, her voyage was over. Since it was not too rough to land the passengers, the 200 Irish people reached the safety of lonely Mount Desert Island, and camped on the shore. At that time the island was inhabited only by roving tribes of Indians. Months might go by before the survivors of a shipwreck could be discovered.

Taking a small sailboat with him, Captain Rowen left the group on the shores of the island, saying that he would soon return with food. It is believed that he had no intention of helping the starving people, as several weeks passed before he did come back, and his return was for another purpose. Meanwhile most of the men decided to leave the island in search of help. Except for the weaker men who were left behind, the women were alone. To this day not the slightest report has ever been heard of the eighty men who gave their lives in a futile attempt to bring aid to the women survivors of the *Grand Design*. That they were massacred by hostile Indians is the usual belief.

The captain finally returned with two small shallops, but brought no food. He began to plunder the ship, and when he had loaded his shallops with everything movable from the *Grand Design*, he invited several of the women to accompany him to one of the settlements farther down the coast, where they would be placed in bonded positions as servants. A number accepted, and when they left the camp with the captain it was a pitiful group of women who remained.

The wreck of the Grand Design, *after a painting by Howe D. Higgins (from Snow's* Secrets of the North Atlantic Islands*)*

Two months more went by, a period in which they lived on mussels and seaweed, gradually becoming weaker and weaker. Death was a common event among the Irish immigrants, occurring almost daily. The Indians paid a visit to the camp, taking what they wished from the women who could not defend their property.

One of the families had placed their fine clothes in the tree branches as a shelter from the snow. An Indian began stealing the attractive clothing which he saw hanging there, when a young woman rushed at him to remonstrate, but by swinging his tomahawk at her, the red man forced her to step quickly out of his way. The Indian continued to rob the family without further interference.

Mrs. Asbell or Isabell Galloway had brought a nursing baby from Ireland with her, but gradually the condition of her body weakened so that the baby suckled blood instead of milk from its mother's breast. The father became so unhappy that he is said to have desired his infant's death; both the baby and the mother survived him, however, as the father soon died from exhaustion. The sorrowing and starving wife was obliged to dig her husband's grave and bury him without help. Mrs. Galloway, at the death of her husband, became acquainted with Mrs. Sherrer, who had also lost her husband.

Shortly after the shipwreck, the woman who later became Mrs. Sarah Porterfield was standing on the beach after being rescued. A little baby was placed in her arms. She asked who the person minding it was, whereupon a twelve-year-old boy spoke up. "Nobody, ma'am, but I," said the little fellow bravely. All the others in his family had perished.

Finally some friendly Indians visited the survivors at Mount Desert Island, and promised that they would let the people of Saint George's know of their shipwreck and suffering. Men from Saint George's finally arrived at the camp, and brought all the survivors back with them. One of the Saint George men, Archibald Gamble, who was also from Ireland, became interested in the Mount Desert widow, Mrs. Isabell or Asbell Galloway. His friend, John McCarter of McCarter's Point, began to feel the need of the friendship of the other Mount Desert widow, Mrs. Sherrer, at the same time, so when the ladies were established at Saint George's, the two men began their courting. Because of the unusual circumstances, Mrs. Galloway quickly accepted the proposal of Archibald Gamble, while McCarter's similar request was granted by Mrs. Sherrer. Down in Pennsylvania, the brother of the late Mr. Galloway was offended when he heard of the marriage, and demanded that he be given Mrs. Gamble's baby boy. The Mount Desert widow wrote to him that she would keep the child until he was old enough to decide for himself. (The boy was afterwards lost at sea.)

The widow experienced many other adventures in her colorful life, being captured by the Indians in 1757, two years after her husband joined Roger's Rangers. The couple had seven children, and their descendants today, including the writer, are numbered in the thousands.

Mrs. Sarah Porterfield also survived the harrowing experiences at Mount Desert. Her father came up from Pennsylvania the next summer to take her back with him, but she had consented to marry a Mr. Porterfield, who lived at Newharbor. They were married in November 1742. When she was an old lady, Mrs. Porterfield wrote out her experiences, ending the story with the thought which she said gave her the courage to live through the terrors of the Mount Desert wilderness:

> *I am now seventy-six years old. My anchor of hope has been for many years cast within the veil. My faith rests on the Rock of Ages, against which the gates of hell can never prevail.*

Today, visitors to Mount Desert Island can walk the Ship Harbor Nature Trail in Southwest Harbor, close to location of the *Grand Design* tragedy.

CHAPTER 7

The Wreck of the General Arnold

One of the most melancholy disasters in the entire history of Plymouth, Massachusetts, was the shipwreck of the armed brigantine *General Arnold* in 1778. More people perished in this marine tragedy than died in that first terrible winter which the Pilgrims endured back in 1620. (Forty-six Pilgrims died during the first winter.)

The *General Arnold* sailed from Nantasket Road, Boston Harbor, on Thursday, December 24, 1778, in company with the privateer *Revenge*. Bound for the West Indies, the two vessels were still inside Cape Cod when a snowstorm began. The superior sailing qualities of the *Revenge* enabled her captain, Barrows by name, to beat around the Race at Cape Cod and escape the worst of the storm so that she does not figure again in our chronicle.

Captain James Magee of the *Arnold*, unable to follow the other craft, sailed for Plymouth but arrived off the Gurnet, the outer arm of Plymouth Harbor, after night had fallen. Although less than a mile from the friendly gleam of Gurnet Light, he anchored his vessel rather than risk the treacherous waters of the inner harbor without a pilot. By midnight the storm had intensified to a gale, and the *General Arnold*, off a lee shore, was now in great danger.

The master prepared his brigantine against the increasing fury of the sea. Sixteen of the vessel's twenty guns were lowered below decks, the topmasts were struck, and the sails snugly furled. Long scopes were given to the cable holding the anchor, and every other possible precaution was taken. The waves rose higher and higher. As the great breakers crashed against her, the vessel quivered and shook until finally the *General Arnold* began to drag anchor. Slowly but surely she drifted toward the shoals of Plymouth Bay, and Captain Magee realized there was little hope of saving his craft.

Uncertain of their fate, the men stood ready for the moment when the brigantine would scrape bottom. Suddenly, with a tremor that jarred the ship from stem to stern, the *General Arnold* grounded on the sands of White Flats. The captain ordered the masts cut away, and the crew disappeared below for axes. An unfortunate incident now occurred.

After what seemed an unnecessarily long interval, Captain Magee heard a loud clamor coming up through the hatchway, and went down to investigate. There he discovered that several members of the crew, instead of coming up on deck with their axes, had smashed into the liquor stores and were drinking heavily. It was truly a desperate situation, with his vessel ashore on a lee beach, the waves getting higher every hour, the ship slowly sinking into the sands, and now his crew drunk below deck.

Captain Magee, however, did not falter. Pleading with some, bullying others, and physically assisting those who needed it, he managed to get his men back on deck, and finally the masts were cut away. All hands were allowed to go below into the cabin where they settled themselves for the night, but few were able to fall asleep. Hour by hour the storm increased in fury, until it reached an intensity seldom equalled in the annals of Plymouth history. For years afterwards other storms of unusual severity were compared with the Magee Gale of 1778. (During the storm at Boston a driver and his oxen froze to death standing up, caught in the great drifts at Boston Neck.)

Rolling and thumping, grinding its way lower and lower into the White Flat sands, the *General Arnold* was enduring a terrific battering from the sea. The seams began to open. Water first trickled, then poured into the crowded cabin where within an hour it had reached a depth of three feet. Since there was nothing else to do but to return to the wave-swept deck of the brigantine, the 105 men and boys started for the companion hatchway and soon reached the comparative safety of the quarterdeck.

It was apparent, however, that there was not room for all of them without extreme discomfort as they had to lie on top of each other three and four deep. Several men were knocked down in the mad scramble for places. To give some protection from the elements, a sail was stretched from the topsail boom on the port side to the starboard quarter rail, and under this tentlike covering the men huddled together. Meanwhile the ship was gradually working itself lower and lower into the sand.

With the coming of dawn, Saturday, there was no letup in the severity of the tempest. The snowfall was so heavy that some of the men, unable to move, were suffocated where they lay. Instead of getting lighter as the day wore on, the sky actually grew darker and darker, while the flakes were so thick that objects a few feet away became invisible. The sea mounted in fury, until each wave which hit the ship drenched the shivering men with icy spray, and the men could do nothing except lie still and endure their suffering.

As the afternoon wore on, the officers gradually abandoned any thoughts of disciplining the sailors and prepared themselves for death. Captain Magee portioned out the remainder of the rum, advising the sailors to pour it down their boots as the alcohol had a lower freezing point than the water which was soaking them. The use of the rum in this manner is said to have saved the lives of several of the men.

But the strain of the unequal struggle with the sea was starting to tell on the men. Captain John Russell, a tall, powerful officer, was the first to die. Capable of tremendous endurance, he had been calling on his followers for patience and fortitude when he suddenly fell heavily on the deck and rose no more.

By now the water on the main deck was ankle deep, and the men prayed for the tide to turn. If the sea rose a foot or two higher, the brigantine would break up. Just as daylight faded, however, the tide began to go out, and the survivors were heartened considerably. Many said later that the receding waters gave them the courage to fight for their existence during the night.

At dead low water the wreck was half exposed on White Flats. Although the spray did not hit the men on the quarterdeck now, another danger threatened. When the wind veered to the northwest around midnight, the weather grew much colder, and the clothes of the men stiffened on them. Many froze to death before morning, and together with those who had fallen overboard or had been suffocated by the snow, more than thirty had now perished.

But the blackness of the night finally ended, and the men looked out on calmer seas. The brigantine's yawl under the port gangboard was put over, and three volunteers offered to row for help. They started away from the vessel with the cries and prayers of the others in their ears, but the three never returned. Those left on the *General Arnold* watched the men row over to the edge of the solid ice, climb out of the yawl, and walk toward a schooner a half-mile away. Disappearing aboard the schooner, they evidently abandoned their comrades to their fate, for they were not seen afterwards.

Bitterly disappointed with the turn of events, the freezing survivors decided to try to attract the attention of the residents of Plymouth and raised a great cry for help. Captain Magee tied a handkerchief to a stick and waved it frantically in an effort to be seen. The people in Plymouth had seen them hours before, however. Small dories which had set out had been trapped in the heavy ice floes, and the attempts at rescue by boat had to be abandoned. A causeway was begun out over the floe to the brigantine but was still a long way from the vessel when darkness fell. Now began the coldest night of all.

When the last glimmer of daylight had gone and there was still no help from shore, the more discouraged of the sailors collapsed on deck and quickly perished. In a few hours only half the 105 who had sailed from Boston were still alive. That night below-zero weather together with a biting, icy wind swept the Massachusetts coast, and the survivors aboard the wreck of the *General Arnold* had to take unusual measures to resist the cold.

Working desperately, the men piled up the bodies of their dead comrades in a protective heap around them to keep out the wind, and then sat down in a circle, their legs crossed over one another. By constantly moving their legs back and forth they kept alive the circulation in their bodies. When one of them fell asleep, he would receive a violent shove from his nearest companion, and thus would be brought back to life. In this way the survivors passed the night.

The first gray streaks of dawn appeared, and Monday's sun rose in a cloudless sky. The *General Arnold*'s quarterdeck that morning was covered with the dead and the dying. Many of the bodies lay just as the men had perished, with their arms and legs bent in grotesque positions. Some were erect, others sitting, some half crouching with their hands on their knees, and still others frozen to death with their hands straight out from their bodies.

The men from Plymouth renewed the building of the causeway at dawn and were making rapid progress out over the ice floe. Two hours before noon they were within hailing distance of the death ship. Soon the sleds and boards were pushed close to the brigantine, and contact was at last established.

It is said that the Plymouth men who stepped aboard the *General Arnold* that bitter morning never forgot the sight which greeted them. The victims were all huddled together in various positions on the quarter-deck, and it was impossible to distinguish between the dead and those still alive.

One of the survivors, Barnabas Downs of Barnstable, was lying help-less on the deck as the rescuers walked around him. This Cape Cod lad was so numbed by the cold that he was unable to indicate in any way that he was still alive. He heard himself referred to as one of the dead and feared that he would be left behind until too late. As one of the Ply-mouth men walked toward him, Downs made a supreme effort and succeeded in rolling his eyes at the man, who noticed the movement. The Barnstable sailor was then taken down over the side and placed on a sled, which was pulled over the causeway to the shore.

Barnabas Downs was taken into one of the Plymouth homes, where a large tank of cold water was waiting. After three hours' immersion in the cold water, he revived enough to suffer excruciating pains as the blood began to circulate through his thawing limbs. He later said that the pain was much worse while he was regaining his circulation than when he was freezing out on the brigantine. All the other survivors were brought ashore and given the same treatment.

When Captain James Magee was brought ashore, he attributed his survival to the fact that he poured the rum down his boots instead of down his throat, as some of the others had done. Those who drank the rum to excess died within a few hours.

Seventy of the dead men were brought to Plymouth, where over a score were placed in the town brook to thaw out their bodies. It was arranged to have a mass funeral at the Plymouth Court House. The strain was so great during the services that the preacher, Reverend Mr. Dobbins, fainted. A large grave to hold the seventy men was prepared in the town cemetery, but not until 1862 was a monument erected to these Revolutionary War heroes.

Many of the men aboard the *General Arnold* came from Cape Cod, but the deep snow prevented word of the disaster leaving Plymouth for sev-eral days. The terrible tidings finally arrived at Barnstable, where twelve of the men lived. Barnabas Downs, Senior, Mr. Oris Bacon, and others

Memorial to the victims of the wreck of the General Arnold, *in Plymouth (photo by Bob Jannoni)*

started out by horseback to Plymouth, but when they reached the scene of the wreck only the young Downs boy was still alive. All the other eleven men had perished.

Downs expressed a desire to be taken back home, but the roads were still impassable for a carriage. John Thacher constructed an improvised ambulance which he slung between two horses. After a featherbed was placed on the sling, young Barnabas was tenderly lowered upon it. The lengthy and painful journey to Barnstable now began, but the boy was in great agony long before the lights of Barnstable were seen that evening. Although given the best of medical attention and care, Barnabas Downs never fully recovered, as he lost the use of his feet altogether and had to walk on his knees for the rest of his life. (Downs later became prominent in his community, and years later Amos Otis penned the story of Downs' terrible adventure aboard the *Arnold*.)

Of the 105 men who sailed from Boston Harbor, only thirty-three were brought ashore alive, and nine of them died shortly afterwards. Fifteen men recovered completely from their experience, while eight others were crippled for life.

At the time it was remarked that the moon-cursers were not present in Plymouth, as later on every article taken ashore from the wreck was restored to its proper owner. To the everlasting honor of the Plymouth men, they had not forgotten their Pilgrim traditions. Elsewhere along the New England coast the records were not always as satisfactory.

Some eighty years after the tragedy a benevolent gentleman of Plymouth noticed the unmarked graves in the Plymouth cemetery, and paid for a monument erected in 1862 to the memory of those who perished in the gale. But for those who had gone aboard the shipwreck that December day in 1778 to rescue the survivors, no monument was needed to remember the occasion, for they never forgot the terrible scenes they witnessed aboard the brigantine *General Arnold*, and their descendants still tell today the story of the "Captain Magee Storm of 1778."

⸻

Captain Magee of the *General Arnold* later had a highly successful career in the China trade, but the 1778 wreck was never far from his mind. According to Samuel Eliot Morison's *Maritime History of Massachusetts*, Magee lived in the old Governor Shirley mansion in Roxbury, Massachusetts. It is said that he hosted yearly Christmas parties for the families of the men from the ship.

When he died in 1801, Captain Magee was buried at Plymouth's Burial Hill. His name is on the obelisk there that lists the victims of the *General Arnold* wreck. One side of the memorial reads, "This monument marks the resting place of sixty of the seventy two mariners, 'who perished in their strife with the storm,' and is erected by Stephen Gale of Portland, Maine, a stranger to them, as a just memorial of their sufferings and death."

A new breakwater was built in Plymouth Harbor in the early 1970s, and the shifting sands that resulted uncovered a portion of a very old wooden shipwreck on White Flats, believed by some to be the *General Arnold*. A dispute over the wreck played itself out in public view. Barry Clifford of *Whydah* fame, with the backing of the Pilgrim Society of Plymouth, claimed that he had found the wreck first. Three local men also claimed that they found it first, and they also battled each other. Eventually the Pilgrim Society and Clifford withdrew their claim to salvage rights, saying they now believed the wreck was that of an old coal barge.

Divers working with Charles Sanderson, one of the local men who claimed to have found the *General Arnold*, later recovered artifacts from the site that included pottery, shoes, cutlery, and rum bottles. Nautical archaeologist Warren Riess headed a team that surveyed the site in 1983, and they concluded that the wreck was indeed "a late 18th century merchant ship, of about 200-ton burden."

The official word from the Pilgrim Society is that the *General Arnold* was repaired and refloated and returned to duty during the Revolution. The wreck that might or might not be the *General Arnold* remains shrouded in mystery.

CHAPTER 8

The Frigate Erfprins

The worst disaster in New England's maritime history is also almost its least known. But few have heard of the Dutch frigate *Erfprins*, yet when that ship went down off Cape Cod in 1783, she carried with her 303 members of the crew.

The *Erfprins* was one of a convoy of three Dutch men-of-war which the Netherlands government provided to escort their newly appointed Minister Plenipotentiary to the United States. The new minister, Pieter Johan van Berckel, the brother of the Pensionaris of Amsterdam, sailed from Texel on either the ship-of-the-line *Overijssel,* carrying sixty-eight guns, or the frigate *de Briel* of thirty-six guns. The *Erfprins*, with fifty-four guns, was the third ship-of-war. The brigantine *de Windhond* completed the convoy, which, according to plan, was to stay a unit during the voyage.

The minister reached his destination, and of his voyage the standard history of the Netherlands navy says that nothing unusual happened except the loss of the *Erfprins*. This is a masterpiece of understatement in view of the magnitude of the disaster. What happened makes a most unusual story.

The *Erfprins* was not the most seaworthy of vessels. It had been one of eight battleships of the Dutch navy, which on July 20, 1781, against heavy odds, furiously fought an English fleet off the Dogger Bank (located about due east of Newcastle, England, and about halfway to Denmark), giving shot for shot, and giving and receiving damage which forced both fleets to retire without victory. The *Erfprins*, the special target of the British, suffered serious injury. In the two years after the Dogger Bank engagement, other ships in the Dutch navy were coppered, but not the *Erfprins*. Does the fact that her wooden hull was left without protection indicate that her seaworthiness was in question?

When the convoy reached the English Channel, the *Erfprins* sprang a leak which necessitated the operation of five pumps. In spite of this overwhelming handicap, Commander Louis Aberson began the long sail across the ocean. The water began to come in faster, so the captain signaled to the squadron commander, Captain Riemersma of the *Overijssel*, for advice. The squadron commander told Aberson that the orders left no alternative; they must all continue across the sea until they reached Philadelphia. The only concession Riemersma made was that each vessel could now choose its own route.

One by one the other ships left the *Erfprins*. It must have been a trying period to the officers and crew members as they watched the brigantine *de Windhond* slide over the horizon and out of sight. Soon the other vessels followed, until the leaking battleship was left alone on the wide expanse of ocean.

The *Erfprins*, left to her fate, sailed along in clear weather for several weeks, but on September 19 in latitude 37 a violent storm hit the ship, causing terrific damage and much suffering aboard the vessel. The foretopmast crashed down on the deck, the mizzenmast went by the board, and the mainmast followed shortly afterwards. Wallowing in the trough of the sea, the *Erfprins* sustained a terrific battering from the waves, which swept headlong against the sides of the stricken vessel. The men on deck pumped furiously, barely holding their own against the water pouring in through the leaking seams.

When the storm died down, the discouraged and disheartened commander ordered the rigging of a jury mast and had the ship made as seaworthy as possible. The sailors pumped on night and day in their efforts to keep the *Erfprins* afloat, but it was a hopeless task. The ship was still out of sight of land, drifting almost at the wind's will, the water now began to gain slowly in the hold of the warship, and there was no help from any other vessels. In this manner the *Erfprins* approached America.

Nine long weeks this voyage of hopeless terror continued. Supplies grew low, water became unfit for drinking, and the sea slowly, steadily gained inch by inch. Storm after storm hit the *Erfprins*, each battering leaving the man-of-war in a more hopeless condition. Finally, by

November 25, 1783, the ship had drifted and sailed to a point only twenty-four miles from Cape Cod. (Evidently this was the last observation which the captain obtained.) That afternoon the vessel reached a position so low in the water that she was making no headway at all.

The Erfprins *(uncredited illustration from previous edition)*

Captain Aberson, knowing that the *Erfprins* would not stay afloat many hours more, decided to try to reach land. Choosing thirty-nine picked men to form his longboat crew, he pushed away from the ship. Three minutes after they left the vessel, the *Erfprins* sank beneath the waves, carrying to their death 303 members of the ship's company.

Rowing strenuously for several hours, the captain and the longboat crew finally sighted a brig outward bound, hailed it, and were soon rescued. Shortly afterwards they were transferred to a Gloucester-bound sloop, which landed them at Cape Ann a short time later.

Just what happened after the Cape Ann landing is not clearly known. The Gloucester records speak of the forty men who brought the news of New England's worst shipwreck, the *Boston Gazette and Country Journal* also reports the incident, but from then on their whereabouts are in doubt. Captain Aberson wrote a long letter to Van Kinsbergen, which was printed in the *Nederlandsche Jaarb* in 1784, but other than brief mention of honors bestowed upon him for saving the forty men, nothing is certain. Whether he ever tried to find others aboard the *Erfprins*, who might have escaped, how he returned to Holland, what parts of the coast he traversed on his journey, we can only surmise. No other members of his crew aboard the ill-fated man-of-war ever reached shore.

CHAPTER 9

The December Storm of 1786

There is an almost unbelievable sequence of freak events and terrible occurrences all along the New England coast because of the December gale of 1786. In Plum Island Sound two men floated for hours on a haystack before they were rescued. Thirteen persons in Boston Harbor were frozen to death, while near Plymouth a shipwrecked party on the Gurnet Beach walked five miles before reaching safety.

The strange story of Samuel Pulsifer and Samuel Elwell is about two men who had journeyed down to Hog Island on the marshes of Rowley to stay for the night. Arriving Monday morning, they spent the forenoon digging clams on the low tide flats. When the snowstorm began, they stopped their work and returned to the island, only to find the storm increasing in violence. Because of the weather they started out at once to return home while the tide was still low, but the snow fell so thick and fast they became completely lost in the blinding storm.

After wandering helplessly through the swirling flakes for several hours trying to find a landmark, Pulsifer and Elwell climbed a nearby haystack to rest their weary limbs. The stack was so warm and comfortable that they agreed to spend the night there and make a fresh start in the morning. When morning came, however, the storm had risen to new intensity, and the tide was coming in around the staddle on which the haystack rested. As it was several hours before high tide, the men began to worry. Higher and higher the sea came, until the staddle began to rock. Pulsifer and Elwell dug themselves places at the top of the stack and there awaited the oncoming tide.

Soon the waters lifted the stack entirely off the staddle, making the men unwilling sailors on as strange a voyage as was ever experienced in Plum Island Sound. The two men could not ascertain in which direction the wind and tide were taking them, but they whirled and twisted back and forth around other stacks and ice cakes with extreme rapidity. Hour after hour passed. Gradually the haystack was going to pieces because of the buffeting of the waves. The men, believing that they would soon be thrown into the icy waters of Plum Island Sound, prepared for death.

Suddenly there was a terrific shock as another larger stack crashed into them. Pulsifer and Elwell leaped into the new haystack in time to watch their former conveyance go to pieces before their eyes. They had been just in time. Now began another strange journey. Hour after hour they floated, never knowing where they were, death always in their thoughts.

Some time later the churning of the sea seemed to abate, and they found themselves grounded at a location later identified as Smith's Cove, Little Neck, Ipswich. They had journeyed on the two stacks at least three miles from the start of their voyage. At first neither Elwell nor Pulsifer made any effort to leave the stack until each realized it was moving out toward the open sea. Pulsifer then jumped to an ice cake and tried to walk ashore in the knee-deep water.

Elwell, almost completely benumbed by the cold, finally climbed on an ice cake and pushed himself ashore. Pulsifer was able to touch the bottom with his feet, but could not move his legs and seemed about to perish a few feet from shore. Finally, grasping his trousers firmly at the knees, he lifted his feet one at a time. In this strange manner he negotiated the short distance to shore, where he fell exhausted.

The men soon realized the importance of keeping up their circulation, and after walking rapidly up and down the shore for a time, they were finally able to run a short distance. Making their way to the top of a hill, Pulsifer and Elwell discovered they were on a small island. A large haystack stood close at hand, into which they crawled for warmth. Later the men climbed to the top of the island again. Pulsifer saw a man walking on the mainland about a mile away but failed to attract his attention. They became utterly discouraged. It had been two days since they had eaten, and there seemed no hope of rescue.

When an hour later three persons were seen walking along near the shore of the mainland, their hopes revived. Elwell, waving his hat and shouting for help, was seen. The persons walking on the mainland were Major Charles Smith of Ipswich and his two sons. Major Smith waded across to the island on a causeway covered with water three feet deep and helped the men back to the mainland. After a short rest of several days at the home of Major Smith, Samuel Elwell and Samuel Pulsifer returned to their homes, thankful that they were still alive after their most unusual adventure.

During the same storm a sloop from Damariscotta, Maine, crashed on the beach at Lovell's Island, Boston Harbor. All the passengers and crew, thirteen in number, reached the safety of the island but looked in vain for shelter. At the top of the hill there was a large rock, which gave them some protection against the fierce blizzard then raging, and there the people huddled in their wet clothing. The temperature in surrounding towns and villages dropped far below zero that bitter night. One by one the freezing cold claimed its victims.

With the coming of dawn, a fisherman on a neighboring island, Thomas Spear by name, crossed over to Lovell's Island. Up by the rock he saw shapeless forms outlined under the snow and found the entire party apparently frozen to death. Among the group were two young lovers, Miss Sylvia Knapp and a young man whose name is not known, who were on their way to Boston to purchase furniture for their new home. The lovers were found locked in death in each other's arms.

Although the usual belief was that all were frozen to death, the *New England Courant* told of one man, Theodore Kingsley of Wrentham, who lived for almost two weeks after the shipwreck before succumbing. Captain Oliver Rouse, a former officer in the American Revolution, was also among the victims. John and Joseph Cowell, brothers, had just returned on the packet from a hunting trip in Maine. Their remains, together with those of a friend, Joseph Robichaux, were taken to Wrentham, where their graves can still be seen. Fifty years to the day after the tragedy, one of their friends wrote a letter of condolence to the family, the manuscript of which is still preserved by Mr. David H. Cowell of Hingham.

The story of the tragedy was told by Frederick William Augustus Steuben Brown, the Boston Harbor poet.* A few verses must suffice:

> *The tempest hid the cheering Light*
> *So thickly flew the snow;*

---

*Brown, an interesting character down Boston Bay, was the signal man at Deer Island, and later the telegraph representative on State Street.

Alas, what horror fill'd the night
With bitter, piercing woe.
At length they gained the sea-beat strand
And rescued from the waves;
On Lovell's Island only land,
To find more decent graves.
Among the rest, a youthful pair,
Who from their early youth;
Had felt of love an equal share,
Adorned with equal truth,
Lay prostrate mid the dire alarms,
Had calm resign'd their breath;
Fast lock'd within each other's arms,
Together sunk to death.

The rock where the two lovers perished, still pointed out to visitors at the island, is now known up and down Boston Bay as Lover's Rock.

Three miles away from Lovell's Island, the brig *Lucretia*, under Captain Powell, was being pushed ashore at Point Shirley by the waves. The brig crashed on the beach about 9:00 in the morning, and five of the men jumped into the raging surf. They succeeded in reaching the deep snow on Shirley Gut Plain and disappeared from the view of others aboard the brig. Floundering around in the waist-deep snow, the men were quickly exhausted, sinking into the drifts. All five perished, including Mr. Sharp, a part owner of the vessel.

Captain Powell and the rest of the crew survived the night aboard the wreck without incident, going ashore after the storm ended the next day. The bodies of the five victims were dug out of the snow the following week. Mr. Sharp, a prominent merchant, was given a funeral at the American Coffee House on State Street, Boston, December 12, 1786. (This edifice was located across from Kilby Street.)

A coasting sloop under the command of Samuel Robbins was thrown up on the sands of the Gurnet Beach, off Plymouth, Massachusetts. Sixteen persons were successful in reaching shore, where they found themselves on the beach at the northern end of the Gurnet Peninsula. Wet and cold, the party separated, some going north and the others south. Those heading south eventually reached the Gurnet Lighthouse, where a rescue party set out to find the others. The survivors who had started to walk northward were finally found in a small hut about two miles from the wrecked vessel. Five refused to leave the hut, preferring to sleep there in their exhausted condition rather than walk the five miles to Mr. Burgess's home at Gurnet Light. They were found safe the next day, when the entire group was given transportation to the town of Plymouth.

This storm covered New England with a white blanket from five to six feet deep. (There is no record in New England history of any other storm with as great a fall of snow.) With its record of freezing cold, shipwreck, and death, the December gale of 1786 was one of the outstanding New England storms of all times.

According to Perley's *Historic Storms of New England*, the winter of 1786–87 was brutal and long. Salem Harbor in Massachusetts was frozen over by the early date of November 20. Thirty to forty vessels were trapped solid in the ice of the Connecticut River, and in Middletown, Connecticut, people were driving horses and sleighs over the frozen river by December.

The incredible story of Pulsifer and Elwell occurred during a storm that began on Monday, December 4. The wreck of the brig *Lucretia* occurred in the same storm, but the gale that wrecked the sloop at Lovell's Island, according to Perley, struck on Friday (December 8) of the same week.

Lover's Rock on Lovell's Island remains one of Boston Harbor's best-known landmarks, thanks to Edward Rowe Snow's dramatic recounting of the 1786 wreck in countless lectures and his narration aboard cruises passing the island.

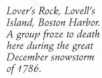

Lover's Rock, Lovell's Island, Boston Harbor. A group froze to death here during the great December snowstorm of 1786.

CHAPTER 10

The Triple Shipwrecks

Until seventy-five years ago a spell of unseasonably warm weather in February would remind the older Salem and Marblehead residents of the wreck of the three East Indiamen back in 1802. It was a tragic disaster with a strange sequel. When such a spell came, the people of that period would gather their children around the fireside to tell of the start of that voyage from Salem Harbor which ended with the triple shipwrecks in the sands of Cape Cod. By now even those children have grown old and passed away, and the present generation knows very little of the wrecks of the *Ulysses*, the *Brutus*, and the *Volusia*.

The winter was very mild until the 21st of February. Ice began to go out to sea from the rivers on January 24, with the temperature at 60 above zero four days later. There had been but little snow, and the people were congratulating themselves on having escaped the extremities of a New England winter. If they had been able to look ahead, they would have been more apprehensive.

Sunday, February 21, started in as a pleasantly warm day, but suddenly the storm clouds gathered and the wind shifted to the northeast. Snow began to fall, and in a few hours a frightful blizzard was sweeping the coast. This storm lasted nearly a week. Out at sea many vessels were caught.

All along the coast, wrecks came ashore. A ship and a schooner slid up on the sand at what is now Revere Beach, Massachusetts, while two vessels crashed on the rocks at Cape Ann. Two schooners and a brig smashed ashore around Boston Harbor. The boats of the Boston pilots suffered during the gale. Pilot Cole's vessel was driven up on the rocks, and the craft of Thomas Knox, Boston Light keeper (from 1783 until 1811), was likewise sent ashore with heavy damage. Another luckless schooner hit Minot's Ledge, while the ship *Florenzo* was lost at Marshfield.

The storm, however, is remembered principally for the loss of the three Salem ships. As has been mentioned, it was a fine Sunday morning when the vessels sailed. The three ships passed Baker's Island Lighthouse, heading for the open sea. The wives and families, together with many friends, had gone down to the wharves to say their farewells, confident that a pleasant voyage was ahead.

At dusk that evening the three square-riggers were still close to each other. Captain James Cook of the *Ulysses*, William Brown of the *Brutus*, and Samuel Cook of the *Volusia* spoke to one another at a point ten miles south-southeast of Thacher's Island, with all three ships sailing east-northeast. The storm which began later that evening necessitated another conference of flags, as the captains dreaded the dangers of snow at sea. They finally agreed to continue the voyage, changing their course to due east. Extra canvas was added in their efforts to get away from land, but the breeze continued light, at times dying away completely. By midnight the storm hit in earnest from the northeast, and the sailors realized their danger.

At 2:30 in the morning Captain Samuel Cook of the *Volusia* became worried and put about for a return to Salem. When he thought he was off Gloucester, the storm was so bad that he could not see a harbor entrance, so he ran before the wind. With reefed topsails, the *Volusia* kept off the coast until late that morning, when the dreaded spectacle of Cape Cod loomed before them on a lee shore. The captain, realizing then that he could not weather the Cape, tried to reach Provincetown Harbor. At this moment a terrific gust of wind swept through the sails of the ship, parted the foretopsail, and tore it to shreds.

The slings of the foreyard were carried away, and the yard crashed down on the deck, rendering the headsails useless. The vessel drove toward shore. Knowing that their chances were slight, the sailors thought of their loved ones at home who had waved farewell just a few hours before; they made their prayers for a safe landing on the dangerous beach ahead.

The *Volusia* hit the Peaked Hill Bars and bumped across the outer reefs, soon becoming a hopeless wreck. The masts were cut away, and

the ship slid over the last of the bars to head for the shore itself, grounding a short distance from safety. The tide was going out, however, so a
more hopeful condition presented itself. Watchers on the beach had
noticed the wreck. If the ship held together until low tide, the men
could reach shore. Hour after hour passed, with the seas gradually going
down. Finally at extreme low water the men scrambled ashore. The
people of Cape Cod who were waiting for them took the sailors to their
homes,where the men of the *Volusia* were soon warm and comfortable.
Later the *Volusia* was successfully got off the beach and sailed away.

When the *Volusia* parted from the other two ships, the captains had
continued their conversations as they sailed along. Finally, they agreed
to keep on a north-northwest course until daylight. At 6:00 A.M. the
Ulysses headed for Cape Ann, while the *Brutus* turned to the southeast.
The storm soon increased to put both ships in its power, with the
Ulysses the first to sight the Cape Cod shore. In spite of all efforts of the
crew, the ship crashed on the northern pitch of Cape Cod shortly after
5:00 in the afternoon. The men from the *Ulysses* leaped down into the
sand just as the waves battered to pieces their proud ship. The *Ulysses*
had struck only a mile from the *Volusia*! While the vessel was a total
loss, the men were all saved.

Highland (Cape Cod) Lighthouse today (photo by Jeremy D'Entremont)

The men of the *Brutus* were not so lucky. The ship had weathered the gale all that day, and when nightfall came the sailors had hopes of final victory over the storm. But it was not to be. Sailor Andrew Herron of Salem fell from aloft and was killed. The *Brutus*, now in the trough of the sea, soon hit the Cape Cod Bar two miles from the lighthouse. To lighten the vessel, a large part of the cargo was thrown overboard, allowing the *Brutus* to come on the beach near the Highland Light. The waves soon had complete possession of the ship. She started to break in two, the mainmast falling toward the beach just as the stern separated from the bow. The sailors climbed over the mainmast to drop nearer to the shore. One by one they reached land, but George Pierce of Marblehead slipped off the mast into the surf, where the undertow soon sucked him down. He was the only one lost at this time.

The trials of the survivors were just beginning. Having reached shore in the blackness of a February night, they had no watchers on the beach to aid them. By this time the swirling snow had created great drifts, obliterating roads and paths alike. Wet and exhausted, the men started their search for shelter. It was the coldest night of the winter, with the temperature far below zero. Captain William Brown was thinly clad and soon succumbed to the elements. First Mate Ruee had tried to save him, but Brown was beyond help. One by one others in the crew succumbed to the cold, sinking to the ground, where they froze to death. At this time the men had reached a point on the western side of the bay between Provincetown and Truro. It was later found that the men had passed a few yards from a man's home, but in the thick snowstorm had failed to see it.

At 4:00 in the morning of Tuesday, February 23, the survivors reached some outhouses and fences, and soon were knocking at the door of the keeper of Highland Light. Only five of them were left. They had walked over twenty miles in the terrible blizzard before reaching the light, crossing and recrossing their steps in their efforts to reach safety. The keeper gave them every possible assistance, and sent his men out into the gale to search for survivors who might still be alive in the snowdrifts.

Benjamin Ober, a sailor from Manchester, was found buried alive in the sand and snow, where he had been watching attempts to locate his body. In the snowdrift for thirty-six hours, so frozen that he was unable to communicate with the men who walked by him, he was in great agony. Finally a little boy saw Ober's hand protruding from the snowdrift, and Ober was immediately taken into a nearby home. But it was too late, for although every care and attention was given him, Benjamin Ober soon passed away.

There is a sequel to this story. During a great easterly storm which swept along the Cape Cod coast seventy-eight years later, the waves washed away part of the sand bank where the wreck of the East India-man *Brutus* had lain, and the skeleton of a sailor was exposed under the beam ends of the vessel. It is probable that the remains were those of George Pierce. Some silver coins were found near his skeleton. When these were moved, there was revealed a watch, the hands of which still pointed at 2:00, the time Pierce had fallen from the mainmast into the sea. Shebnah Rich, who wrote the history of Truro sixty years ago, comments on the story, saying that the wheels of the watch and the wheels of life stood still, having been wrapped in their sandy winding sheet for seventy-eight years.

A number of huts, or "charity houses," were built along the Cape to provide shelter for shipwreck victims. In *Cape Cod*, Henry David Thoreau wrote that he learned that a particular hut in Truro had been destroyed by high winds in January 1802. "If it had remained," he wrote, "it is probable that the whole of the unfortunate crew of that ship [the *Brutus*] would have been saved, as they gained the shore a few rods only from the spot where the hut had stood."

CHAPTER 11

The Storm of October 1804

One of the outstanding October gales of all times swept across New England on the morning of October 9, 1804. The tempest brought heavy rain in the southern part of New England, while the people in Massachusetts and to the north experienced a snowstorm. The wind blew from the southeast, and then early in the afternoon veered to the north-northeast, increasing in intensity until sunset, when its terrific force blew down houses, barns, trees, and hundreds of chimneys. Before midnight the worst of the gale had passed, although the snow and wind continued for two days.

It was one of the worst October storms ever witnessed in Massachusetts, the fall of snow averaging from five to fourteen inches. At Concord, New Hampshire, the snow was two feet deep, but in Vermont only five inches fell. Farmers were among the worst sufferers. Fruit orchards were blown down everywhere. Cattle and sheep died by the hundreds, with thousands of fowl perishing. At Thomaston, Maine, a sixty-acre timber lot was almost completely blown down. Such great sections of timber were destroyed that entirely new views were possible; houses and other buildings never before visible from a distance could be seen across valleys and townships. The change was so pronounced in certain sections, according to Perley, that the surroundings seemed to have become entirely different, people feeling that they were in a strange place.

The South Church in Danvers lost its roof, while in Peabody over 30,000 unburned bricks were ruined by the gale. The spire of the Beverly meetinghouse broke off.

In Boston, the wind blew the battlements from a new building upon the roof of a residence occupied by Ebenezer Eaton, who had left the house with his wife just in time. Four others were crushed in the ruins, one dying later. The roof was ripped off King's Chapel, dropping it to the ground two hundred feet away. The handsome steeple of the Old North Church was toppled over into the street, landing partly on a building nearby and demolishing it. No one was inside. Paul Revere's buildings over his copper furnaces were destroyed.

Shipping in the harbor suffered considerably, with several persons losing their lives. The schooner *Dove* was wrecked on Ipswich Bar, all seven on board perishing. The sloops *Hannah* and *Mary* were driven on Cohasset at about the same time. Captain Gardner of the *Hannah* was swept off the deck and drowned, but the others aboard were saved. The crew from the *Mary* were successful in reaching shore alive. The ship *Protector* hit on Cape Cod five miles south of Cape Cod Light, with a cargo valued at $100,000. Only one man was lost.

The Reverend William Bentley of Salem said that this gale was the heaviest blow ever known in that town. He could find no record of previous storms in which wharves, ships, trees, houses, fences, and outhouses were so totally destroyed. "I cannot refuse to adopt the belief that the late storm was the most severe ever felt in this part of America. All the accounts which I have seen represent nothing like it," were the words Bentley wrote in his diary.

The steeple of Boston's Old North Church, one of the casualties of this storm, was replaced by a new one that was fifteen feet shorter than its predecessor. The second steeple in turn fell victim to Hurricane Carol in 1954 and was replaced by a replica of the eighteenth-century steeple.

CHAPTER 12

The September Gale of 1815

The most severe storm of the nineteenth century, the September Gale of 1815, centered its destruction in Providence, Rhode Island, although the effects were felt all over New England. Beginning around 8:00 on the Sunday morning of September 23, the wind swept Narragansett Bay with a force seldom approached, causing death and disaster for miles around. By 10:00 utter confusion reigned around the wharves of Providence as large vessels, torn from their moorings by the wind and tide, swept across streets and wharves which in normal times would be ten and twelve feet above the usual high tide.

The great bridge connecting the two parts of Providence was swept away as the vessels crashed into it and continued up the cove. After the storm four ships, nine brigs, seven schooners, and fifteen sloops were found from five to six above the usual high tide mark. One sloop stood upright before the door of a Mr. Webb, while a ship was found in the garden of General Lippet.

On the west side of the river, the water rose nearly to the tops of the first floors of the residences. On the east side, the water swept up Weybosset Street three feet deep. Masts, cotton bales, coffee, grain, and wreckage of boats were all carried along Providence's main street as the water rose higher. The Second Baptist Church collapsed when the tide came up around the foundations, while the meetinghouse of the Reverend Mr. Williams barely escaped the same fate as the tide began to recede. Along the higher ground, lumber, candles, grain, flour, household furniture, and endless other articles were heaped in hope-less confusion. Those who witnessed the storm in Providence later said it was a sight of such widespread desolation and havoc that it defied description.

The Exchange and Union Banks, leading investment houses, were lit-erally inundated. The ship *Ganges*, forced up the river by the tide, crashed into the Washington Insurance Building, smashing her bowsprit into the third story of the edifice. India Bridge at India Street was swept away, as was Mill Bridge at the foot of Constitution Hill. More than 500 buildings, valued at $1,500,000, were completely destroyed. It is impos-sible to estimate the loss of life in Providence during the 1815 gale, but it was extremely heavy. After the storm a force of 300 armed men were stationed in the town to prevent looting.

At Bristol, Rhode Island, every vessel in the harbor was driven ashore. The post office and several other buildings were carried away. A grist-mill at Glenrock Village was destroyed, while a similar fate befell the Point Judith Lighthouse.

Buzzard's Bay also felt the full force of the hurricane. No rain fell there, but the tide was eight feet higher than usual, with tremendous damage as a result. At New Bedford all the vessels except two went ashore. A merchant named Russell, who was in his store when it was swept away, had an unusual experience. The store crashed into a vessel and Russell leaped aboard. The vessel soon smashed to pieces, but Rus-sell escaped unhurt. The storm carried away the salt works, one small building sailing for several miles before grounding at a location usually nine feet above the high tide mark.

At Stonington, Connecticut, the tide rose seventeen feet higher than usual, and swept across the town. Twenty ships in the harbor were either sunk or driven ashore. At New London the tide was higher than ever before in its history. Wharves were everywhere demolished; that of M. Ledyard was entirely destroyed with the merchandise upon it. Groton and Norwich also suffered heavily, the market house in the lat-ter place being carried away.

The storm seems to have spent itself before reaching northern New England, as no portion of the coast north of Cape Cod suffered from the gale except the area between Boston and Cape Ann. In Boston the only building entirely destroyed was the Glass House, a huge rickety affair which blew down around 11:00 Saturday morning. It immediately took fire and was completely consumed. About sixty chimneys were blown down, three or four of the smaller chimneys of the State House among them. Twenty stately trees on Boston Common were leveled, and five of Paddock's famous elms shared the same fate. In Chelsea the well-known elm near the ferry, seventeen feet in girth, which had a portico built about it, was blown down. The Danvers pear tree, which Governor Endicott planted in the seventeenth century, lost half its branches.

Shipping damage in Boston Bay was severe. About sixty vessels were included in the list of those affected by the gale in Boston Harbor alone, while at least an equal number met trouble elsewhere along the Massachusetts coast. Salem, Marblehead, and Gloucester suffered severely. Compared to Providence and other locations in southern New England, however, the Massachusetts towns were very fortunate.

Oliver Wendell Holmes remembered well the September Gale of 1815. His story follows:

> The wind caught up from the waters of the bay and of the river Charles as mad shrews tear the hair from each other's heads. The salt spray was carried far inland, and left its crystals on the windows of farm-houses and villas. I have, besides more specific recollections, a general remaining impression of a mighty howling, roaring, banging, and crashing, with much running about, and loud screaming of orders for sudden taking in of all sail about the premises, and battening down of everything that could flap or fly away. . . . It was hard travelling that day. Professor Farrar tried with others to reach the river, but they were frequently driven back, and had to screen themselves behind fences and trees, or "tack" against the mighty blast, which drove them like a powerful current of water.

In that September gale which occurred when he was a small boy, Oliver Wendell Holmes suffered an unusual loss.

> It chanced to be our washing-day,
> And all our things were drying
> The storm came roaring through the lines,
> And set them all aflying;
> I saw the shirts and petticoats
> Go riding off like witches;
> I lost, ah! bitterly I wept,—
> I lost my Sunday breeches!

The Hurricane of 1938 took many more lives in New England, but the September Gale of 1815 is often ranked second on the list of the region's storms in terms of sheer destructiveness. This storm did have some effect north of Cape Ann. In Wells, Maine, a man was killed by a tree felled by the wind, and much damage was done to buildings in Newburyport and Portsmouth.

It was recorded in Harvard, Massachusetts, that the following year "frosts occurred during every month of the year," earning 1816 the title of "the year without a summer." It was certainly a punishing two years weatherwise for the Northeast.

CHAPTER 13

The Loss of the Royal Tar

During the summer of 1836 a circus and menagerie toured the Canadian province of New Brunswick and the surrounding areas. At the close of a successful season the entire circus embarked on the *Royal Tar*, a steamer bound from New Brunswick to Maine. It was a new vessel, named for King William IV of England (who ruled from 1830 to 1837), and built at Saint John that spring.

Captain Thomas Reed was in command of the Portland-bound *Royal Tar* as she sailed out of Saint John Harbor on Friday, October 21, 1836, with a strange cargo of assorted animals. The shows were billed as Dexter's Locomotive Museum, and Burgess' Collection of Serpents and Birds. The circus carried a brass band and included horses, two camels, Mogul the elephant, two lions, one Royal Bengal tiger, a gnu, and two pelicans. The 164-foot vessel soon reached the open sea and headed south.

When the steamer began her voyage that Friday morning, the weather had been fine in every respect, but before the sun set a high westerly wind started to blow. Continuing several days, the wind forced the *Royal Tar* to seek shelter in Eastport Harbor, where the steamer remained until the following Tuesday. She left port that afternoon, but the rising winds again forced her to seek shelter, this time behind Fox Island.* The *Royal Tar* anchored about two miles off Fox Island Thoroughfare to fill her boilers.

---

*Now known as North Haven.—*Ed.*

Evidently the water in the boilers was much lower than had been believed, for when the pilot's son tested the lower cock, he found it dry. The boy told his father, who mentioned the fact to Mr. Marshall, the second engineer-in-charge. Both father and son were made to understand that they were mistaken in believing that the boilers were dry, as everything was in order. It was later learned that the regular engineer had been up all night working on the boilers. Tired, he had entrusted his position to the second engineer, who in turn had given the task of watering the boilers to the fireman.

A few minutes after the discussion, the empty boiler became red hot, setting fire to two wedges supporting the elephant stall. The fire gained headway rapidly, for by the time Captain Reed looked down the grating, the flames were beyond control. Realizing that the *Royal Tar* was doomed, he ordered the men to slip anchor, hoist a distress signal, and lower the boats.

Taking charge of the jolly boat, Captain Reed came alongside the *Royal Tar*, where two able men, Mr. Sherwood and Mr. Fowler, joined him. Sixteen other men jumped into the long boat, cut the ropes to drop their craft into the water, and started for shore. The strong wind rapidly swept them leeward in the direction of land, which they reached safely four hours later.

A man in the circus escaped from the pandemonium, which had broken loose on deck, by jumping into the water and swimming to the jolly boat. It was a strange tale he told the others of wild animals and frightened people milling together on the burning ship, man and beast alike frantic in their desire to escape the spreading flames.

The revenue cutter *Veto* was seen in the distance, approaching rapidly. Captain Dyer of the cutter soon drew near, and Captain Reed in the jolly boat ordered his men to row over to the *Veto*, then lying to windward. The men refused, infuriating Captain Reed.

"I was captain of the big boat," said Reed, "and damn me if I will not be captain of the small one, and if any man refuses to run for the cutter I'll throw him overboard." Without further interruption, the jolly boat now made for the cutter, where the passengers received treatment.

The revenue cutter's pilot arrived near the *Royal Tar* with the *Veto*'s gig, but the flames of the burning vessel so frightened him that he dared not approach closely enough to effect the rescue of anyone. Passing around in back of the stern, the pilot saw the passengers and crew hanging over the sides, clinging to the ropes. Terrified by their cries for help,

The Royal Tar *ablaze off Fox Island Thoroughfare off Isle au Haut*

he lost his nerve and steered back to the cutter without saving a single person. The cutter itself, with a heavy deckload of gunpowder, was unable to approach any closer to the burning steamer.

Working desperately to construct a substantial raft from the deck boards of the *Royal Tar*, a group of men aboard the burning ship managed to launch a makeshift boat, which supported them fairly well. Just as they were about to push off from the vessel, the huge form of the elephant loomed directly over them, balanced for a terrifying moment at the taffrail, and smashed down through the air to land on the raft, sinking the float and drowning the men. The body of the elephant was found floating a few days later near Brimstone Island. It was said that every animal belonging to the menagerie was lost. Other accounts mention that when the horses jumped overboard, they swam round and round the burning vessel until they sank, instead of making for shore where they might have been saved.

Captain Reed now took charge of the revenue cutter, as the regular captain was not aboard.* Steering the cutter in closer to the *Royal Tar*,

---

*Snow is not correct on this point. See the notes at the end of the chapter—*Ed.*

he went across in the jolly boat for those still left on board. By this time some of the passengers had been on the wreck for almost two hours, hanging to ropes in the water. One by one the ropes would burn through, dropping the victims into the sea to their death. Another element of delay had been the elephant, which had appeared at the rail several times as the jolly boat drew near, seeming ready to leap.

One of the passengers, Mr. H. H. Fuller, clung to the rope over the stern until his strength failed him; then he twisted the line around his neck to prevent slipping into the sea. Four others grabbed hold of his body, causing terrific pressure on his throat. Lifting his leg high out of water, in some way he transferred the rope from his neck to his leg. A woman grabbed hold of his other leg and clung desperately to him. They were still in this awkward position when rescued a short time later.

Of the ninety-three persons on board, thirty-two passengers and members of the crew perished. One of the most unusual deaths was that of a man who lashed his small trunk to a plank, which he slid off into the sea successfully. Fastening $500 in silver to a money belt around his waist, he mounted the taffrail and leaped into the sea. What he did not realize was the tremendous weight of the $500 in silver! When he plummeted down through the waves, he was so heavy that he never rose to the surface again.

The passengers were high in their praise of the acts of Captain Reed, who did much to reduce the loss of life aboard the *Royal Tar*. One of the prominent passengers on board was quoted as follows:

> *Captain Reed took charge of the stern boat, with two men, and kept her off the steamboat, which was a very fortunate circumstance, as it was the means of saving from 40 to 50 persons, and to him all credit is due for his deliberate and manly perseverance throughout the whole calamity.*
>
> *It is impossible to describe the appalling spectacle which the whole scene presented—the boat wrapped in flames, with nearly 100 souls on board, without any hope of relief, rending the air with their shrieks for help; the caravan of wild beasts on deck, ready to tear to pieces all that might escape the flames.*

Shortly before sunset the last rescue boat with a single survivor on board left the *Royal Tar*. The passenger was a woman who had seen her sister and daughter perish before her eyes. After taking aboard the unfortunate woman, the revenue cutter started for the Isle au Haut to land the survivors. (The location of Isle au Haut is west of Vinalhaven, south of Deer Island, and southwest of Swan's Island.) The passengers then obtained a schooner to take them to Portland while the master and crew went to Eastport on another vessel.

On November 3, 1836, Captain Reed was presented with a purse of $700 for his heroic work during the fire. A few years later he was appointed harbormaster at Saint John. He became a picturesque figure around the Saint John waterfront, where he was often seen with his faithful dog walking at his side.

Peter Dow Bachelder's book *Shipwrecks & Maritime Disasters of the Maine Coast* paints a vivid and detailed picture of the wreck of the *Royal Tar*. But as Bachelder writes, much of what happened during the vessel's final hours can never fully be known.

Roy Heisler of the Vinalhaven Historical Society points out that while Edward Rowe Snow obviously used a variety of 1836 news stories and reports as all researchers would, "he must have missed the newspaper's (*Argus*'s) retraction of the erroneous rumor in its first story regarding Captain Howland T. Dyer of the *Veto*." Dyer was indeed the regular captain of the *Veto*, and he played no small part in the drama.

In fact, as Bachelder's book emphasizes, Captain Dyer's performance was apparently quite heroic. He brought the *Veto* very close to the burning steamship, so close that the schooner twice caught fire itself. Dyer was seriously wounded and burned during the ordeal. An undated article at the Vinalhaven Historical Society from the *Rockland Courier-Gazette* quotes a person (possibly Captain Reed) on the *Royal Tar,* who reported, "In about half an hour we saw a schooner coming to us, which proved to be the United States revenue cutter *Veto*, Capt. Dyer, who rendered us every assistance in his power. He ran the cutter close to the burning steamer, then in a sheet of flames succeeded in taking out 40 passengers who must have perished, had not the cutter come to our aid."

In his official report on the disaster, Captain Ezekiel Jones of the revenue cutter *Morris* said that he had talked to many of the survivors about Captain Dyer, and that "they all look upon him as their preserver." In their retraction, the *Argus* said that Dyer's conduct was "in every respect noble and praiseworthy."

Interestingly, after his revenue cutter experience, Howland Dyer became keeper at Brown's Head Lighthouse on Vinalhaven, serving from 1843 to 1864.

The story of Mogul the elephant leaping into the water and crushing some passengers on a makeshift raft may be apocryphal. What actually seems to have happened is that when the elephant crashed through the *Royal Tar*'s railing, he took several passengers with him into the ocean.

To date, the remains of the *Royal Tar* have not been located. In his 1963 book *True Tales of Terrible Shipwrecks*, Snow wrote, "My cousin, the late Willis Snow, once kept the lighthouse in the Fox Island Thoroughfare [Goose Rocks Light]. During his free time he made several trips to the scenes of the wreck of the man-of-war *Albany* and the *Royal Tar* . . . but he never did find the hull of the *Royal Tar*." Snow believed that a fairly large sum of money was waiting to be found in a chest on the "Circus Ship."

Poet Wilbert Snow imagined the *Royal Tar* a reappearing ghost ship in "Fate of the *Royal Tar*." An excerpt:

> *They remembered and believed, for many a year*
> *On that autumn night a crowd would appear*
> *Looking out toward Eggemoggin Reach to behold*
> *The* Royal Tar *rising in a circle of gold.*
> *And some saw a sign that the flood of Noah's warning*
> *Would yield to fire on the Judgment Morning.*
> *But other folks went to bask in the glow*
> *Of the one great horror they would ever know.*

Snow's daughter, Dolly, holding an elephant bone said to be from the wreck of the Royal Tar. *The bone was later stolen during one of Snow's lectures. (From Snow's* True Tales of Terrible Shipwrecks*)*

CHAPTER 14

The Triple Hurricanes of 1839

Perhaps the only account of three gales in one month is that of the triple hurricanes of December 1839. The first two weeks had been unusually mild, suggesting September or October weather. At midnight on Saturday, the 14th, snow began to fall and the wind veered to the southeast. By noon of the 15th a bad storm had set in. All along the coast, vessels were blown ashore or capsized at their anchors. Many crews cut away their masts in time, while others steered their craft ashore on sandy beaches, thus saving their own lives. At 2:00 the next morning, the storm went down a little after the wind had swung to the northeast.

When the gale ended, the whole of the Massachusetts shore was covered with wreckage from scores of vessels, and no accurate survey of the loss of life was ever made. The harbors of Boston, Salem, Newburyport, Gloucester, Cohasset, Lynn, Marblehead, and Provincetown were filled with disabled vessels. On land many buildings were blown down and hundreds of chimneys were toppled over.

The tide in Boston swept across Boston Neck, isolating the city and making it a temporary island. The force of the tide was so strong that there was no apparent fall of the sea for three hours after high water. In East Boston, a corner of the Maverick House roof was ripped away, as was the roof of the car barn there. The schooner *Davenport* was pushed high and dry on Rainsford's Island, Boston Harbor.

Perley avers the scene in Gloucester Harbor has never been equaled in any other New England port. Of course Perley wrote before the 1938 hurricane, but the 1839 storm was nevertheless an awesome sight. Sixty vessels were there during the gale, and one by one they broke loose and drifted across the bay. By Monday morning only a single mast was left standing in the harbor. Twenty-one vessels were driven ashore, three schooners went down, and seventeen others were broken up into kindling wood. Twenty vessels still were straining at their moorings out in the harbor, all but one having had their masts broken or cut away.

About forty lives were lost around Gloucester Harbor. The worst disaster was at Pigeon Cove, where twenty people were drowned from a schooner. It is believed that Henry Wadsworth Longfellow obtained the idea for his poem "The Wreck of the Hesperus," by watching the wreckage and bodies that came up on the beach after the storm. Not satisfied with the poetic possibilities of any name on the ships wrecked at Gloucester, he noticed the results of a peculiar disaster when he returned to Boston. A schooner from Gardiner, Maine, had driven into a four-story building on the waterfront, with the schooner smashing her jib boom through the fourth story. While he was down near the wharves, Longfellow looked up at the unusual accident and noticed the name of the vessel. It was the schooner *Hesperus*.

Gloucester Harbor during its worst storm, December 15, 1839

The schooner *Deposit* came ashore at Ipswich, but the surf was so heavy that no boat could live in the angry sea. The waves broke over the wreck all night long. By morning two sailors had died. Keeper Greenwood of Ipswich Light* and a friend, Marshall, tried to approach the vessel. Tying one end of a rope to a dory and the other around his waist, Greenwood swam out to the wreck and then signaled for Marshall to climb into the dory on the beach. Marshall launched the dory just as a wave started to recede, and Greenwood pulled his friend out to the schooner. The exhausted captain was first lowered into the dory, and after several narrow escapes from swamping, was landed safely on the shore. Two others of the crew were then rescued.

The second of the December hurricanes hit the coast on Sunday, the 22nd. Terrific damages resulted in many sections of New England. In Boston Harbor the schooner *Davenport*, which had just been floated from Rainsford's Island, was again thrown up on the beach there. The brig *Pocahontas* was another victim of the storm.

The *Pocahontas* was bound from Cadiz to Newburyport but crashed against the sandbar off Plum Island. Her masts were carried away by the gale, and the anchors dragged. Stern first she drove up on the reef, 150 yards from the beach itself. Soon after daylight the next morning, Captain Brown of the hotel on Plum Island discovered the disaster and notified the people of Newburyport. When the vessel was first seen, there were three men still on it, one of them at the taffrail and two others clinging to the bowsprit. Several of the bolder men ashore hauled a dory three-quarters of a mile to the beach near the wreck, but finally gave up their efforts to launch it after several vain attempts. A short time later another view of the ship disclosed one man still clinging to the bowsprit, the other two having vanished.

Just before noon the man at the bowsprit lost his hold and was seen no more. A few minutes later the wreck washed ashore on the beach. A man found lashed to the vessel was still breathing, but soon expired. Thus young Captain Cook, who perished within sight of his own home, lost his life along with ten others. Seven bodies washed ashore in all, and were buried in the Old Hill Burial Ground at Newburyport.

During the middle of the week the weather moderated, but on Friday another storm, believed by some to be worse than either of the other two, smashed along the coast. The ship *Columbiana*, loaded with ice,

---

*Ipswich Range Lights—*Ed.*

smashed against Boston's Charlestown Bridge. She ripped through the structure and crashed against Warren Bridge, tearing down the drawtender's house. If the mate, then at the wheel, had not luffed the *Columbiana*, she probably would have carried away Warren Bridge as well.

With the third hurricane, December had finished its gales. As a result of these three storms, over 300 vessels were wrecked, at least a million dollars' worth of property was destroyed, and more than 150 lives were lost. Perley remarked of the three storms:

> *How many widows and orphans afterwards sat at the windows of their cottages at Mount Desert and many other places looking for the sails that they knew so well, yet not daring to hope that they would see them again!*

*Celia Thaxter
(from the collection of
Jeremy D'Entremont)*

In his book *Shipwrecks North of Boston, Volume One: Salem Bay*, Raymond H. Bates, Jr., wrote of an earlier storm in that same year. On August 30, 1839, fourteen ships at anchor were wrecked in Salem Harbor alone.

During the terrible storm of December 22, 1839, a young girl named Celia Laighton watched the *Pocahontas* pass by White Island in the Isles of Shoals off New Hampshire, where her father was the lighthouse keeper. Celia soon learned that all aboard were lost. Celia (Laighton) Thaxter later gained widespread fame as a poet and author, and the memory of this incident inspired her poem "The Wreck of the Pocahontas." Here is an excerpt:

> *Like all the demons loosed at last,*
> *Whistling and shrieking, wild and wide,*
> *The mad wind raged, while strong and fast*
> *Rolled in the rising tide.*

It was reported that the keeper and his wife from the Plum Island Lighthouse were away on the mainland and were unable to return to their station during the storm, leaving the lighthouse dark. Some have suggested that this contributed to the wreck, but this can't be known with any certainty.

CHAPTER 15

The Fire on the Steamer Lexington

Commodore Cornelius Vanderbilt's 205-foot steamboat *Lexington* was one of the most popular vessels on Long Island Sound during the early part of the last century. Built in 1835 to accommodate New York–bound passengers from Boston to Providence, the *Lexington* made a new record on her first run, reaching New York from Providence in eleven and one-half hours, June 2, 1835. Some famous steamboat races took place during this period, inhabitants of towns and cities flocking to the waterfront to watch the steamers go by. Perhaps the most outstanding race of the period was the occasion when the *Lexington* lost to the *Richmond*.

The *Lexington* soon established herself as one of the leading steamers on the Sound. In 1840 she was running regularly between Stonington, Connecticut, and New York City. On the afternoon of Monday, January 13, Captain George Childs sailed the *Lexington* away from her New York pier on what was destined to be her last voyage. Backing out of the dock, the *Lexington* threaded her way up the East River through Hell Gate, and into Long Island Sound. The last streaks of sunset were lost in the western sky by this time, and the boisterous January winds began to lash the afterdeck.

Gathered in various parts of the steamer were coastwise travelers, merchants, and round-the-world sea captains, discussing national affairs and local matters. A few tables for the card players had been set up, and those who enjoyed the games were busy at their chosen pastime, while the returning sea captains gathered around one of the stoves to talk over

Survivors of the Lexington *disaster, Hillard and Cox, are shown as they floated on the bale of cotton. Cox later dropped to his death.*

their homecoming. Some of these master mariners who had been away from their loved ones for several years were happy with the thoughts of the coming family reunions.

Suddenly a single cry full of alarm and terror was heard echoing through the *Lexington*. "Fire, fire," came the shout, which was picked up and repeated everywhere. Soon the passengers all knew the dreadful news. The worst marine calamity possible, a fire at sea, had broken out. A vessel may weather a thousand storms, but disaster is inevitable aboard a burning ship unless the fire is brought under immediate control.

Second Mate David Crowley rushed to the scene of the blaze near the smokestack, and quickly organized a fire bucket brigade. Pail after pail of water was thrown in vain at the growing blaze, which by now had assumed terrifying proportions. The men fought on until their burned and blackened bodies could stand no more. As the flames forced their relentless way ahead, Captain Childs finally told the bucket brigade to drop back, as the *Lexington* was doomed. The steamer was now running for the nearest shore.

Across Long Island Sound at Southport, Connecticut, Captain Meeker of the sloop *Merchant* watched the burning boat sail up the coast.

Attempting to sail his sloop to the rescue, he ran her aground on the outer bar. It was not until several hours later when the tide turned that Meeker arrived at the scene to render assistance, but by that time few were alive to be helped.

Another small boat put out from the Long Island shore, but the speed of the *Lexington* was so great that the other vessel gave up and returned to port. The water had been rough, and the smaller craft was in danger of capsizing.

Finally the captain realized that he would have to abandon ship. In a calm voice he cried out, "Gentlemen, take to the boats." According to some, this started a rush for the lifeboats while the steamer was still making too much headway for the launching of a lifeboat into the rough seas. Regardless of this danger, the panic-stricken passengers put over a lifeboat from the forward part of the steamer. The small boat, caught in the waves, was swamped instantly. If the passengers had waited until the engines stopped, they could have launched the boat into comparatively calm seas.

The testimony of a passenger, Captain Hillard, under oath, follows:

It was about an hour after supper that I first heard the alarm of fire. I was then on the point of turning in, and had my coat and boots off. I slipped them on. I then discovered the casing of the smoke pipe, and I think, a part of the promenade deck, on fire. There was a great rush of the passengers, and much confusion, so that I could not notice particularly. The after part of the casing was burning, and the fire was making aft. I thought at the time that the fire might be subdued; but being aft at the time, could not, therefore, see distinctly. . . .

I shortly after went on the promenade deck; my attention had previously been directed to the passengers, who were rushing into the quarter boats; and when I went on the quarter deck, the boats were both filled. They seemed to be stupidly determined to destroy themselves, as well as the boats, which were their only means of safety. I went to the starboard boat, which they were lowering away; they lowered it until she took the water, and then I saw some one cut away the forward tackle fall; it was at all events disengaged, and no one at the time could have unhooked the fall; the boat instantly filled with water, there being at the time about twenty persons in her; and the boat passed immediately astern, entirely clear. I then went to the other side; the other boat was cleared away and lowered in the same manner as the first, full of passengers. This boat fell astern entirely disengaged, as the other had done, but fell away before she had entirely filled with water.

By this time the fire had got under such headway, that I pretty much made my mind up "it was a gone case.". . . The fire by this time began to come up around the promenade deck, and the wheel-house was completely filled with smoke. There were two or three on the promenade deck near the wheel-house, and their attention was turned to the life boat; it was cleared away. I assisted in stripping off the canvas, but I had no notion of going in her, as I had made my mind up that they would serve her as they had done the other boats. . . . The smoke was so dense that I could not see distinctly what they were about. I think that the communication with the fore part of the boat was by this time cut off; from the first hearing of the alarm, perhaps twenty minutes had elapsed. The engine had now been stopped about five minutes. I recommended to the few deck hands and passengers who remained, to throw the cotton overboard; and told them they must do something for themselves, and the best thing they could do was to take the cotton. There were perhaps ten or a dozen bales thrown overboard which was pretty much all there was on the larboard side which had not taken fire. I then cut off a piece of line, perhaps four or five fathoms, and with it spanned a bale of cotton, which, I believe, was the last one not on fire. It was a very snug, square bale, about four feet long and three feet wide, and a foot and a half thick. Aided by one of the firemen, I put the bale up on the rail, round which we took a turn, slipped the bale down below the guard, when we both got on to it. The boat then lay broadside to the wind, and we were under the lee of the boat, on the larboard side. We placed ourselves one on each end of the bale, facing each other; with our weight it was about one-third out of the water. The wind was pretty fresh, and we drifted at the rate of about a knot and a half.

The two voyagers decided not to lash themselves to the bale, but coiled the rope up in the middle. They then pushed away from the burning craft, as it was getting unbearably hot. Shoving the bale around to the stern, they finally left the burning *Lexington* around 8:00 that night. Captain Hillard found a stick in the water, which he adapted for a paddle. In this manner he kept the bale facing into the sea.

When the men pushed away from the ship, there were few living persons still aboard the *Lexington*. Most of them had either perished in the swamping of the boats, or had jumped into the ocean. The two men sat astride their bale of cotton, the waves sloshing against their bodies until they were wet up to the waist. Every half hour Hillard glanced at his watch. The wreck did not sink until 3:00 the next morning. It was then so cold that the men kept up their circulation by violently beating their arms against their wet bodies. An hour later, whether because of their vigorous efforts or not, the great bale rolled over. The men clambered up on top of the other side, the paddle was lost, and conditions rapidly became worse. Now riding an unmanageable bale of cotton, the men were desperate. Cox soon lost courage at the turn events had taken, and lapsed into a coma. Hillard tried to revive him, but in vain. Suddenly the bale gave a quick lurch. Cox rolled off into the water and failed to come up. That was the last Captain Hillard ever saw of Benjamin Cox, the *Lexington*'s fireman.

Back in Southport, Captain Meeker had finally got his sloop off the bar. Sailing in the direction which the *Lexington* had taken, he came upon Captain Hillard lying across the bale of cotton. Hillard was taken aboard the sloop, where he was given every possible attention. A short time later Captain Meeker fell in with two other survivors, one on another bale of cotton, and the second floating with the help of a section of the guard rail. They were quickly revived and told their stories.

The man who had been taken from the second bale was Captain Manchester, a pilot of the *Lexington*, while the other was Charles Smith, a deckhand. Captain Manchester said that when the fire broke out he had put the wheel hard-a-port to steer the *Lexington* to land. When orders came later to abandon ship, he saw a small raft floating by the side of the vessel, and jumped down on it. Several others were already there, however, and his added weight made the raft sink, so Manchester climbed back aboard the burning ship. He next noticed a bale of cotton tied to the rail, with a man whom he recognized as a Mr. McKenna sitting on it. Another person threw McKenna into the water, but Manchester pulled the man back and the third party left them. The bale now drifted away from the blazing ship. McKenna gradually weakened as the long night advanced, dying early the next morning. The seas washed him overboard. Captain Manchester's body was freezing when the sloop hove in sight, and he was barely able to wave at his rescuers.

The story Deckhand Smith told Captain Meeker gives us a vivid picture of the last moments of the *Lexington*. Asleep in his bunk at the time of the fire, Smith heard Captain George Childs call out to the engineer, asking if he could stop the engines. The engineer shouted back that the fire prevented this being done.

Smith had then gone aft, where he found Captain Childs in serious trouble. The lifeboat had been launched full of passengers, and the bow tackle cut away. The boat had swung, filled with water, and was then hanging by the stern tackle. Childs stepped down into the stern sheets, shouting to Smith to hold onto the stern tackle. Just then someone else cut the tackle, and the lifeboat fell free, swamped, and went over. That was the last seen of anyone in the small boat, and Smith believed that the captain of the *Lexington* perished in a futile attempt to save the lives of his passengers in the lifeboat.

The deckhand then went over the stern to climb on the rudder. Hanging by the nettings, he was able to kick in three cabin windows, and lowered himself down by them to stand on the rudder itself. Several others followed him. The bales of cotton now started to fall into the sea as the ship eased lower in the water. There were only ten or twelve people then alive on the craft, all men. The *Lexington* began her final plunge, thought Smith, around 3:00 in the morning. All those still alive grabbed for drifting timbers. Deckhand Smith located a large section of the guardrail, and with it kept afloat until he sighted the *Merchant* and was picked up.

The three survivors were soon landed ashore, and it was believed no other persons were still alive from the disaster. But this was not the case. The remarkable story of David Crowley, the second mate, was not learned until later. When the three men were safely put ashore at the Southport wharf, Crowley was floating on a cotton bale some miles away. He had actually seen the *Merchant* rescue two of the survivors, whereupon he had tried to wave to the captain, but could not get his attention. The *Merchant* sailed away, and the course of the bale brought Crowley to a point off Faulkland Island. As the cold was beginning to affect him, he tied his waistcoat around his head for warmth.

Crowley had hoped the bale would touch the island, but the tide carried him out to sea again. As soon as the wind and surf went down, he stretched out on the bale and soon fell asleep from exhaustion. Why he did not freeze to death he never could understand, but he awoke with the morning sun shining in his face, completely refreshed by his slumbers. All that day he drifted on, hoping and praying for rescue. As darkness fell, the bale suddenly bumped ashore, and Crowley sat up to find himself on a beach at the foot of a high bank. Sliding off the bale, he managed to crawl to the top of the hill, where he saw a light shining from a house in the distance. Step by step he forced his weary body toward the beacon in the darkness, finally arriving at the door of the home. He was admitted just as the son of Mr. Huntington (or Hutchinson, according to some accounts), the occupant, finished telling the story of the *Lexington*'s disaster. It was said afterwards that he presented a weird appearance, with his waistcoat tied around his head while he stood explaining his adventure. He was given immediate care and later recovered completely.

It was later brought out at the inquest that the *Lexington* had been on fire before, on the January 2 run. At that time the deck did not catch fire, since only a small box had ignited. Another point discussed at the inquest was the proximity of the sloop *Improvement* at the time of the fire. Less than five miles away, Captain William Tirrell of the *Improvement* decided for himself that the boats of the *Lexington* would take off all the passengers. It was estimated that over half of the 150 lost would have been saved if Captain Tirrell had sailed over and investigated the disaster.

Among those who perished was Dr. Charles Follen of Lexington, formerly a professor at Harvard College. (Follen Street, in Cambridge, is named for him.) A liberal in Austria, Follen fled to America because of his convictions. Another person lost was Robert Blake of Wrentham, an outstanding citizen in his community.

The steamer's loss made a tremendous impression up and down the Atlantic Coast. Pictures of the burning vessel were sold by the thousands. As a commentary on the age, we include part of a sermon by Reverend S. K. Lothrop, preached shortly after the disaster:

> The steamboats of Long Island Sound have, till recently, been in general managed with distinguished skill and care, and all necessary, nay, even a scrupulous attention paid to the safety and comfort of the passengers. Of late years, however, the growing competition and the increased facilities for carrying freight, afforded by the rail-roads to Providence and Stonington, have produced an unfavorable change, and taken from the boats the high character of safety and comfort that once attached to them. . . . Until the fate of the Lexington is forgotten, most persons will be willing to pay something extra if they can be insured a safe, comfortable passage. It is to be hoped that this melancholy catastrophe will direct public attention to the subject, so that the

reckless exposure of human life, which has marked some portions of the travelling in New England will end.

But it was many years before marine regulations were of such uniformity that they insured stringent enforcement of the safety laws. Man learns slowly and forgets quickly, especially when it is something which involves much thought and planning.

———————— ∼ ————————

In his book *The Sea Hunters*, Clive Cussler wrote that poet Henry Wadsworth Longfellow was nearly on board for the fateful voyage of the *Lexington*. An argument with his editor over changes in his poem "The Wreck of the Hesperus" had caused him to miss the boat by seconds.

A young artist named Nathaniel Currier, who later achieved lasting fame after teaming with James Merritt Ives, produced a widely circulated lithograph of the *Lexington* disaster.

Two years after the wreck, a salvage attempt was made, and the *Lexington* was lifted by heavy chains. As it reached the surface, the vessel broke apart and sank once again into about 130 feet of water. A large melted hunk of silver coins was salvaged before the steamer was again lost.

The *Lexington* was definitively located in 1983 by the National Underwater and Marine Agency. Clive Cussler and other researchers found the vessel largely with the help of an eyewitness account by the lighthouse keeper at Old Field Point, who described seeing the flames die out about four miles north and slightly west of Old Field Point at Port Jefferson. Artifacts recovered from the site were donated to the Vanderbilt Museum in Centerport, Long Island, New York.

The steamer is split into three sections virtually in the path of the Bridgeport to Port Jefferson ferry.

CHAPTER 16

The Immigrant Ship Saint John

The most serious shipwreck to occur in the outer reaches of Boston Harbor was that of the British brig *Saint John* in the year of 1849. One hundred and forty-three persons perished in this disaster, which took place inside of Minot's Ledge October 7 of that year. The *Saint John* had left Galway, Ireland, for Boston, September 5, running into heavy weather off Cape Cod a month later.

The storm itself was well remembered around New England for many years. Rain began to fall October 6 late in the afternoon, and by midnight a violent storm from the northeast set in. Many other vessels were wrecked at various locations along the coast, while in Chelsea, Massachusetts, the walls of the partly constructed Universalist Church on Chestnut Street blew down with a terrific crash. Many other cities and towns in Massachusetts were swept by the gale, and damage was exceedingly heavy.

When the weather turned thick, Captain Oliver of the *Saint John* ordered the crew to heave to, heading northeast. At 4:00 the next morning they wore ship and stood south. Several hours later Captain Oliver reached a point off Minot's Ledge Light, and noticed the British brig *Kathleen* anchored just off Cohasset.

Hoping to gain the protection of a landlocked harbor, Oliver ran before the wind, dropping anchor near the newly completed but unlighted Minot's Ledge Lighthouse. The wind increased, the waves grew higher, and soon the *Saint John* began to drag her anchors.

Although the frightened crew cut away the masts, it was soon apparent that the brig was doomed. Slowly but inevitably the Irish immigrant ship neared the rocks. Suddenly a wave higher than the rest loomed before the terrified passengers and crew. Of gigantic proportions, the breaker rolled in toward the vessel, carrying the brig with its screaming cargo toward the rocky ledge.

Hundreds were watching the disaster from the Cohasset shore, while many others stood at the Glades House in Scituate. As they saw the vessel ready to pile up on the Grampus, they knew that the brig was doomed. They also realized that since the waves were too high to launch a lifeboat, few would be saved from the *Saint John*. The men of Cohasset and Scituate could do nothing except wait for the elements to subside.

Ripping and grinding its way over the outer rocks, the *Saint John* wallowed in the trough of the sea, buffeted by each wave as it swept by. Directly in its path was the Grampus, the grave of many a sturdy ship. With a tearing crash, the *Saint John* struck the ledge and began to break up.

The towering breakers swept over the vessel, twenty and thirty feet high, each wave carrying several victims to their death until only a few remained alive aboard the wreck. The ringbolt holding the jolly boat in place snapped, dropping the small boat into the ocean. Twenty-five persons jumped into the frail craft, which capsized, throwing its occupants into the sea. Only the captain and one boy managed to swim back to the ship, while all the others perished. A great wave now swept the long boat some distance from the ship, and a number of passengers drowned trying to swim to it. The captain and eleven others reached it, landing at the Glades an hour later after a dangerous trip through the high waves.

Meanwhile the seas were going down rapidly, and a rescue boat from shore started for the wreck. Rowing through the waves, they passed the captain and the others in the longboat, and decided from the fact that only twelve were in it that all others aboard the *Saint John* had been rescued. So the lifesavers rowed on by the wreck and headed for the British brig *Kathleen*. They had not seen the survivors aboard the *Saint John* because of the high waves.

Two incidents should be mentioned here. An Irishman, Patrick Swaney by name, was aboard the *Saint John* with his eleven children, and they were all swept overboard by the same wave. Swaney, with his youngest child at his breast, swam toward the longboat. When he had almost reached his destination, a gigantic wave engulfed him, and neither he nor the child was ever seen again. Since all his other children had perished, that was the end of the Swaney family. A fourteen-year-old Irish lad had secreted himself aboard the immigrant ship at the start of the journey because his two sisters were going to America. When the crash came, he jumped into the jolly boat, swam back when it was swamped, and was later helped into the longboat. On reaching shore he discovered that both his sisters had been lost.

The great shipwreck off Cohasset attracted the attention of Henry David Thoreau, who was planning to visit Cape Cod. When the regular boat failed to run because of the storm, Thoreau went by land, stopping at Cohasset. On the train he noticed many Irish people on their way to the scene. Arriving at Cohasset, he made his way through Cohasset Common. As Thoreau walked by the graveyard, he saw an immense hole freshly dug there, where the bodies of the victims were to be placed.

Reaching the ocean, Thoreau found the sea still breaking violently over the rocks. More than twenty-six bodies had been recovered from the vessel. A woman who came to Boston without her baby months before had been expecting her sister to bring the child with her on the *Saint John*. On hearing of the tragedy she went down to the scene for particulars. The men in charge advised her to examine the remains of those who had come ashore. As the mother opened the lid of one of the coffins, she found her own child in her sister's arms, both cold in death. The poor lady died three days later as a result of this terrible shock.

The men who worked straight through all the excitement made a deep impression on Henry David Thoreau as they continued collecting the seaweed as if nothing else mattered. Separating bits of cloth and sticks from it, the men piled up the kelp and rockweed undisturbed by the possibility of turning up a dead body at any time. Much debris filled the cove. A man's garments were arranged on a rock, then came a woman's scarf, a gown, and a straw bonnet. A large section of the brig forty feet long lying behind one of the rocks attracted Thoreau, and he climbed down to where he could examine the wreckage. Quoting from his story, we read:

> *I was even more surprised at the power of the waves, exhibited on this shattered fragment, than I had been at the sight of the smaller*

fragments before. The largest timbers and iron braces were broken superfluously, and I saw that no material could withstand the power of the waves; that iron must go to pieces in such a case, and an iron vessel would be cracked up like an egg-shell on the rocks. Some of these timbers, however, were so rotten that I could almost thrust my umbrella through them. They told us some were saved on this piece, and also showed where the sea had heaved it into this cove which was now dry. When I saw where it had come in, and in what condition, I wondered that any had been saved on it. A little further on, a crowd of men was collected around the mate of the Saint John, who was telling his story. He was a slim-looking youth, who spoke of the captain as the master, and seemed a little excited. He was saying that when they jumped into the boat she filled, and the vessel lurching, the weight of the water in the boat caused the painter to break, and so they were separated. Whereat one man came away saying,—"Well, I don't see but he tells a straight story enough. You see, the weight of the water in the boat broke the painter. A boat full of water is very heavy,"—and so on, in a loud and impertinently earnest tone, as if he had a bet depending on it, but had no humane interest in the matter.

Another, a large man, stood near by upon a rock, gazing into the sea, and chewing large quids of tobacco, as if that habit were forever confirmed with him.

Further, we saw one standing upon a rock who, we were told, was one that was saved. He was a sober-looking man, dressed in a jacket and gray pantaloons, with his hands in the pockets. I asked him a few questions, which he answered; but he seemed unwilling to talk about it, and soon walked away. By his side stood one of the lifeboat men, in an oil-cloth jacket who told us how they went to the relief of the British brig, thinking that the boat of the Saint John, which they passed on the way, held all her crew. . . . There were one or two houses visible from these rocks, in which were some of the survivors recovering from the shock which their bodies and minds had sustained. One was not expected to live.

We kept on down the shore as far as a promontory called Whitehead, that we might see more of the Cohasset Rocks. . . . We afterwards came to the lifeboat in its harbor, waiting for another emergency; and in the afternoon we saw the funeral procession at a distance, at the head of which walked the captain with the other survivors.

Many years after the last bruised and battered body of the immigrants had been placed in the Cohasset cemetery, the Irish people of Boston visited the graveyard to dedicate a graceful granite shaft in memory of the shipwrecked victims. Because of this act of the Ancient Order of the Hibernians, Patrick Swaney and his eleven children, as well as the others who perished, will probably not be forgotten.

In his book *The Story of Minot's Light*, Snow wrote about Captain Michael Neptune Brennock, a Cohasset diver who later served as a lifeguard during the construction of Minot's Ledge Lighthouse in the 1850s. Snow described Brennock's rescue of a woman passenger of the *Saint John* from the surf. He launched a lifeboat to pick up what he believed was the body of a lifeless woman, but it turned out she was very much alive and Brennock later reported that she had "married twice since."

The nineteen-foot granite Celtic Cross raised in Cohasset Central Cemetery, overlooking Little Harbor, is inscribed: "This cross was erected and dedicated May 30, 1914, by the A.O.H. [Ancient Order of Hibernians] and the L.A.O.H. [Ladies Ancient Order of Hibernians] of Massachusetts to mark the final resting place of about forty-five Irish immigrants from a total company of ninety-nine

Minot's Light during a storm

who lost their lives on Grampus Ledge off Cohasset October 7, 1849, in the wreck of the brig St. John from Galway, Ireland. R.I.P."

A memorial service is held at Cohasset Central Cemetery every October by the Ancient Order of the Hibernians Division One of Plymouth, Massachusetts, and the Massachusetts State Board. In 1999, the 150th anniversary of the tragedy was marked with a variety of events in Cohasset, including Irish music and dancing and a special Sunday mass celebrated partly in Gaelic. Irish villagers traveled to Cohasset to observe the anniversary.

Only one of the survivors of the wreck, a woman named Mary Kane, remained in Cohasset. She married James St. John, a father of five children. Their great-great-grandson was present at the unveiling of the Boston Irish Famine Memorial in 1998.

CHAPTER 17

The Minot's Light Storm

The storm which began on Monday, April 14, 1851, developed into a gale which proved to be one of the severest of the century along the shores of Massachusetts. Damage to shipping was estimated in hundreds of thousands of dollars, while property all along the coast was destroyed. Many of the residents of New England remembered the gale for one reason, the total destruction of Minot's Ledge Lighthouse off the shores of Cohasset, Massachusetts.

The light had been built because of the many shipwrecks in the area south of Boston. In 1847 Captain Daniel Lothrop made a survey of the shipping losses in the vicinity from 1817 to 1847. He found that thirty-nine ships had been wrecked off Cohasset during that period with the loss of many lives, so the lighthouse was built.

Completed January 1, 1850, the tower was constructed on iron stilts, which rose to a height of sixty feet above the water. (The entire height of the tower was seventy-five feet.) In the spring of 1850 several great storms weakened the lighthouse, causing the keeper to resign his position, but a new man was found willing to accept the responsibility and danger.

With the coming of 1851 John W. Bennett, the new keeper, realized that the tower was in danger. He wrote several letters asking to have the lighthouse strengthened. But since the man who built the tower, Captain William H. Swift, scorned any suggestion that the light would fall, nothing was done.

A terrific tempest swept the Atlantic in March, and the tower swayed four feet in the gale. Damage was great, but the storm finally went down. The assistant keeper, Joseph Wilson, visited Boston on leave a few days later. During his stay in the city a friend asked him whether it would be difficult to hire another capable man for the position in the event that Keeper John W. Bennett gave up his post at the lighthouse.

"Yes, sir," he replied. "I shall stay as long as Mr. Bennett does, and when we leave the light, it will be dangerous for any others to take it." The young man, only twenty, was feeling rather happy that the winter was over. He was looking forward to being at the light the coming summer, with the warmth and sunshine making up for the winter of terror he had recently experienced. But the summer never came for Assistant Keeper Wilson.

While he was in Boston, he was also asked what he would do if the light should fall. He answered that he was quite confident of reaching the shore. In view of what actually happened three weeks later, his remarks take on special significance. His final statement was that he would stay at the light as long as the tower stood. When the time came, that is exactly what happened.

The head keeper, John W. Bennett, spent the next few days at the light tightening and strengthening the braces. He found the dory smashed beyond all hope of repair, however, and made arrangements to go to Boston to purchase a new one as soon as Assistant Keeper Wilson returned from his leave. A relatively calm spell was enjoyed the first week in April, but around the 8th of that month easterly winds began to blow. Bennett decided to leave the light when the east wind diminished somewhat, and on the morning of Friday, April 11, he flew the signal for the boat to come out. Leaving the weakened structure in charge of the two assistant keepers, Joseph Antoine and Joseph Wilson, Head Keeper Bennett sailed away from the lighthouse never to return. It was the last time he saw either man alive.

Arriving on the mainland, Keeper Bennett proceeded to the Custom House in Boston, where he interviewed Collector Philip Greely concerning the purchase of his new boat. The next day he returned to Cohasset and made an effort to reach the light, but the easterly wind had increased so that a heavy sea was running at Minot's Ledge. Sunday the wind grew stronger, and by night the surf was seen hitting fairly high against the structure on the lonely ledge. Late Monday the wind had developed into a gale which intensified to hurricane force by

Wednesday morning. The exact course of the storm on April 16, 1851, was east-northeast.

On the mainland, the storm was causing considerable destruction up and down the coast. Scituate Harbor was damaged to the extent of $5,000. Several houses on Pleasant Beach in Cohasset were entirely swept away. A large three-story hotel was floated right out from its underpinning, with almost a score of guests escaping in time. A few moments after the occupants had left the building, the sea broke over it, smashing the hotel into four great sections in a comparatively short time. The storm raged all along the coast from New York to Portland, Maine. The feeling was general that the storm brought a higher tide and greater gale than any since December 1786, when thirteen people froze to death on Lovell's Island in Boston Harbor after their ship had been wrecked.

The tide at Dorchester, Massachusetts, rose seven feet higher than usual, while a Brighton man crossing the Cambridge Bridge was blown into the Charles River but saved himself from drowning. The old railroad depot at Wilmington Junction and two barns at Tewksbury were demolished, with a house and many chimneys blown down at Danvers.

Church steeples suffered in many localities. That of the new Baptist church in Charlestown was blown down, the steeple crashing on a Mr. Locke of Lexington, who died shortly afterwards. The steeple of the Catholic church in Pawtucket, one of New England's tallest, was blown down. East Boston's new Episcopal church at the corner of Decatur and Paris Streets was moved from its foundations on Tuesday night and blown down altogether the following day.

Deer Island in Boston Harbor was in the direct path of the tempest. The new seawall was destroyed, and the water swept right across the island to carry three buildings out to sea. The boys at the Deer Island school had a narrow escape, as they were caught in their dormitory with the water steadily rising around them. The instructor waded through water three feet deep to warn them of the danger. By midnight the water had risen to a height of five feet, and the roof of the building fell in. The instructor and the boys feared they would be drowned as the waves battered the house, but by dawn a team of oxen arrived and took them to higher ground. A few hours later the boys watched their dormitory swept out to sea. The passage through Shirley Gut was widened to twice its former size.

Winthrop, Massachusetts, across Shirley Gut from Deer Island, was heavily hit by the gale. In the Point Shirley district, Taft's Hotel was inundated, the waves breaking completely over the structure to destroy the front of the hotel. The occupants fled to higher ground, stopping with a Mr. Wyman for the night. At the height of the storm, the roof of the Taft barn was carried away, crashing on a pleasure yacht on the back beach, completely demolishing the craft. At Pleasant Beach, Isiah Baker had a public house. Mr. Baker was able to escape with his boarders before the building broke up completely. Several vessels were pushed ashore onto the beach, with a number of sailors drowned. The Fay family, then living at Winthrop Beach, were rescued just in time as their house was hit by the surf.

Derby Wharf in Salem was ruined. The railroad track at Collin's Cove and the bridge between Forrester Street and Northey's Point were carried away, and the sea rushed into the tunnel. In Beverly the sea washed over Tuck's Point and over Water Street, while the tide in Gloucester was said to have been the highest in fifty years. Michael Duley's store there was carried away.

The Merrimack River rose twenty-two inches higher than the record of December 1839, flooding warehouses and cellars on the lower side of Water Street, Newburyport. Twenty thousand dollars' damage was sustained in that town. Below South Street the river swept over the whole length of the turnpike road to Plum Island.

The brig *Primrose* went ashore off Plum Island. Captain Bokman, not able to take an observation for several days, supposed the craft in Boston Bay. The *Primrose* hit a reef near the Emerson Rocks, and began to break up. For three hours rescuers tried to make fast lines thrown from the brig. At 2:00 in the afternoon the rope was made fast, and the nine shipwrecked men made their way to safety.

At Newcastle, New Hampshire, the ocean washed across the roads, making an island of Jaffrey Point. Several families, believing that another deluge had come to destroy the world, did nothing to escape, as they felt they were doomed. The next day, however, the tide went down, and they returned to their regular pursuits.

Many schooners were driven ashore at Rockport, Nahant, and Salem Harbor. Seven vessels were wrecked at Marblehead, while it is known that a number of mariners were drowned off Marshfield.

The city of Boston actually became an island during the Wednesday high tide as the water swept across the neck, cutting the city off from the mainland completely. On Harrison Avenue the water was four feet deep, and the tide flowed entirely across Washington Street near the corner of Waltham Street. In downtown Boston the waves swept right up State Street, with the area around the Custom House three feet under water. Broad Street was partially submerged, the waves continuing up Central and Milk S treets. It is said that Merchants Row was reached by the great tide. The record high tide submerged both the Charlestown and Chelsea bridges. The evening Transcript for April 16, 1851, reported that no cars were operated over the Old Colony Railroad line that morning.

> *The rails have been washed up, so that they lie crosswise hundreds of feet in many places. . . . This is believed to be the highest tide ever known in Boston. It began to recede slowly about twelve o'clock. Thousands of spectators flocked down to the wharves to witness the grand spectacle which the waters . . . presented.*
>
> *Great apprehensions are felt in regard to the lighthouse at Minot's Ledge. The weather is still too misty to distinguish if it is still standing.*

At the time this article was written, however, Minot's Light was still fairly upright. The two heroic keepers had continued to carry out their tasks in spite of the terrific odds against them. They kept the bell ringing and the lamps burning for the ships in distress outside the ledge. Their worst night was about to begin. The storm seemed to have spent its fury, but at is so often the case, the great seas grew even higher as evening came.

No one will ever know the exact circumstances of the tragedy which befell the two brave keepers out on the rock. The following explanation is offered as a possibility. It is, however, an account in which all the known facts are put together in a sequence that may be considered reasonable.

We know that several families living at the Glades in Scituate saw the gleam of Minot's Light about 10:00 that fateful Wednesday night. Thus we may naturally assume the light was still standing at that time. The two men, realizing their danger would be greatest around high tide at midnight, prepared a message for the outside world in case they failed to survive the storm. Casting the bottle containing the message out from the lighthouse, Wilson and Antoine now made their plans for what proved to be their last night in this world.

The wind had abated appreciably, but the great tide was slowly rising, sending wave after wave through the upper framework of the tottering structure. There was still that terrifying surge of hundreds of tons of foaming surf just below them. The doomed tower, rocking perceptibly back and forth, seemed about to crash at any time. Higher and higher the billows swept, until almost every wave smashed against the keepers' quarters sixty feet above the ledge. Probably around 11:00 that night the central support snapped completely off, leaving the top-heavy, thirty-ton lantern tower to be upheld by the already weakened outside piling.

The large five-and-one-half inch rope hawser, which had been fastened into position by Keeper Bennett, ran from the top of the tower to a seven-ton granite rock located about two hundred feet in the lee of the lighthouse. Keeper Bennett used this cable to get on and off the tower whenever a turbulent sea was running.

Many believe that this cable, pulled by the huge rock as the boulder in turn was pushed toward shore by the sea, was a contributing factor in the destruction of the edifice. Keeper Bennett usually slackened the

Boston Custom House during the Minot's Light storm (from Snow's Boston Bay Mysteries and Other Tales*)*

hawser when a storm came up, but it is a question whether this was beneficial to the lighthouse. If the rock started moving, the slack would soon be taken up.

With the central support cracked off, the tower became more and more dangerous. The cable attached to the rock probably had the same effect that a rope would have tied to the top of a high tree after it is almost chopped through, with the granite block creating a pull like men trying to bring the tree down. Inch by inch the granite block moved toward the shore, gradually increasing the strain on the eight remaining iron supports. Without question the lighthouse slanted at an angle of twenty degrees from the perpendicular by midnight. The previous afternoon a man with a telescope, standing on the beach at Cohasset, was peering anxiously in the direction of the ledge. He detected a decided list toward shore when he occasionally saw the structure through the mist, and felt that the lighthouse was doomed.

Just before 1:00 on the morning of April 17, 1851, because of the combined forces of wind, sea, and straining hawser, the Minot's Ledge Lighthouse toppled over into the sea. One by one the pilings broke, snapping like pipe stems, until only two or three remained. There the tower rested for a time.

The tower at Minot's Light topples over into the sea during the storm of April 16–17, 1851

The keepers realized that the end was near. Wishing in some way to communicate with their loved ones ashore, they seized the heavy hammer and began to pound furiously on the lighthouse bell. We know that this signal was heard, for many residents at the Glades later recalled the sound of the bell which came over the water to them even above the roar of the surf at 1:00 that wild morning.

With the tower so bent over that the storeroom and capping received the full force of each breaking wave, the remaining supports soon gave way, and the great tower plunged beneath the ocean waves. The government had made a costly mistake. The sea reclaimed the ledge for its own.

But what of the two keepers?

Letting themselves down by the hawser into the water, the two men, each with a life preserver strapped to his back, dropped into the boiling surf. We believe that Antoine and Wilson did come down the hawser, for the stay was later found, and from its appearance it seemed probable that the lanyard connecting it to the lighthouse had been let loose. It had been tied in such a way that only human hands could have loosened it.

The body of Joseph Antoine was washed ashore soon afterward at Nantasket. The writer believes it possible that young twenty-year-old Wilson tried to live up to his expressed determination to reach land.

A short distance from the Glades lies Gull Rock. Here it was that Joseph Wilson was washed ashore, more dead than alive, terribly chilled and bruised by the battering of the icy waves. He crawled up to the top of the rock, and discovered he was not on the mainland. This disappointment, after his long swim from the lighthouse, was too much for Wilson, and he sank, exhausted, in a cleft of the Gull Rock far above the reach of the outgoing tide. He probably died before morning of exhaustion and exposure. It is not all conjecture, however, for when the body of Joseph Wilson was discovered, the position and condition indicated that the young man reached the rock alive.

When Keeper Bennett had been prevented from going out to the tower, he went to his home on White Head, near the Glades. As the storm increased, the water swept across the shore and surrounded his residence, forcing the keeper to leave his home. Restless and uneasy about the fate of his fellow workers out on the lighthouse, he wandered along the beach. Around 4:00 the next morning, perhaps at the very time when his assistant, Wilson, was near death on Gull Rock, John Bennett began to notice debris coming ashore. He went down to the edge of the sea. To his amazement Bennett recognized some of his own

clothing which he had left at the lighthouse. Wreckage was also coming in, and he gathered two or three fragments from the rolling breakers. His worst fears were realized when he saw the pieces of timber
were actually from the light itself, proving that without question it had
fallen.

Captain William H. Swift visited the ruins of Minot's Light on April
22, 1851, and made a sketch of the ledge with the broken piling. He also
drew the lighthouse tower itself, as it lay in the water with only a part
of the side showing. He probably experienced the bitterest moments of
his life when he stood on the rolling deck of the boat and sketched the
symbol of his costly failure.

The gale which caused the destruction of the lighthouse off Cohasset
has since been referred to as the Minot's Light Storm of 1851.

Minot's Ledge Lighthouse was rebuilt. A fine stone beacon, rising to
a height of 114 feet, was erected on the site of the old tower, and after
a wait of nine and a half years, the welcome gleam of its rays flashed
out on November 15, 1860. (The tower was first lighted by Keeper
Joshua Wilder.) Although many fear that this tower may some day fall
into the sea, the keepers feel that nothing less than an earthquake can
ever shake it from its foundations.

During the many yearly storms at the new lighthouse, the surf often
goes over the very top of the tower, and one may well imagine the
lonely lives the keepers pass on the ledge. As the gales roar in from the
depths of the Atlantic with gigantic waves sweeping up the sides of the
tower, the men in the lighthouse often think of that night, now so long
ago, when two brave men stood side by side to keep their last faithful
watch that ended in eternity.

The year 1851 was monumentally bad for New England shipping interests.
Less than six months after the Minot's Light Storm, the Yankee Gale of 1851
lambasted the Gulf of St. Lawrence and much of the New England fishing fleet.
More than nineteen vessels from Gloucester alone were lost in the storm,
and it was estimated that a total of 160 lives were lost in the region. The
Yankee Gale is considered the worst marine disaster in the history of Prince
Edward Island.

The second (1860) Minot's Ledge Lighthouse was renovated in the late
1980s. A short time later the Cohasset Historical Commission oversaw the

installation of a replica of the top portion of the lighthouse at Government Island, incorporating some of the blocks removed from the lighthouse. The replica lantern atop the blocks contains a third-order Fresnel lens that was used in Minot's Ledge Light from 1964 to 1971.

In 1997 a group of Cohasset residents began a campaign to erect a granite memorial at Government Island to Joseph Antoine and Joseph Wilson, the young assistant keepers who lost their lives in 1851. The monument was finished and dedicated on May 21, 2000. The event was a joint effort of the Minot Ledge Light Keepers Memorial Committee, the American Lighthouse Foundation, the First Coast Guard District, and the towns of Cohasset and Scituate. The ceremony included the playing of taps echoing from a distant location.

CHAPTER 18

The City of Columbus

One of the most terrible marine disasters in the annals of Massachusetts steamship navigation was the loss of the Boston and Savannah liner *City of Columbus* at Martha's Vineyard in 1884, with the death of 100 passengers and members of the crew.

When she sailed from Nickerson's Wharf in Boston (across Northern Avenue Bridge in South Boston), the steamer had eighty-seven passengers and a crew of forty-five. The *City of Columbus* possessed the highest rating possible, with an A-1 classification and was amply provided with fixtures, life preservers, and boats as required by law. It was a happy group of travelers who sailed away from Boston that January afternoon, for they were leaving the wintry weather for the South's warm sunny climate.

As the steamer rounded Cape Cod, the night was clear and cold. The *City of Columbus*, all her lights visible, continued down the coast. The weather was getting colder, with a strong wind blowing from the northwest. By 1:30 in the morning the captain, constantly on his feet since the ship had sailed, believed it safe to turn in. The dangerous part of the journey, around Cape Cod, lay behind, and the vessel was now halfway through Vineyard Sound. Captain S. C. Wright told his first mate, Edwin Fuller, the course to follow:

> When [Tarpaulin] Cove bears north, change the course to west southwest.

It later developed that the man at the wheel, Quartermaster Mac-Donald, had not heard the low-voiced instructions the captain gave the first mate. Captain Wright then retired to his cabin in the rear of the pilot house, but for some reason did not go to bed. He sat down on the floor with his back against a stanchion. The wind was now north-northwest. Robert Bennet Forbes, master mariner of the nineteenth century, said later in referring to the ship that "any ordinary landsman without chart or compass could have taken her clear of all danger." The passage in the Vineyard Sound at this point is almost five miles wide, but the tired and overconfident mate did not realize that the combined force of wind and tide near Menemsha Bight was slowly dragging the great steamer to disaster.

At a few seconds before quarter of four that morning, the lookout was pacing the deserted deck forward of the wheelhouse when he suddenly noticed a buoy on the starboard side of the ship. Shouting a warning at the top of his voice, he received no answer from the pilot-house, so he rushed toward the man at the wheel. First Mate Fuller, however, hearing the cry, excitedly ordered Quartermaster MacDonald to port his helm.

The shouting aroused Captain Wright, who was still sitting on the floor of his cabin. Rushing into the wheelhouse, Wright cried out, "Hard to port!" and ordered the engines stopped. It was too late, for in less than thirty seconds the *City of Columbus* crashed on the hidden rocks of the Devil's Bridge at Martha's Vineyard, and disaster followed.

At this location there was a murderous double ledge which projected out under water. The outer reef where the ship hit was locally known as the Devil's Back. And such it proved on that luckless night of 1884. The ship remained afloat barely four minutes after she hit, for the captain now made his greatest mistake.

"I . . . saw the buoy on the port side about two points forward of beam and about three hundred yards distant," said the captain later. (The hull was found inside the buoy.) "She immediately struck. I ordered the engines reversed, and she backed out about twice her own length. The steamer stopped immediately, and I ordered the jib hoisted and endeavored to head her for the north, but she filled forward and listed to port so that the plank sluice was about four feet under water." Thus the captain ordered the vessel backed off the rocks which had ripped open the ship's bottom, and she sank at once. (In 1887 the *Gate City* hit the same ledge, but stayed on, and no one was lost.)

The *City of Columbus* crashed on the ledge at 3:45 that morning, and by ten minutes past four most of the men, women, and children on the liner had perished. Number six lifeboat was launched but capsized at once. The crew lowered another boat, which was crushed against the side of the ship. Four men later reached shore in it, however. Some of the men managed to set adrift one of the life rafts, but all aboard were swept off and drowned. Although a few survivors reached shore holding spars or woodwork, most of the others sank to their death in the icy waters.

The remaining twenty or so persons in the rigging suffered all the tortures that living people could endure. Frozen onto the shrouds because of the surf which lashed around them, and numbed by the zero wind which swept through their thin garments, the survivors, all men, waited for daylight. An hour after dawn the sufferers were glad-

A dramatic illustration of the wreck of the City of Columbus, *from the* Police Gazette *of February 9, 1884 (courtesy of the Martha's Vineyard Historical Society)*

dened when they saw smoke from a steamer which appeared around the west end of Cuttyhunk Island, dead to the windward of them. Four miles away, the ship was within easy view, and the watchers in the rigging counted the minutes before the vessel could arrive to save them. But their hopes were in vain. To their dismay, the steamer continued on her regular run up the coast, ignoring the now thoroughly discouraged victims. The ship had been the steamer *Glaucus*, commanded by Captain Bearse.

The keepers of the Gay Head Lighthouse had noticed a light out near the end of the Devil's Bridge and were organizing a crew to go to the wreck. Gay Head Lighthouse Keeper Horace N. Pease had been called by his assistant at 6:00 that morning. Realizing that a shipwreck had taken place, Pease ordered Assistant Keeper Frederick Poole to make up a crew to row out to the scene. By dawn the attempt was begun. Poole had recruited lifesavers from the Gay Head Indians. Despite the heavy surf, the lifeboat was launched into the breakers, but it soon overturned. All man reached the beach safely. Now soaking wet, their clothing was beginning to freeze. Poole ordered the men to remove their shoes and start out again in their stockings so their feet would not freeze. This time the lifeboat was successfully launched, and the dangerous waves were conquered. After an hour's struggle with the oars, the volunteers reached the scene of the wreck. Since the lifeboat would have capsized had it approached too close to the mast, the survivors, still clinging to the rigging, were told to jump into the water, where they would be picked up.

One by one the men in the shrouds jumped into the icy waves, and each one was quickly rescued by the lifesavers. The overcrowded lifeboat now started for land, but another danger awaited the survivors. As the boat neared the shore, a breaking wave swamped the craft, and she capsized just off the beach. No one was drowned because of the quick work of the Gay Head Indians, who pulled the shipwrecked victims out of the surf.

Meanwhile Keeper Pease had notified the residents of the adjoining village of Squibnocket that a shipwreck had taken place, and soon their volunteer life-saving crew was on the way to the wreck. They reached the scene and had rescued several persons when a whistle in the distance drew their attention to the revenue cutter *Dexter* steaming toward them under forced draft. The Squibnocket lifeboat started for shore with its load of humanity, leaving nineteen forms clinging to the rigging.

When two boats were sent over to the wreck from the revenue cutter, seventeen more survivors dropped into the sea and were saved. Only two persons could now be seen clinging to the rigging. As it appeared that they were afraid to leave the wreck, young Lieutenant Rhodes of the *Dexter* volunteered to swim over to the *Columbus* to rescue the men. With a rope around his waist, Rhodes jumped into the January seas. Swimming through the water, he was hit by some floating wreckage and had to be hauled back to the *Dexter*. Shortly afterwards the wind went down, and Lieutenant Rhodes made a second attempt, this time using the dinghy. After trying unsuccessfully several times, Rhodes made the dinghy fast to the rigging, and began to climb the futtock shrouds. When he reached the two men, he found that both had frozen to death in the ratlines. Cutting the bodies down, Rhodes dropped them into the water, later rowing back to the revenue cutter with them. He left the wreck alone in the sea, with its icy rigging glistening in the sun and the bow of the *City of Columbus* barely showing above the waves. One hundred lives had been sacrificed to carelessness. (Estimates of the number of drowned run from 99 to 107.)

Several of the men who were active either on the wreck or ashore have left their personal testimony of the disaster. One of these individuals was Quartermaster Roderick A. MacDonald, the man at the helm when the vessel struck. His testimony follows:

> *I went on duty at midnight. Heavy winds, clear, could see lights plainly, a little hazy on land. Wind a little on starboard bow. The usual course on passing Tarpaulin Light on Naushon is southwest by west, which should take us clear of the Sow and Pigs Lightship. We generally intend to steer in midchannel. The captain went below about three-quarters of an hour before the vessel struck, and gave me the course a quarter or half an hour before he went below. It was southwest by west. The second mate was in the pilot house when the course was given. The second mate told me a short time before she struck not to go to leeward of that course. . . . The light shone out plain enough but you could not judge the distance from the light. It appeared closer than usual but I was not in command of the ship. That is the course I always steer through there.*

Quartermaster MacDonald, after the crash, was successful in swimming to the lifeboat, which had floated some distance from the wreck, and took charge of operations to reach the island. Time after time the crew tried to row directly for the shore, where they would have drowned in the great breakers, but MacDonald prevailed upon them to keep off until the calmer waters of Menemsha Bight were reached. By this time one of the passengers in the lifeboat had died of exposure, but the craft was landed safely near the home of an Indian named Ryan, where the survivors were given the best of care.

The aftermath of the shipwreck of the *City of Columbus* included many touching scenes. Among the bodies found was that of a young woman with a tiny pair of shoes frozen to her breast, her child having been separated from her in the terrifying moments after the crash.

Captain Bearse of the *Glaucus* was later called before the investigation committee and asked why he had not bothered to sail over closer to the wreck of the *City of Columbus*. He admitted that he recognized the ship on the Devil's Bridge as the *City of Columbus*, but since he knew she had been supposed to pass that particular point hours before, he figured all the survivors had been removed from the ship. He said at the investigation that he looked through his telescope at the wreck and could see no movement of any kind. Although the United States Marine Inspectors exonerated Captain Bearse, Robert Bennet Forbes condemned their

An artist's rendering of the wreck of the City of Columbus *off Gay Head (courtesy of U.S. Coast Guard)*

STORMS AND SHIPWRECKS OF NEW ENGLAND

action as "lame and impotent." Captain Forbes said that it was because of a deplorable dullness of mind and vision that Bearse did not sail close enough to see the men in the rigging, where he could have saved the lives of many who subsequently perished.

Captain S. C. Wright, the master of the *Columbus*, was deprived of his license as pilot and his certificate as shipmaster. Many years later a prominent Boston sea captain was ashore at Savannah, Georgia. As he walked up the pier, stepping between bales of cotton and other cargo piled up ready for shipment, he heard a voice hailing him. Stepping closer, the Boston mariner recognized the former master of the *City of Columbus* working as a stevedore on the wharves of Savannah.

────────────── ～ ──────────────

Some of the Gay Head Wampanoag Indians who assisted in the rescue efforts were awarded medals by the Massachusetts Humane Society, and these medals have been handed down to the present generation on the island. It is also said that some of the homes at Gay Head (now officially named Aquinnah) contain furniture made from pieces of the *City of Columbus*.

A joint resolution of Congress praised Lieutenant John U. Rhodes of the revenue cutter *Samuel Dexter* for his heroism in the *City of Columbus* rescue efforts, and also thanked the entire crew. Also, U.S. President Chester A. Arthur authorized Rhode's promotion by twenty-one numbers in grade, and the Massachusetts Humane Society presented him with a gold medal.

There were attempts to salvage items from the *City of Columbus* soon after it was wrecked. The ship's safe was successfully raised, but it proved to be almost empty. It was reported that the hull soon disappeared, virtually swallowed up by the sands around Devil's Bridge.

In a 1958 article for *Yankee Magazine*, Snow wrote about a memorial service for the victims of the *City of Columbus* disaster held at Gay Head Lighthouse in January of that year. At that point, Snow wrote, there was only one man still living who had actually walked the decks of the *City of Columbus*—Francis Forrester Haskell of Haverhill, Massachusetts.

Among the relics shared by Snow when he lectured across New England was a pair of baby's shoes, said to have been worn by a tiny victim of this 1884 tragedy. The shoes are now in the collection of the Peabody-Essex Museum of Salem, Massachusetts. The quarterboard from the *City of Columbus* is exhibited in the carriage shed at the Martha's Vineyard Historical Society's museum in Edgartown.

CHAPTER 19

A Nantucket Rescue

The evening of January 19, 1892, was a typical wintry night on the Nantucket coast. The sky was dull and overcast, with an occasional squall to vary the monotony. The weather was nearer zero than the freezing point, and the northerly winds were biting across the sand dunes around the Coskata Life-Saving Station. The regular patrols departed and returned; Keeper Walter N. Chase took a final glance along the coast as darkness descended, but there was no vessel in distress near his station.

A short time later, however, the three-masted schooner *H. P. Kirkham* struck far off shore on the Rose and Crown Shoal. The vessel, commanded by Captain McCloud of Liverpool, Nova Scotia, settled into the sand, forcing the men to take to the rigging. The location is not visible from the Coskata Station, which is on the inner or western side of Coskata Beach. At daylight Keeper Chase receive a telephone call from the keeper of Sankaty Head Light, who said that he had seen rockets from the vicinity of the Rose and Crown Shoal, and at dawn could make out a vessel's masts on the Bass Rip, ten miles away.

Keeper Chase called his crew at once, and they hauled the lifeboat across the sands to the outside of Great Point, where they successfully launched the craft into the foaming breakers. Meanwhile Keeper Remsen at Sankaty Head Lighthouse telephoned Vineyard Haven for a tug to proceed to the scene of the shipwreck. The lifeboat sailed the long distance to the *H. P. Kirkham* without incident, finding it five miles farther

Late nineteenth-century image of Sankaty Head Lighthouse (U.S. Coast Guard)

out than on the Bass Rips as reported by Keeper Remsen. Since the starboard rail of the *Kirkham* was submerged, the men would have to be removed from that side. The lifeboat was then anchored with a long scope, and the hawser was taken over the weather bow. The boat dropped down with the current, carefully aided by skillful handling of the oars, and after several attempts the heaving stick was thrown into the rigging of the schooner.

The keeper shouted across to the sailors to bend a line to the heaving stick; this was done at once, and the end of a topsail clewline was taken aboard. The boat was slowly hauled toward the schooner. The frenzied sailors, anxious to leave their sinking ship, tried to haul in on their end of the line, but Keeper Chase passed his boat knife forward to the stroke oarsman, telling the schooner's sailors: "Pull that boat one foot nearer and we cut the line." Chase was six feet four, and very impressive; the sailors obeyed him instantly, letting go the hawser.

The end of the line tied with a bowline was thrown to the wreck. The first sailor to reach it put his leg through the loop, and Keeper Chase ordered him to jump overboard and hang on. Cautiously he followed directions. He jumped and was hauled aboard as the boat slacked away.

Then the lifeboat was brought in for the next man, and continued until every one of the seven men, who had been on the wreck for fifteen hours by this time, was in the boat.

The troubles of the lifeboat crew and the sailors they had rescued were not over, however. No land could be seen, but when on the crest of the waves, the men could barely make out the top of Sankaty Head Lighthouse. They weighed anchor and threw overboard the mast and sail as they would be of no further use in the long journey home against wind and tide. Three hours of hard rowing brought the lifeboat across the shoal, and the boat was then anchored to await the southern tide, which would set them toward land. At sunset they began rowing again, but six hours after leaving the wreck they had actually covered less than a mile. The location of the wreck was now nothing but sea and waves; the *Kirkham* had vanished.

The situation was very grave. They watched, hopefully at first and then in despair, for the Vineyard Haven tug, but it never came. Every few minutes they would ship a sea, after which frantic bailing would keep the lifeboat from swamping. At 9:00 P.M. the southern tide was done, and they had not landed. There was nothing left to do but to anchor again, as the northern tide would carry them out to sea again.

The men said afterwards that the period from 9:00 until 3:00 the next morning was the longest in their lives. Terrible scenes were enacted in the overcrowded lifeboat. The cross sea made the men violently sea-sick, while the waves threatened every minute to swamp them. When the tide changed, the wind went down and the men were visibly encouraged. The snow squalls ended and the sun came out. With the moderating weather and the favorable tide, the men rowed for Sias-conset, where they landed at 10:00 in the morning, having spent twenty-six hours at sea.

During the long night when the men did not come home, Keeper Chase's wife kept the watch at the station. Her thoughts during the period when the lifeboat failed to return can only be imagined. The crew had actually been given up for lost by friends along the shore who could not sight the small dory from any vantage point on the island. Dawn enabled the discouraged onlookers to sweep the ocean with their telescopes, and the lifeboat was finally sighted. This rescue and subsequent fight against a head-on sea brought acclamation from all New England, praise which the heroic rescuers deserved. The crew members under Keeper Chase were Jesse H. Eldredge, John Lyman, Charles B.

Cathcart, Josiah B. Gould, George H. Flood, and Roland H. Perkins. It had been an epic rescue of the sea.

In the month of January 1893, the keeper and his associates were presented with medals awarded them by the government, the presentations being made in the Unitarian Church. There was one sad note to the occasion, however. Surfman Roland H. Perkins, who had suffered severely from exposure during the long night out at sea, steadily grew worse after his return. Failing to rally, he died as a result of his part in the successful efforts to save the lives of those aboard the *H. P. Kirkham*, and his medal was given to representatives of his family, who were present at the church.

───────────── ～ ─────────────

When the Nantucket lifesavers were awarded their medals for heroism, the rescue was described in the government report as "one of the most remarkable rescues in the history of the life-saving service."

CHAPTER 20

The Bad Luck of the Jason

In many cases it seems that ships are like people. Some persons are born lucky while others are always having accidents from time to time. There have been barks, brigantines, or full-rigged ships which appear to have had their share of ill fortune. Sailors would fall from the rigging, or the vessels would strand while coming into the harbor, and if there happened to be any blow worth mentioning, there would be this particular ship right in the middle of it.

When accident after accident occurs in the lives of certain people, they are said to have bad luck. And so it is with ships of the sea. The story of the *Jason* is hard luck and bad luck from the start of its voyage to the finish. Even the sole survivor of the wreck died a short time later.

The ship *Jason* sailed from Barry, England, in February 1892, with a load of coal for Zanzibar. Three days out a great black object loomed across the bow of the *Jason*, crashing into the coal ship with terrific force. It was the steamer *Trilawie* from St. Ives. Temporary repairs were made, after which the *Jason* was placed in drydock at Queenstown. Another start was then made for Zanzibar.

While rounding the Cape of Good Hope, the ship encountered a terrific gale during which one of the men furling sail lost his hold and fell overboard. The *Jason* reached Zanzibar, discharged her cargo, and began a voyage for Calcutta. In the harbor of Calcutta one of the crew fell from a Hindoo craft and was drowned.

After loading a great cargo of jute at the Calcutta port, the *Jason* sailed for Boston. For once conditions seemed to favor the ship, with fair winds and pleasant weather. But the fair winds gave way to strong gales, which in turn developed into a hurricane. At the height of the storm the ship was laid over on her beam ends, all masts went by the board, and the vessel became a hopeless mass of wreckage. In the midst of the confusion the captain of the ship broke his leg.

After three days the storm went down. With a jury mast rigged, the *Jason* sailed for the nearest port, Mauritius, where she arrived ten days later. Six months were needed this time to repair the *Jason* and give her a new cabin. Almost everything was made over except the hull itself, which they decided had come through pretty well. They later found out how weakened the hull actually was.

The captain, with his broken leg, was sent back to England with his wife. There are those who say a woman should not be aboard a ship as she brings bad luck, but the worst luck aboard the *Jason* occurred after the lady had left for England with her husband.

Again the *Jason* attempted an Atlantic crossing, this time with a new captain. Hardly had they left port when another sailor fell out of the rigging and was killed. The jute cargo below decks swelled so much that the ship had to return and leave some of it behind. This caused a further substantial delay, but finally a start was made for America.

The new captain, McMillan by name, arrived with his ship off the New England coast the first day of December 1893, almost two years after the *Jason* had left England. Thick weather prevailed, with the captain uncertain as to his exact location. Falling in with a New York pilot boat, he was given his bearings, and shaped his course accordingly. Although he did not realize it, he was then approaching Cape Cod in such a way that he was doomed should an easterly set in. Cape Cod has a natural trap for sailing vessels from which very few escape. It is a triangular area made up of Pollock Rip Shoal, Chatham, and Highland Light. Once inside this area with a strong northeast breeze, the ship's doom is sealed, for there is not room enough to wear around and avoid the shoals to leeward or weather the Cape hard on the starboard tack.

A driving rain now began with the wind from the northeast, and the rain shortly turned to sleet and snow. Nauset Three Lights was the first landfall the *Jason* made, late in the afternoon of the 5th of December. The ship was on a lee shore and the captain realized there was no hope. The men worked hard to get out their boats and prepare for the disaster which they knew was coming.

Back on shore the vessel had been under close observation for hours. The telephone which runs from one Cape Cod life-saving station to another was constantly ringing that afternoon as the *Jason* made her way up the coast. Captain Charles first reported the ship off his Orleans station. Every station crew from Nauset Beach to Race Point hauled out their boat and gear and awaited the inevitable.

Down at Chatham, Captain Hezekiah F. Doane at Old Harbor Station was the first to report. "She's gone by me," said Doane.

The next to be heard from was Captain Charles at Orleans. "I've missed her," he said as he watched the *Jason* edge on up the coast.

Captain Daniel Cole at Cahoon's Hollow came through later with "She's gone by our station."

Finally came the last report. "I've got her," shouted Captain David Rich from Pamet River over the wire. [His name was actually John Rich —*Ed.*] "She's stranded off the beach."

The crew of the Pamet River Station rushed the beach cart to the scene. By this time the shore was piled high with wreckage, and the slatting of the *Jason*'s sails could be heard even above the storm. Unable to launch a lifeboat into the sea, the men fired their gun out to the vessel, but there was no response. Unknown to them, most of the sailors on the *Jason* had already perished when the mizzenmast fell into the sea. The ship, presumably weakened from her previous encounters,

A lifeboat returns from the wreck of the ship Jason, *December 1893. (Photo by John R. Smith)*

broke in two almost as soon as she struck. One person, a young man named Samuel Evans, had been too late to climb the mizzenmast with the others, and a great sea swept him overboard. His life belt secure, he swam to a nearby bale of yellow jute, grasped it, and knew no more until the men picked him up on the shore. (Jot Small says that the boy told him he had floated ashore and then grasped the jute bale to prevent the undertow from pulling him back.)

"Be I saved?" asked the lad, as he came to.

"Yes," was the answer, "but you're the only one." Twenty-six others had been engulfed by the storm. The great jute cargo littered the beach for miles, with many of the residents reaping a rich harvest because of the disaster. The foremast of the *Jason* continued to show out of the

Samuel J. Evans, sole survivor of wrecked ship Jason *(courtesy of Provincetown Museum)*

water day after day, prompting the observation that if the crew had chosen the right mast, many of them would have been saved. In the clear weather which followed, scores of pictures were taken of the broken ship, her stern showing out of water many yards from the bow. The broken rigging and tattered sails of the *Jason* presented a fascinating but awesome sight to the thousands who viewed her from the shelter of the mainland. It is said by some that part of the *Jason* can still be seen at low water off the shore, but not for many years has any of her cargo washed up on the beach.

Samuel Evans, the sole survivor, returned to England with the memory of the strange voyage of the *Jason* in his thoughts. When he sailed again shortly afterwards, it is said that he fell from his bunk and was killed. There are those who believe that every man aboard the *Jason* when she left England was doomed the moment the vessel sailed out of the harbor and Evans' death was delayed only a short time longer than the others.

Without question some shipwrecks are recalled more frequently than others as the years go by. The *Jason* is one of them. From time to time grizzled old sea captains, talking of the ways of the ocean, have mentioned the *Jason* among the shipwrecks they easily recall. This sad tale of the bad luck and subsequent disaster of the *Jason* holds an unusual place in the minds of the people of Cape Cod.

Nineteen of the victims of the *Jason* wreck are buried in Wellfleet Cemetery. William Evans, father of survivor Samuel Evans, wrote to the U.S. Life-Saving Service to express his gratitude "for their successful endeavors to save the life of our beloved son."

The location of the *Jason* is said to be just offshore of Truro's Ballston Beach, in thirty feet of water. In his 1928 book *Shipwrecks on Cape Cod*, Isaac Small wrote, "Out there today when the tide is low, protruding through the sands of the bar and the white caps that wash them, are the broken fragments of the sunken ship looking like tombstones in the village churchyard."

CHAPTER 21

The Monomoy Disaster

An event which excited much popular sympathy over the entire country in the year 1902 was the disaster which befell the Monomoy life-saving boat as she neared the beach at Monomoy Point, south of Chatham, Massachusetts, on the morning of March 17. Together with the subsequent rescue of the sole survivor, Surfman Ellis, by Captain Elmer Mayo, the event created an unusual amount of interest, especially around New England.

Two coal barges, the *Wadena* and the *Fitzpatrick*, had been stranded several days before on the Shovelful Shoal off Monomoy Point, and several men were rescued by the Monomoy life-saving crew. The weather moderated, allowing wreckers to go aboard and plan the task of lightening the vessels. On the evening of March 16 the weather grew heavy, so that all but a few of the men were taken ashore by the tug *Peter Smith*.

The next morning when the barge *Wadena* flew a distress signal, Captain Eldridge organized a lifeboat crew to reach the craft. At several places on the shoals the seas were extremely rough, but the surfboat reached the lee of the barge without further incident. With a line made fast, plans were formed for the return journey. Five men were on the barge, all of whom excitedly asked to be taken ashore. It is believed that the workers on the *Wadena* were in a partial state of panic and fright from their perilous position.

Four of the five men lowered themselves into the boat successfully, but the captain of the barge, who was a heavy man, let go his hold when he was a few feet above the lifeboat and fell, breaking the after thwart. The painter or rope was cut as soon as the five men had been placed in position in the lifeboat, and the trip to safety began. Getting out from the lee of the *Wadena*, the lifeboat was hit by a great wave, which partly filled the craft. This made the bargemen frantic, and they leaped to their feet in the lifeboat, throwing their arms about the bodies of the surfmen. One after another the seas struck the little lifeboat, until it finally filled and capsized with its thirteen occupants. Twice the lifeboat was righted by the surfmen in the water, but each time the seas overturned her.

The five bargemen were the first to drown since they could not get back to the overturned craft. The surfmen clung desperately to the bottom of the boat, but soon their strength began to fail. Surfman Chase was the first to perish, and then Nickerson and Small disappeared. Only five remained. Ellis, who was the sole survivor, later wrote down his experience. We quote now from his journal:

> *Captain Eldridge, Surfmen Kendrick, Foye and Rogers and myself still managed to hold to the boat. Every sea which struck the boat swept completely over us, almost smothering us. Kendrick was the next one of our crew to perish, and poor Foye soon followed him.*

Marshall W. Eldridge and crew outside the Life-Saving Station (courtesy of the Chatham Historical Society)

Captain Eldridge and Surfman Rogers and myself were the only ones left and we expected that we, too, would soon share the fate of our comrades.

Rogers was clinging to the boat about amidships, while Captain Eldridge and myself were holding on near the stern. Captain Eldridge called to me to help him get a better hold, and I managed to pull him on to the bottom of the boat, when a sea struck us and washed us both off. I managed to regain a hold on the bottom of the boat, and looking around for Captain Eldridge, I saw that he was holding on to the spar and sail which had drifted from underneath the boat, but was still fast to it. The seas were washing me off the boat continually at this time, and when I last saw our brave captain, he was drifting away from the boat holding on to the spar and the sail.

My strength was fast going, and when poor Rogers begged me to help him climb further up onto the boat, the only thing I could do was to tell him that we were drifting toward the beach, and that help would soon be at hand and to hang on.

Rogers had lost his strength, however, and failing to get a more secure place on the bottom of the boat, feebly moaning, "I have got to go," he fell off the boat and sank beneath the waters.

I was now alone on the bottom of the boat, and seeing that the center board had slipped part way out, I managed to get hold of it, and holding it with one hand had succeeded in getting my oil clothes, undercoat, vest, and boots off.

By that time the overturned boat had drifted down over the shoals in the direction of the barge Fitzpatrick, which was also stranded on the shoals, and when I sighted the craft I waved my hand as a signal for help. I soon saw those on the barge fling a dory over the side into the water, but could see nothing more of the dory after that until it hove in sight with a man in it rowing towards me.

The man in the dory was Captain Elmer F. Mayo, who at the time of the Monomoy disaster was aboard the barge *Fitzpatrick* in company with Captain Mallows of Chatham and the barge captain. There had been a fourteen-foot dory alongside the barge, which was hauled on deck the night before. The only oars aboard were too long for the dory, so Mayo cut them down.

Mayo knew nothing of the tragedy until he noticed Surfman Ellis drifting along, clinging to the overturned lifeboat. Realizing that a terrible catastrophe had occurred, Mayo stripped down to his underwear, let over the dory, and climbed down a rope into the little craft.

With improvised thole pins and oars so large he could hardly hold them, Mayo fought his way toward the lifeboat. Surfman Ellis saw the dory just as it reached him. It was a difficult feat to take Ellis from the water, but as both men were experts at the task of life saving, it was successfully accomplished. Mayo realized that Ellis could not stand the exposure much longer, and headed the dory for shore at once. Only his expert knowledge of the shoals and rips around Monomoy allowed Mayo to reach the shore, where Surfman Walter Bloomer rushed into the breakers to assist in beaching the dory. The two men were quickly cared for.

Mayo's feat had been one of outstanding heroism, earning for him the title "Hero of Monomoy." Both the United States and the Massachusetts Humane Society recognized Mayo's gallantry, awarding him medals for his rescue.

The people of New England quickly responded to a call for help for the widows of the Monomoy lifesavers. William U. Swan, then of the Associated Press, publicized the story throughout the nation, and a benefit meeting was held at the Tremont Theatre, Boston, where Ellis,

Surfman Ellis and his rescuer, Elmer Mayo

Mayo, and Mayo's dory were on view. In a comparatively short time a fund of several thousand dollars (actually $36,583.52) was raised for the widows of the men who sacrificed their lives that wintry morning off Cape Cod.

Keeper Marshall W. Eldridge and his crew were doing what they saw as their duty, but an official report by the Life-Saving Service stated that the men who gave their lives trying to save those aboard the *Wadena* may have died needlessly. "There was no more skillful or fearless crew on the whole coast," the report stated, "and since it appeared that the *Wadena* remained safe for days after the disaster, there was a general conviction that the men were practically a sacrifice, on the one hand to the needless apprehensions and senseless panic

Mack Memorial, with Chatham Light in the background (photo by Brian Tagne)

of the men from the barge, and on the other to their own high sense of duty, which would not permit them to turn their backs upon a signal of distress."

Seth Ellis was also presented a gold life-saving medal for his efforts. He became the acting keeper of the Monomoy Station soon after he survived the disaster, and within a few weeks he was leading a rescue. Both Ellis and his savior, Elmer Mayo, died in 1935.

A memorial obelisk was erected in 1903 near the Chatham Light Station, paid for by the mother and sister of William Henry Mack, twenty-nine-year-old owner of the *Wadena* who perished in the disaster. The inscriptions include Alfred Lord Tennyson's poem "Crossing the Bar."

A ceremony was held at the memorial on March 17, 2002, the centennial of one of the worst days in Cape Cod's twentieth-century maritime history.

CHAPTER 22

The Larchmont Disaster

Often we find that history teaches, but man disregards the lesson. It is the same way with marine disasters. When the *Portland* sank in 1898 carrying the only passenger list, tremendous agitation developed for requiring an extra list to be left ashore whenever a passenger vessel sailed from port. Yet in 1907, more than eight years after the Portland storm, the Joy liner *Larchmont* left her pier in Providence, Rhode Island, with the only passenger list available. Evidently the steamship lines of that period had learned nothing from bitter experience, continuing a policy which had caused such indignation with the general public. But the period of which we write has gone; today maritime regulations are better than in any other period in the nation's history.

It was at 7:00 on February 11, 1907, that the *Larchmont* left Providence, about half an hour behind her regular schedule. The wind was about northwest, blowing almost forty miles an hour, when Captain G. W. McVey took the steamer down the river. As the *Larchmont* approached Sabine Point, McVey gave charge of the wheel to Quartermaster Staples, under the supervision of Mr. Anson, the First Pilot.

Captain McVey now proceeded on his usual tour of the ship, after which he called on the ship's purser. At about quarter of eleven he passed through the pilothouse, where he conversed briefly with the man at the wheel. The pilot was in command of the course to be steered. The steamer's headlight, masthead light, and sidelights were all burning brightly and everything was in satisfactory order.

Shortly before 11:50, when Watch Hill Light bore four miles northwest, Quartermaster Staples, at the wheel, saw the lights of a schooner ahead. The vessel was yawing and luffing, making it hard to figure her course. As she appeared on the port side of the *Larchmont*, Staples swung his wheel hard-a-port, but evidently the schooner, later identified as the *Harry Knowlton*, luffed just at that time, for the schooner's red lights disappeared completely. The *Knowlton* was even then headed directly for the doomed *Larchmont*, crashing a moment later into the steamer's port side just forward of amidships.

As the schooner bore down on the steamer, several short, rapid blasts of the steam whistle were sounded from the wheelhouse of the *Larchmont*, bringing Captain McVey from his cabin into the pilothouse just as the schooner loomed up and smashed against the steamer. Captain McVey's own story follows:

> *Realizing that this was a severe blow, I at once rang the bell to call the engineer so as to have him report to me the conditions of affairs below. Failing to get any response, I at once sent Mr. Wyman, who had appeared on the scene, and Mr. Staples, the quartermaster, to get the desired information.*
>
> *At this time the boat became enveloped in steam, and everybody appeared panic-stricken except the crew. I at once from my station in the pilot house ordered everybody to their stations as I realized by the starboard list of the boat that she must be in a sinking condition.*
>
> *Almost immediately after this Mr. Wyman and the quartermaster reported to me that the* Larchmont *was in a sinking condition and I think told me that it was the request of the chief engineer that I should beach the boat as soon as possible.*
>
> *I at once proceeded to the pilot house, rang the necessary bells to start the engines ahead, but could receive no response and I turned again to the deck to superintend the clearing away of the boats.*
>
> *At this time the* Larchmont *had a very heavy starboard list, in fact, I think her freight deck was under water which brought my own boat which was the forward starboard boat quite near the water.*
>
> *At this time there were no passengers in the vicinity of my boat, and knowing that the only way to save lives in the proper manner was to lower my boat and go around to the other side of the* Larchmont, *I proceeded at once to have my boat lowered into the water and at this time the ones who got into my boat were the only ones that were on my side*

of the ship, unless some one might have been aft, hidden by the star-board paddlebox. . . . We at once proceeded around the bow of the sink-ing Larchmont *to get on her port side to be in a position to save life.*

The wind and sea, however, prevented Captain McVey's boat from helping those still aboard the *Larchmont*. In fact, it is doubtful if there were many on the *Larchmont* who could be helped by that time. When the captain had launched his lifeboat into the bitterly cold waters of Long Island Sound, five other lifeboats and two life rafts had already left the ship. It is true that one or two shady forms could be discerned through the steam and spray still standing on the deck, but they made no efforts to jump into the boat. All this time the *Larchmont* had been steadily settling in the water; she soon started her final plunge and dis-appeared into the icy February seas, carrying with her an unknown number of victims. Since it was then two minutes past 11:00, the entire incident covered a period of twelve minutes.

The six lifeboats and the two rafts were now left floating in the rough seas. As the night wore on, the survivors noticed the gleam of a light-house beacon far in the distance, and rowed for the welcome flash. The icy waves, driven by a wind which at times reached fifty miles an hour, swept over the boats and rafts until every person was coated with freezing spray. As it was practically impossible to do anything toward

The steamer Larchmont, *which sank after a collision near Block Island, February 11, 1907*

reaching land except drift before the wind, the passengers and crew still alive did what they could to face the icy gale.

Block Island was in the direct path of the survivors. Keeper Elam P. Littlefield of the Sandy Point Lighthouse [better known as Block Island North Lighthouse—*Ed.*] had been aroused by the barking of his dog Leo. Getting up to quiet the animal, Littlefield was startled by a knock against the window pane, and pulled upon the door. A boy fell across the threshold, muttering, "More coming, more coming."

It was then five minutes of six in the morning of February 12. Keeper Littlefield aroused his wife and five children, after which he telephoned the New Shoreham Life-Saving Station. Two guests at the lighthouse volunteered to help, and the first trip down to the beach was made. Purser Young of the *Larchmont* was brought back. "The *Larchmont* has gone down, 200 have perished," Young gasped, as oil was applied to his face. His body was completely encased in ice. One after another the survivors were brought into the old Sandy Point Lighthouse, until it resembled a hospital. Bedspreads were torn into strips for bandages to be used on frozen arms and legs. The keeper's eldest daughter, Addie Littlefield, took charge of the newcomers. It was a race with death to keep many of the sufferers alive, but only one man, the Turkish fireman of the wrecked vessel, succumbed. The work of the keeper was made easier by the arrival of the New Shoreham Lifesavers. Keeper Littlefield drove along the beach with his team, stopping here and there, while the victims were place aboard and rushed to the lighthouse.

A lifeboat came through the breakers with one live man, who jumped ashore. Left in the boat were ten dead men, all but one of whom had slowly frozen to death. This man had cut his own throat to end his agony. The survivor was quickly taken to the impromptu hospital and cared for. After the living had been attended to, thirty-eight bodies were brought to the station. The young boy who had first arrived at the lighthouse, Fred Heirgsell, now began to tell his story of the disaster, and it chilled the hearts of the keeper and his family. He described how the others had frozen to death. According to his account, he too was about to fall asleep when the lifeboat grated on the shore. He was barely able to reach the lighthouse when he was encouraged by the barking of a dog, whose commotion had already aroused the lighthouse keeper. Summoning his remaining strength, Fred Heirgsell rapped on the window pane, and the last he remembered was falling across the open doorway. Others told equally harrowing tales of exposure and suffering.

A recent photo of Block Island North Lighthouse at Sandy Point. The same lighthouse was standing at the time of the Larchmont *disaster. (Photo by Jeremy D'Entremont)*

Captain McVey landed at Block Island around 6:30 that morning, with his hands and feet terribly frozen. He was later taken home to Providence, where he was placed under a doctor's care. Although it had been a bitter experience, he had been subjected to much criticism for his actions. But it is always easy to criticize in times of extreme trouble and danger, and the majority of sea captains with whom I have talked have believed he did what they would have done.

The schooner *Harry Knowlton*, after striking the *Larchmont*, was abandoned by her captain, Frank T. Haley, and his crew three miles from Block Island. They rowed to safety at the Life-Saving Station of Weekahaug. A prominent Rockland sea captain expressed his opinion on the cause of the disaster as follows:

> *I have talked with both captains, and feel that it was a case of stubbornness on the part of the schooner's captain. According to his sworn testimony Captain Haley saw the steamer's red lights less than one hundred yards away from him, but he told his helmsman to keep her on her course. Technically he was right, as a schooner does have the right of way, but it was a case of bull headedness, as the* Knowlton *was yawing considerably.*

The disaster which befell the *Larchmont* was the last major marine calamity in the vicinity.

――――――――――― ～ ―――――――――――

The original name of the *Larchmont* was the *Cumberland*. In 1902, near Boston, she was rammed by another vessel and badly damaged. After extensive repairs, the steamer was bought and renamed by the Joy Line.

The estimates of the number who died in this tragedy range from 109 to around 300. The *Larchmont* today rests in about 130 feet of water, three miles southeast of Watch Hill. It is a popular site for divers. Gary Chellis of Atlantis Dive Charters in New London, Connecticut, describes visiting the wreck:

> *Diving the* Larchmont *is truly a trip back in time. It is still 1907 on the wreck. Swimming around you see the paddlewheels. One still stands up after all the years on the bottom, and one is leaning over and will be on its side soon. They are huge. One of the smoke stacks lies near the boilers. Most of the wood structure is gone. What is left of the* Larchmont *is pretty broken up as the result of being hit by nets from the fishing boats over the years. Another area that I find fantastic is in the broken piece of the bow. The anchor still is in the chock. This is not a dive for a novice diver. The water is 130 feet deep and is very dark.*

Unfortunately, says Chellis, "The *Larchmont* does not lend itself to good photos because of the low visibility on the wreck."

CHAPTER 23

The Fairfax–Pinthis Disaster

At 5:00 in the evening of June 10, 1930, the Merchants and Miners passenger liner *Fairfax* sailed from Boston Harbor on her regular run down the coast. A heavy fog soon settled over Massachusetts Bay, so Captain A. H. Brooks ordered the ship to proceed at a moderate rate of speed, from ten to twelve knots.

At 6:58 that night the Shell Oil tanker *Pinthis* hove in view half a point on the *Fairfax*'s starboard bow. Captain Brooks, hearing one blast of the whistle, ordered the helm hard aport and backed away full speed. The *Fairfax* quivered from stem to stern as the engines changed their direction, but it was too late. The two ships came together with a sickening crash, and the *Pinthis* caught fire. Eleven thousand barrels of oil [gasoline] spouted high into the air to come down on the two steamers. Locked with the *Pinthis*, the *Fairfax* also broke out in flames, her decks soon a mass of roaring fire.

The *Pinthis* started to sink at once, pulling away from the *Fairfax* as she began her final plunge into the foggy sea. Captain Brooks now cleverly maneuvered the *Fairfax* in order to get the fire on her decks into the lee, thus preventing it from spreading. The crew showed their splendid discipline by rushing to the scene with the fire apparatus, extinguishing the blaze with quickness and dispatch. Several marines and sailors who were passengers helped the ship's company in beating out the flames and maintaining general order.

Immediately after the collision the captain ordered an S.O.S. radioed.

The radio operator later testified that although he had directions to send the S.O.S., he found the calls were not going out and cancelled the appeal on his own responsibility. Later, when the radio worked properly, he did not again send the S.O.S., but radioed many personal and private messages. The reason for the radio operator's inexcusable behavior has never been clearly explained.

Shortly afterwards the captain anchored the *Fairfax*. Blazing oil from the tanker lighted up the sea for miles around. The Coast Guard Cutter *Tampa* was a short distance away, but Captain Brooks said that he did not request her aid because with the sea on fire the cutter was unable to approach.

To escape the flames two boys, John V. Eubank, nineteen-year-old quartermaster, and Joseph Poco, Negro pantry boy, dived through the burning oil, swam under water until they reached a clear area, and dived again and again until they arrived at the edge of the flames. Locating one of the *Pinthis* lifeboats so wrenched and broken as to be almost sinking, they made it serviceable by stuffing the largest holes with clothing which they tore from their bodies. Having bailed the boat dry, the two boys drifted along until picked up by the two-master *Dacia*, which took them into Boston.

The steamer Fairfax, *which collided with the* Pinthis, *June 10, 1930*

One of the woman passengers on the *Fairfax,* who was terribly injured and had been told that she could not live, kept repeating over and over the words, "Tell Ellsworth that I love him. Tell Ellsworth that I love him." She died shortly afterwards.

There was much criticism of the handling of information in connection with the collision. In spite of the relative nearness of Boston to the scene of the catastrophe, the entire incident was shrouded in mystery for several hours. Hundreds of relatives and friends of those aboard the *Fairfax* crowded around the Boston pier of the steamship company, anxious for information of their loved ones. Ambulances waited in vain. Even at 2:00 A.M. the Scituate Coast Guard had not been notified of the disaster a few miles off their station. It is said that the *Tampa* radioed to the *Fairfax* asking what was wrong and received a reply that all was well.

Meanwhile the *Fairfax* had contacted her sister ship, the *Gloucester,* which proceeded to the scene of the collision. Fifty-six passengers transferred to the rescue ship were later safely landed ashore. There were forty-seven lives lost in the disaster, including those who perished from both ships.

For days after the accident, the waters off Scituate were the scene of a spectacular phenomenon. An enormous cloud of fire and smoke billowed high into the heavens day and night, unceasingly raising its gigantic signal message of warning so all might notice. The cloud of smoke gave a strange sensation to those who witnessed it. Even stranger, however, must have been the feelings of those who stood on the deck of the *Fairfax* that June evening when they watched the huge unwielding bulk of the *Pinthis* bear down at them out of the fog.

David Ball's book *Night of Terror at Buoy No. 4* provides us with more detail of the *Fairfax-Pinthis* disaster, but as he wrote, "The ensuing investigation failed to determine all the facts and there is no way now to unravel all the details. Too much time has passed."

Ball's book describes a nightmarish half-hour of panic, heroism, and tragedy. Eyewitness accounts from the *Fairfax* told of crewmembers fighting the flames, helping passengers, and going into the burning ship to retrieve medical supplies. Ball tells us that the name of the dying woman mentioned by Snow, the one who kept repeating, "Tell Ellsworth that I love him," was May Dearborn. Ellsworth Dearborn was listed by newspapers as a survivor.

Eubank and Poco from the *Fairfax* drifted for almost twelve hours in the lifeboat before they were picked up by the crew of the *Dacia*. Most of those aboard the *Pinthis* died at once in the explosion. Others apparently died later in the water, including Captain Albert Jones. If aid had been summoned sooner, some would have undoubtedly survived.

The repaired *Fairfax* was later sold three times, operating under the names *Chung Hsing, Pacific Star,* and *Bintang Sumadra.* The vessel was broken up in 1956.

The *Pinthis* today lies upside down in about a hundred feet of water, six miles east of Scituate's Fourth Cliff, and is a popular diving site. Diver Keith McDonald reported the following in October 2000:

> *The wreck still resembles a ship, but there are quite a few areas on the* Pinthis *where the riveting has rusted away sufficiently to fail, allowing the most steeply angled side plates to fall away and settle on the bottom. These failures have provided wreck divers numerous entry points. . . . Sea life is always abundant, and anyone that frequents the* Pinthis *is familiar with the pair of wolf eels that have made their home under the ship's rudder, laying in the sand about thirty feet from the former port side of the vessel. Additionally, the wreck is known for its large col-*

Smoke from the burning oil a week after the Fairfax-Pinthis *disaster*

lection of bright red twelve-legged starfish and sea robins. The hull of the wreck has been described as "a sea of frilled anemones," and there's no doubt of the appropriateness of this because descending onto the wreck, it is clearly a ship, but it more closely resembles a submerged parade float whose "skin" is made from flowers. Crabs and lobster are fairly abundant with the amount of fallen steel plating on the bottom, and the open interior areas of the wreck are swarming with fish of all types and sizes.

Some artifacts recovered from the *Pinthis*, including a steam whistle and a porthole, are now on display in the Maritime and Irish Mossing Museum in Scituate.

Wreckage of the Pinthis *today, in the waters off Scituate (photo by Keith McDonald)*

CHAPTER 24

The New England Hurricane

New England's 1938 hurricane was unparalleled in the entire history of the United States in the widespread destruction which it created, the gale of September 21 causing more property damage than had ever occurred before in a single storm anywhere in the world. Although the exact number can never be known, there were from 682 to 700 persons who lost their lives in the tempest which swept over the New England shores and countryside. (Six hundred eighty-two is the estimate of those who wrote *New England Hurricane*.)

Residents of every part of New England thought that their section was the hardest hit, but without question Rhode Island has that unfortunate distinction. Providence, as in the 1815 hurricane, suffered more comparatively than any other city its size. Since Rhode Island was directly in the path of the terrific upheaval of the elements, more than 300 men, women, and children in this state died before nightfall on that memorable day. Entire beach settlements were obliterated, the actual contours of the state's geographical boundaries changed radically, and downtown Providence, the metropolis of Rhode Island, was inundated to a depth of ten feet!

The Providence Weather Bureau early that afternoon reported winds of forty miles an hour, and hurricane warnings were received by the *Providence Journal* at 3:10 P.M. Forty-mile winds, however, were not too uncommon for the autumnal season, so the people paid little heed to reports of trouble ahead. Only the historians remembered the terrible

1815 disaster. Later that September afternoon, however, when slates began to fly from the roofs, knifing down into the streets below, and when windows started to crash inward and church steeples to sway back and forth, the nonchalant attitude of the average bystander changed first to one of extreme concern and then to utmost horror. By this time the gale had begun an ominous vibrating whine of warning and danger. Shortly after 5:00 P.M. the Providence Weather Bureau gauge registered eighty-seven miles an hour.

The newspapers were among the first to feel the effects of the storm. The *Evening Bulletin* never reached the streets with its hurricane extra because all power failed at 5:16 P.M. Just as the edition was about to be printed, the newsroom lights faded and went out, and the workers were forced to give up their efforts.

Narragansett Bay was then being subjected to a 121-mile-an-hour gale, which was pushing the waters of the Atlantic toward Providence. Reaching the center of the city around 5:00, the gale within a half hour filled Union Street in the business section of Providence with six feet of water, marooning thousands on upper floors of the banking and industrial buildings. Hundreds of automobiles sank out of sight in the deep water of the Providence streets. People struggled for their lives as they fled from streetcars, buses, and autos. Chimneys fell on three different cars in separate parts of the city, killing a person in each case. Four men were drowned in the city itself. At the height of the tide, the water rose to a point 13 feet 9 inches above mean high water, as compared with the mark of 11 feet 9 1/4 inches in the 1815 hurricane. (A geologist has suggested that the 1815 hurricane may have been equally as high as the 1938 blast, the difference being caused by the settling of the land around the building.)

Outside of the city, in Charlestown Beach, Watch Hill, Mataunuck, and other locations, scores of people were drowned. Great waves thirty feet high with breaking crests came roaring through the villages, sweeping all before them, and leaving death and desolation in their wake.

At the amusement center on Rocky Point the roller coaster was shattered and the large dining hall and bath houses became a mass of wreckage. At Misquamicut ten women attending a church social were swept out to sea when the building collapsed, and were never seen again.

At about 7:30 in the evening the tide in Providence began to go down, but Rhode Island had been laid in ruin. The state had lost its electricity and its transportation, while telephone connections were broken, and even water was at a premium. A few days later the Department of Commerce issued warnings that all coastal charts were worthless because of the great changes the hurricane had caused. Without question no living person had ever seen disaster to equal this Rhode Island destruction.

Every storm or hurricane has its ridiculous story, and the 1938 storm was no exception. At the height of the gale, when hundreds were fighting for their lives as the rising tide swept through the state, the phone in the *Providence Journal* offices rang vigorously. A woman wished to register a complaint with the paper because a tree had fallen across her property, and the forestry department had refused to do anything about it!

The *Boston Post* published the *Providence Evening Bulletin* for nine emergency editions, the fine work done by this Massachusetts daily paper creating considerable favorable comment. In addition to the *Bulletin*, the *Post* printed an issue of the *Fall River Herald*. The *Providence Evening Bulletin* resumed its regular edition on October 3, 1938.

Devastation in New Bedford was considerable. The New Bedford Yacht Club was smashed to kindling wood, while out in the harbor the wife of Keeper Arthur Small of the Palmer Island Light was drowned. She had tried to row over to help her husband when the gale hit, and her rowboat overturned. Although Mrs. [Mabel] Small was lost, Keeper Small survived the gale.

Lighthouses themselves, ancient guardians of the deep, could not stand against the hurricane. The Whale Rock Lighthouse fell into the sea, taking the [assistant] keeper [Walter B. Eberle] to his death. This iron-plated beacon located at the entrance to Narragansett Bay had survived hundreds of ordinary storms and gales since its erection in 1822,* only to crash in the hurricane of 1938.

Five persons were carried to their death from the keeper's dwelling at Sandy Point Light [officially known as Prudence Island Light] on Prudence Island. The keeper himself survived as he was on another part of the island at the time, but his wife and son perished. (The September Gale of 1869 severely damaged this lighthouse.)†

---

*Whale Rock Lighthouse was actually built in 1882.—*Ed.*

† According to most accounts, Keeper George T. Gustavus was swept out to sea but survived when another wave returned him to the shore, where he was pulled to safety by sixteen-year-old George Taber.—*Ed.*

A priest, the Reverend Mr. T. F. McKitchen, was trapped with his mother by the gale at Conimicut Point. Escaping in a small skiff, Father McKitchen realized that his dory was being swept away from land in the gathering dusk, and was about to administer the last rites of the church to his mother when the current shifted, and the skiff soon grounded at Annawamscutt Beach in Barrington. A little girl at Conimicut Point rode through the storm on a kapok mattress, finally coming ashore after four hours at Narragansett Terrace. Both her parents had perished.

New Bedford in the aftermath of the hurricane (postcard from the collection of Jeremy D'Entremont)

At Mackerel Cove on Conanicut Island, seven small children, four in one family, were drowned when their bus was caught by the ocean. The driver was trying to move the frightened youngsters to safety when three enormous waves swept the road, engulfing everything in their path.

The noted Herreshoff shipyards were destroyed. The only possession of the Bristol Yacht Club after the gale went down was a flagpole, as the club and all its other possessions were swept out to sea. Bailey's Beach at Newport was wiped off the map by the giant hand of the storm, and Newport Beach suffered the same fate.

The state of Connecticut was in the direct path of the storm. Hartford experienced heavy damage around the state capitol. The Park River overflowed into the business district, while the Connecticut River at midnight had risen to almost twenty-five feet. Seven thousand people were forced to evacuate their residences in the city.

At Stonington, Connecticut, the passenger train *Bostonian* encountered first a cabin cruiser on the tracks, and then a house. The track ahead had washed out, and so all the passengers were placed in a coach and diner for the night. As the night wore on, the passengers ate food from the diner and seemed to enjoy their unusual experience. They were cut off from the world for almost twenty hours.

An early 1900s postcard of Whale Rock Lighthouse, which was destroyed in the 1938 hurricane (from the collection of Jeremy D'Entremont)

In Bridgeport, thirty passengers and the crew of the ferryboat *Park City*, which ran to Jefferson City [Port Jefferson], encountered the gale fifteen miles from land. With her engines dead, she drifted helplessly until the storm went down. She was later towed back into Bridgeport by the *Galatea*, a Coast Guard patrol boat.

New London experienced the brunt of the hurricane. The spectacular sight of the barkentine *Marsala*, a training ship, tossed against a railroad trestle was matched by the lighthouse tender *Tulip*, which reposed on the railroad tracks when the gale went down. Barges, tenders, yachts, and motorboats were jammed in helpless confusion into the New London streets. Whole sections of the city were devastated. Fires broke out, threatening to destroy the entire city, but the wind shifted so that the flames were put under control.

As in the 1635, 1723, and 1815 gales, Massachusetts was hard hit by the 1938 hurricane. (The state lost 100 persons.) The people of the state, however, fell to work and with unyielding enthusiasm soon were able to overcome the worst effects of the storm. Provincetown, Massachusetts, was prepared for the worst, but aside from a schooner which parted from its moorings, the majority of the fishing fleet rode out the storm. Fear as to what might happen at high tide, 10:00 P.M., was dispelled when the gale diminished before that time.

Marion, Massachusetts, lost its Beverly Yacht Club. Tabor Academy was flooded to its second floor; the schooner *Tabor Boy*, however, rode out the storm without too much damage. The entire personnel at the school helped the townspeople to save their belongings. Fairhaven suffered severely. Seven deaths were reported in this area, and five boat yards at the waterfront were put out of business. Many vessels were left stranded on the Fairhaven-New Bedford bridge when the tide went down, leaving them high and dry.

Twelve residents of suburban Fall River died. The City Hall roof was blown off and the sides of the water tower were blown in. The Shell oil tanker *Phoenix* was torn from her moorings at Fall River and was pushed by the gale to Somerset, disrupting telephone service when her dragging anchor broke a cable.

The Boston and Albany tracks were undermined in Adams, Massachusetts, and when the street caved in at McKinley Square in that town, two automobiles were catapulted into the excavation.

With all trains at a standstill and all wires down between Boston and New York, unusual methods were resorted to for necessary transportation and communication. Boston talked with New York via London. In eight days airlines between Boston and New York carried 8,000 passengers. One of Uncle Sam's giant battleships carried mail between the two cities. On October 1, train service was resumed.

The hurricane force lasted two hours at high intensity around Boston; the peak of the storm was about 6:47 P.M. Boston Common was greatly damaged, as was the famed Arnold Arboretum. Churches were hard hit in Greater Boston, with over a score suffering substantial damage. The anemometer at the Blue Hills Observatory registered 180 miles an hour before blowing away.

City Point seemed to draw the gale's worst blasts around Boston. A million dollars' worth of sailboats, motor yachts, expensive pleasure cruisers, and excursion steamers were in the path of the storm. Three great yacht clubs, the Columbia, South Boston, and Boston Yacht Clubs, all had their fleets anchored in the area between Thompson's Island and the mainland, but when the gale had gone down around midnight on September 21, only a handful had ridden out the storm. The rest were battered into hopeless masses of unidentifiable wreckage, and were

Wreckage from the 1938 hurricane at City Point, Boston

heaped up in a jumbled pile against the City Point Public Landing and the Columbia Road Breakwater—hundreds of thousands of dollars' worth of vessels gone forever.

One of the epic stories of the storm is the fight which Captain Fred Esterhill and his younger brother Eddie put up against the gale. Realizing that the hurricane was coming, they went down to the landing pier just in time to watch their sixty-foot excursion motorship *Francis* break loose from her moorings and start toward them. As luck would have it, the *Francis* ended her dash from her moorings by hitting the end of the pier, whereupon the two courageous brothers jumped aboard the vessel, Fred rushing to the pilothouse and Eddie taking charge of the engine room. They soon had the *Francis* under way and ran her across the harbor, keeping the motorship headed into the wind, which at one point registered 100 miles an hour. The brothers won their fight with the gale, and the *Francis* was one of the few vessels in the vicinity to ride out the hurricane of 1938.

Captain Lawrence H. Dunn of the Boston Harbor Police and the crew of the police boat *Michael H. Crowley*, risked almost certain death when, at the height of the worst hurricane in at least 100 years, they attempted the rescue of eight men caught at the end of a piling jetty near the Boston Fish Pier. Running the *Crowley* into the teeth of the gale, Captain Dunn edged the sturdy vessel up to the men, who were clinging desperately to the piles. Watching their chances, the crew maneuvered the motorboat at opportune moments between the waves, and the men were saved from death. Only an expert mariner could have accomplished this feat.

The state of Vermont had never before seen such a wind as swept up in the Green Hills [Mountains] that evening, and even the most secluded villages and towns nestling in the comparative security of the deep valleys were ravaged. Maple sugar groves and almost the entire apple crop suffered terrific losses, but there were only seven deaths because of the gale.

The White Mountains of New Hampshire, as well as the seacoast, received some damage, but the force of the gale did not approach that of the southern New England states. Apple crops, bridges, and highways were considerably affected.

Maine was able to escape the worst effects of the hurricane, as the storm veered off inland. However, the forests of Maine had thousands of trees blown down, and for many years afterwards the fire hazard there was great.

The beautiful trees of New England suffered irreparable damage in the hurricane. Millions crashed to earth. Many of the historic trees were damaged, including the Governor Winthrop willow in Winthrop, Massachusetts. It has been estimated that it will be more than half a century before New England's forests can recover from the 1938 storm.

Of course in damage created, the 1938 hurricane, as compared with the 1635, 1723, or 1815 storms, caused far greater damage. But the writer believes that the three other storms, had they occurred today, would have created devastation almost equal to New England's worst hurricane, that of September 21, 1938.

The 1938 hurricane remains the most destructive storm in New England's recorded history. The statistics are staggering: peak steady winds that reached 121 miles per hour and a gust of 186 miles per hour recorded at Great Blue Hill, a storm surge of seventeen feet above normal in Rhode Island, fifty-foot waves off Gloucester, rainfall of ten to seventeen inches in the Connecticut Valley, approximately 700 deaths and 1,700 injuries, 63,000 left homeless, 8,900 homes and 2,600 boats destroyed (and many more damaged), and an estimated 2 billion trees lost. The estimates of the cost of the damage vary widely, but it was least in the hundreds of millions of dollars. According to *Time* magazine, converting the storm to 1998 dollars would have made it the sixth costliest storm in U.S. history.

In his 1976 book *A Wind to Shake the World: The Story of the 1938 Hurricane*, Everett S. Allen wrote, "I shall not forget one man whom I interviewed, who cried out, even after all these years, 'That was when I stopped believing in God!'"

The only storm to rival this one in the decades since has been the February Blizzard of 1978. In his book *Tales of Terror and Tragedy* (1979), Snow wrote that the 1978 storm caused damage that amounted to nearly $1 billion in New England. He ranked the 1978 storm as one of the region's five greatest, along with those in 1635, 1723, 1815, and 1938.

CHAPTER 25

Maine and New Hampshire

For centuries the men of Maine have sailed the seven seas. During the period from 1790 to 1850, three out of every five sailors in New England drowned at sea, and the men in Maine were no exception. Wrecks have occurred by the hundreds along the Maine coast. The loss of the *Royal Tar* and the *Portland*, as well as many other ships which either hailed from Maine ports, or had Maine sailors aboard, are mentioned elsewhere in the book.

New Hampshire, although having a short coastline, has been the scene of many great shipwrecks, while nearby Boon Island and the Isles of Shoals have had harrowing experiences.

THE PLYMOUTH PINNACE

One of the earliest shipwrecks of which we have definite knowledge is that of a pinnace from the Plymouth Colony, which was wrecked at Damariscove over three centuries ago. The sequel to the story of the shipwreck is of interest.

Governor William Bradford tells us that in March of 1624 the Pilgrims went to quite a little trouble having "new-masted and rigged their pinass," sending the vessel on a fishing trip to Damariscove. Here she was "well-harbored in a place where ships used to ride, there being also some ships already arrived out of England." Shortly after this a violent storm hit the Maine coast, and the pinnace was driven against the rocks, "which beat such a hole in her bulke, as a horse and carte might have gone in, and after drive her into deep water, wher she lay sunke. The master was drowned, the rest of the men, all save one, with much adoe; all her provision, salt, and what els was in her, was lost."

As it was a sturdy vessel, the Pilgrims agreed to have the Plymouth pinnace repaired and refitted. Casks were placed around the ship at low water and she was floated to a cove where carpenters and coopers worked on her for some time. Finally she was ready to leave and after a substantial amount was paid, the craft sailed for Plymouth, at which port she eventually arrived. Bradford, however, was not reconciled to the expenses presented by the first Maine wreckers in history, and ends his comments on her as follows:

> But she cost a great deale of money, in thus recovering her, and buy-ing riging and seails for her, both now and when before she lost her mast; so as she proved a chargable vessell to the poor plantation.

THE INDUSTRY

One of the wrecks recounted around the firesides during the last cen-tury was that of the *Industry*, built at Packard's Rock, in what is now Cushing, Maine. She was commanded by David Patterson, 2nd, who had previously coasted for some time with Reuben Hall.

No one ever learned what happened to the *Industry*. She was launched late in the fall, and sailed for Boston on her first trip in November 1770. Wreckage began to come ashore along Cape Ann some time later, but no one from the *Industry* was ever seen again. Those on board included Major Fales and his son from Massachusetts, George Briggs, John Porterfield, Robert Gamble, John Mastick, David Malcolm, Alexander Baird, Samuel Watson, Mrs. Benjamin Packard and her child, and Aba-gail Patterson. The captain's brother had been lost two years before at Mosquito Harbor with seventeen persons, all perishing.

THE ALBANY

The British sloop-of-war *Albany* was wrecked on the Northern Trian-gles, between Mussel Ridges and Green Island, just before the close of the American Revolution. Joshua Thorndyke, who previously had been a prisoner on the *Albany*, heard of the shipwreck and sailed out to the

Edward Rowe Snow and others examining wreckage, possibly of the Industry, *at Kennebunkport (from Snow's* New England Sea Tragedies)

scene with two friends, Mr. Elwell and Isaac Orbeton. There they found that all of the cannon aboard had gone down through the broken bottom of the vessel to rest on the rocky ledge, where they remained for many years visible at low tide. Even today, it is said, cannon can be retrieved from the Triangle Ledges off the Maine coast.

When the crew of the *Albany* abandoned ship, they rowed away in an open boat for Castine, but became lost in the "vapor," necessitating a landing at Matinicus. Three of the men froze to death before the boat reached shore, and the others were in a pitiful condition. Taken into the homes of the island inhabitants, the men of the enemy were given the best of attention. While dressing the frozen hand of one of the British sailors, Aunt Susan, one of the interesting personalities on the island, noticed tears coming from the young man's eyes. He admitted that he had been one of a party of raiders who shot and killed her heifer on the island some months before. On Matinicus Island today there are many coins taken from the clothing of the bodies of the British sailors frozen to death and buried there.

THE ADAMS

In the month of August 1814, the United States frigate *Adams* ran up on a ledge near the the Isle of Haut [Isle au Haut]. A tent was erected for the accommodation of sailors ill with scurvy, while the guns and other articles were brought ashore. British prisoners were aboard, and Captain Morris arranged to have Robert Knowlton and his brother of Deer Isle, Maine, transport them to Thomaston. While on the way the prisoners rebelled, but the two men soon quelled the uprising, landing the prisoners a short time later at that part of Thomaston now known as Rockland.

Later the frigate was floated off the rocks, and proceeded up the river to Hampden. While she was in port there, word came of the capture of Castine by the British, whereupon the gallant Captain Morris blew up his vessel to prevent the *Adams* from falling into the hands of the enemy. All the sailors aboard were successful in reaching the American lines.

THE NEW YORK

The steam brig *New York*, commanded by Captain Harrold, left Portland, Maine, August 22, 1826. On the following Thursday evening at 9:00 the brig caught fire while eight miles off Petit Manan Light, and Captain Harrold soon saw that he would have to abandon ship. (This same vessel had blown up several years before, with the loss of many passengers.) There were aboard fourteen passengers and a crew of eigteen, all of whom took to the boats, reaching Petit Manan about 11:00 that night. The *New York* was entirely consumed by flames.

A Miss Sarah Tucker of Kennebunk was among those on board. When interviewed later she said, "I lost everything except what I had on, which was the meanest I had, my habit, my shawl, and bonnet."

THE SARAH

In the year 1835 the packet *Sarah* sailed from Boston to Eastport, Maine, on its regular run, but the master, Captain Pierce, mistook Mount Desert Rock Lighthouse for the gleam of Moosepeak Reach Light [Moose Peak Light—*Ed.*], wrecking the vessel on one of the islands off Jonesport.

Daniel Goulden, one of the young passengers, could not swim. A capable Negro woman volunteered to get him ashore, and told the boy to climb on her shoulders after she jumped into the water. Goulden jumped and clung to her as she swam toward the beach. They both reached shore safely, but sixteen of the others were lost.

Some time later the ballad "The Loss of the Sarah," appeared, which had a substantial sale in Eastern Maine.

In Fannie Eckstrom and Mary Smyth's fine collection *Minstrelsy of Maine*, "The Loss of the Sarah" is quoted in full. We reproduce two of the verses:

> *Ye landsmen all, now pray draw near,*
> *a lamentation ye shall hear;*
> *A ship was lost on the sea,*
> *It was the* Sarah's *lot to be.*
> . . . .
>
> *Thirty and two were the* Sarah's *crew*
> *And landsmen were all counted too;*
> *Sixteen survived to reach the shore,*
> *Sixteen are lost, they are no more.*

THE BOHEMIAN

The steamer *Bohemian* sailed from Liverpool on February 4, 1864, with a passenger list of 218 and a crew of 99. Captain Borland made a brief stop at Londonderry before starting out across the ocean. Stormy weather delayed the vessel several days, and so it was late on the afternoon of February 22 that she made Cape Elizabeth, Maine.

A peculiar condition of haze confused Captain Borland into believing that he was quite a distance off the shores of Cape Elizabeth, but actually he was approaching Alden's Rock. Realizing that he needed help, he sent up rockets and blue lights to attract the attention of a pilot, also slowing his speed to a knot and a half. The ship's gun was fired.

Suddenly, without warning, the *Bohemian* crashed against Alden's Rock (about halfway between the Hue and Cry Ledge and Cape Elizabeth Light), and slid over. A hasty examination revealed that the engine compartment had sprung a bad leak, and so the captain headed the *Bohemian* for land, at the same time ordering all lifeboats over. The crew took their stations in orderly fashion, but the passengers became excited, milling around the boats in confusion. When the number 2 lifeboat had been loaded, the pin broke, dropping everyone into the sea. This particular accident caused the greatest loss of life.

The other lifeboats were successfully launched, although only partially filled with passengers. Captain Borland ordered the rowers to return to the ship, as there were more than eighty still aboard. They refused, heading at once for shore, where they all landed safely. Three hours later, however, others brought the lifeboats back to the *Bohemian*, and the remaining survivors were taken ashore without accident.

The fact that it was Washington's birthday caused an unfortunate interpretation of the ship's distress rockets and the firing of the ship's gun. Several pilots had heard the cannon's firing, and had seen the rockets in the air, but concluded that some patriotic festivities were being celebrated in honor of George Washington. They gave the matter no further thought.

Later Captain Borland testified that the peculiar haze made the land look many miles farther away than was actually the case. He had two lookouts on the forecastle and one aloft. He had tried to reach shore, but the fires in the engine room were drowned within ten minutes, and

A mural of the wreck of the Bohemian, *by Alzira Peirce, which hangs in the South Portland (Maine) Post Office (photo by Jeremy D'Entremont)*

his proud ship, the *Bohemian*, went down near Richmond's Island within ninety minutes after the accident.

There had been considerable mail aboard, and divers were sent down to recover it. Every sack except a mailbag destined to Philadelphia was eventually brought to the surface.

A tradition has it that John F. Fitzgerald, famous Boston mayor, was aboard the *Bohemian*. When the writer asked Mr. Fitzgerald for details of the wreck, the eminent Bostonian replied that he was not the Fitzgerald in question. A John Fitzgerald of New York was the person aboard the *Bohemian*.

THE ANNIE C. MAGUIRE

Thousands who journey down to Portland Head's historic lighthouse look out on the dangerous ledge which juts out into the Atlantic there, and read the inscription painted on the natural rock: "In memory of the ship Annie C. Maguire wrecked here, Dec. 24, 1886."

The wreck of the Annie C. Maguire, *December 24, 1886 (from the collection of Jeremy D'Entremont)*

Captain Thomas O'Neil had lost his bearings, and the vessel crashed on the ledge off Portland Head on Christmas Eve. Fifteen members of the crew, together with the captain, his wife, and his son, were brought ashore in a boatswain's chair by young Joseph Strout, son of the keeper of Portland Head Light. The *Annie C. Maguire* stayed on the ledge until a snowstorm swept the coast a few days later, when she broke up and went to pieces.

THE GALE OF 1888

In the Rockland, Maine, *Courier-Gazette* for Tuesday, November 27, 1888, appears a telegram addressed to S. M. Bird:

> *Hingham, Mass., Nov. 26*
> *Sch. H. C. Higginson ashore on Nantasket Beach. Will be total*
> *loss. Captain and two men lost. Wire instructions.*
> *E. C. ROAD, Mate*

There were many similar messages sent from scores of coastal points along the Atlantic Coast after the great November gale of 1888 had run its course. There are still old men living who witnessed both the 1888

Rocks with inscription about the Annie C. Maguire, *near the Portland Head Lighthouse (photo by Edward Rowe Snow)*

and 1898 blows who claim the 1888 was the more severe of the two storms. Regardless of which was the greater storm, the 1888 gale was particularly hard on Maine ships.

The *Higginson* had sailed from Hillsboro, Nova Scotia, for Newburg, New York, but adverse winds had driven her off her course. Captain A. N. Fales had gone out with his summer sails on because his winter canvas was in the hands of the sailmaker. The two sailors lost with him were strangers who had signed on just before the schooner sailed. Four others besides the mate were saved.

During the storm a hay schooner was abandoned at Webster's Head on the northern part of North Haven, while the schooner *Mountain Fawn* went ashore at Naskeag Harbor. The *Golden Eagle of* Gouldsboro crashed at Owl's Head and went to pieces, a total loss. The *Maud S.* of Ellsworth smashed against the rocks nearby, but was later pulled off and repaired. In Rockland Harbor the *William McLoon* broke from its moorings and hit the end of Atlantic Wharf, finally becoming a complete wreck.

A Maine schooner, the *G. W. Rawley*, went ashore at Edgartown, and was condemned and stripped. The *Robert Ripley*, with 500 bushels of corn and flour, went ashore in the storm at Dolliver's Neck.

THE PORTLAND GALE

Rockland suffered greatly during the Portland storm. At the height of the gale, one could not see across Rockland Harbor. Over twenty vessels met trouble. The schooner *S. F. Mayer* and the *Fannie May*, a lobster boat, were wrecked in the harbor. The schooner *Georgietta* was ashore at Spruce Head; the *Alida* was on Ash Island Bar. Captain Leslie Blake's *Anna W. Barker* was ashore at Southern Island. A twenty-ton schooner hit the beach at Martinsville, soon breaking up. *Carrie C. Miles* was damaged at Northport. The *Woodruff* was also there in distress. The *Ella F. Crowell,* the *James A. Brown,* and the *E. G. Willard* were all at Vineyard Haven. The *Bertha E. Glover* of Owl's Head was also at Vineyard Haven. The *Idella Small* was ashore at Bay View, Massachusetts.

The steamer *Hurricane* went to pieces in a short time when caught in Rockland Harbor. Mrs. H. A. Bain, now of Riverside, California, observed that it was astonishing to see how quickly the steamer broke up into kindling wood.

THE PEMAQUID SHIPWRECKS

A gale which caused great damage all along the eastern seaboard hit New England September 17, 1903. Two shipwrecks occurred at Pemaquid Point, Maine, both of them resulting in loss of life. The *George F. Edmunds* of Gloucester hit on the east side of the rocks. Her captain, Willard F. Poole, was master and owner. The schooner had left Gloucester seven weeks before, but ran into bad luck, catching less than a barrel of mackerel. Finally deciding to return home, Captain Poole sailed by Monhegan and was headed for Boothbay Harbor. He missed the way in the gale, however, crashing on the ledges of Pemaquid. He and thirteen of his men were lost, only two of the sailors being rescued.

The other vessel was the little two-masted coaster *Sadie and Lillie*, which hit close by. Weston Curtis of Pemaquid, who saw the wreck, managed to get a line out to the schooner, and two men made their way safely to shore. The last to leave his ship, Captain William S. Harding, of Prospect, Maine, began the hazardous trip in over the lines. Just as the captain was buried in the swirling seas halfway to shore, the lines sparked and jammed, and Captain Harding drowned before the eyes of the helpless watchers ashore.

THE CATAWAMTEAK

One of the outstanding schooners along the Maine coast was the *Catawamteak*, on which many fine Maine captains and seamen have sailed. The writer's grandfather, Captain Joshua N. Rowe, was among those who considered it a privilege to command her under sail. (He was also aboard the clipper ship *Crystal Palace* when she made her record run to Melbourne from Boston in 1854.) The schooner was wrecked on Cape Cod, July 28, 1911. Floated off successfully, the *Catawamteak* continued on her sailing career for many years. George M. Cook of Friendship, Maine, saw the *Catawamteak*, loaded with stone, sink after a gale about three miles west of Monhegan Island.

THE FLORA D. THOMPSON

An unusual rescue story involving one of America's destroyers and a schooner was enacted in Maine waters in 1915.

On the evening of December 9, 1915, the sloop *Flora D. Thompson*, with seven men aboard, anchored off the Kennebec River near the Seguin Island Lighthouse. Before morning a gale came up, and the *Thompson* parted her cable, beginning to drift out to sea.

Discovered by watchers from the Hunniwells Beach Life-Saving Station at daylight on December 10, the *Flora D. Thompson* was then slowly drifting farther away, the only deterrent being a sea anchor made of the cookstove taken from the galley and thrown overboard. A surfboat was quickly dispatched to the scene, many miles at sea, and on the journey the lifesavers fell in with the new destroyer *Conyngham* on the way to undergo her trial runs on the course off Rockland, Maine. The captain of the *Conyngham* agreed to help, so proceeded to the scene and threw a line aboard.

The *Conyngham* now began the tow toward shore. Approaching Seguin Island, the *Flora D. Thompson* started to settle in the water, so all hands, including four women and children, were removed as the *Thompson* went down. They all were shortly afterwards transferred to the tug *Cumberland*, which had appeared on the scene.

The wreck of the Charles H. Tuckey *and* Mary E. Olys *at Goat Island, 1920 (photographer unknown)*

THE GOAT ISLAND SHIPWRECKS

The double shipwreck of January 7, 1920, at Goat Island, Cape Porpoise, was one of the unusual occurrences along the coast that year. The *Charles H. Tuckey* came in on the wrong side of the spindle, striking the ledge, and the *Mary E. Olys* tried to pass to starboard of the *Tuckey*. The *Olys* also went aground, but hit much more heavily than the *Tuckey*, for within five minutes she had broken to pieces. The *Tuckey* was later floated, but only kindling wood remained of the other vessel.

THE WANDBY

One of the mysterious ships of the early 1920s was the British steamer *Wandby*. She had gone on a long voyage to the White Sea, where the *Wandby* completely disappeared from contact with the outside world. Sailing as far north as latitude 71 degrees, she returned to civilization to find the insurance agents had paid off on the vessel, and every member of the crew had been mourned as lost, many of them discovering that funeral services had been held in their memory.

After this unusual experience the *Wandby* sailed to American waters. Around the year 1921 she was off the coast of Maine. Sailing from Portland one day, she headed for what the captain believed to be Cash's Ledge (about 100 miles to the eastward of Newburyport, Massachusetts), but it was actually Kennebunkport where the *Wandby* ran aground.

THE CITY OF ROCKLAND

On September 2, 1923, the steamer *City of Rockland* ran up on the reef off Parker's Head on Dix's Island in the Kennebec River. The popular steamer had sailed with 300 passengers from Bath at 7:30 in a dense fog, going ashore a half hour later. Attention of those on land was attracted by long, repeated blasts of the steamer's whistle, and soon surfboats from the Popham Beach Coast Guard Station arrived.

As they jumped from the lower deck, the passengers were caught by the coastguardsmen and placed in the surfboats and lifeboats from the *City of Rockland* for the short trip to Dix's Island. Most of the passengers crowded around a gigantic bonfire which had been built on the beach. Blankets and food were brought ashore from the ship. The castaways were good natured and made the best of it. The children, while sliding

down the sloping sides of the steamer into the boats, enlivened the proceedings by their songs, singing at the top of their voices, "Yes, We
Have No Bananas," or "Barney Google," the favorites of the period.

Later the *City of Rockland* was floated off and taken to Salem by Captain Betts. She was burned for her fittings between Little and Great
Misery Island in Outer Salem Harbor, October 29, 1924.

THE CASTINE

On the morning of June 8, 1935, the steamer *Castine* went ashore on
the Bay Ledges near Vinalhaven. Since Captain Leighton Coombs had
his engines stopped at the time because of the dense fog, the situation
was not regarded as too serious until the vessel began to careen at an
alarming angle. When she reached an angle of forty-five degrees, more
than a score of passengers were thrown into the waters of the Penobscot. Four of them drowned.

Many vessels responded to the distress signal which Captain Coombs
sounded, among them the steamer *North Haven* and several lobster fishermen. Aboard the *Castine* were seventy-five members of the Limerock
Valley Pomona Grange.

The steamer *Castine* quickly broke in two, and proved to be a total
loss. The forward part of her hull, however, was used in the building of
an unusual cottage on the shore at Treasure Island, Vinalhaven.

THE ISLES OF SHOALS

Crashing against the ledges of Smuttynose Island, one of the Isles of
Shoals, in January 1813, a Spanish ship went to her doom. At the height
of a blinding snowstorm the richly laden craft struck, leaving no living
soul to tell the story of the ship. She was believed by some to be named
the *Sagunto*, while others claimed that her name was not known. (The
Sagunto was later said to have reached Boston Harbor.) Several sailors did
reach shore, but were unable to get to the home of Captain Sam Haley,
who always kept a light burning in his window during a storm. It seems
even more tragic when it is realized that the men who had escaped from
the wreck walked some of the distance toward the house when their
strength gave out and they fell exhausted to the ground. Their bodies
were found after the storm. Two of them actually reached the stone wall
in front of Haley's house but they could not climb over the wall.

The surf brought ashore many boxes of raisins and almonds. A silver watch was later found, having stopped at 4:00, possibly the time its owner was lost. On the back of the watch were the initials P. S.

Fourteen bodies from the wreck were found and buried in a little plot of land on the island where the rude stones may still be seen. Celia Thaxter often visited the graves of the Spanish sailors at Smuttynose Island, and part of her poem (from her brother Oscar's book, *Ninety Years at the Isles of Shoals*) is quoted here:

> *O sailors did sweet eyes look after you*
> *The day you sailed away from sunny Spain?*
> *Bright eyes that followed fading ship and crew,*
> *Melting in tender rain?*
>
> *O Spanish women, over the far seas,*
> *Could I but show you where your dead repose!*
> *Could I send tidings on this northern breeze*
> *That strong and steady blows!*
>
> *Lonely, unknown, deserted, but for me,*
> *And the wild birds that flit with mournful cry,*
> *And sadder winds, and voices of the sea*
> *That moans perpetually.*
>
> *Dear dark-eyed sisters, you remember yet*
> *These you have lost, but you can never know*
> *One stands at their bleak graves whose eyes are wet*
> *With thinking of your woe.*

The writer, while flying over the Isles of Shoals at Christmas time dropping packages on New England lighthouses,* has often looked down at Smuttynose Island and thought of the Spaniards buried there and of the women who waited in vain for their men to return. Celia Thaxter's words always came back as the plane roared across the island. In January 1942, 129 years after the wreck, as an officer in the Army Air Corps, the writer was convalescing in a hospital in Oran, North Africa.

---

*Captain Bill Wincapaw inaugurated this practice back in 1929.

One of the ladies who attended him was from Malaga, Spain, sixty miles up the Mediterranean from Gibraltar. She was a Spanish refugee from Franco's government. Of a historical frame of mind, the lady had remembered the ship, with some of her ancestors aboard, which had never returned to port in 1813, and the writer thus became the first one to tell her (in doubtful French) of the story of the Spaniard's shipwreck at the Isles of Shoals.

The paddle-steamer Katahdin, *which ran into difficulty off Maine and New Hampshire during the blizzard of January 1886 (uncredited photo from Snow's* Great Gales and Dire Disasters, *1952)*

THE KATAHDIN

The experience of the paddle-steamer *Katahdin* during the blizzard of January 1886, on the route from Bangor to Boston, gives an idea of what the *Portland* must have gone through before she foundered in the 1898 gale.

On January 9, 1886, the *Katahdin* left Bangor for Boston. Running into a heavy gale off Cape Porpoise, her master, Captain Homer, decided to take no chances and ran to sea. Reaching the vicinity of Boon Island, he tried for its shelter and failed. All night long the terrific blast from the northeast continued and the *Katahdin* kept her head into the wind. The fuel was entirely consumed, however, and a shipment of spoolwood, excellent for fuel, was also used. Finally the ship was driven to a position near the Isles of Shoals. By this time all the spare fixtures had been thrown into the fires and the dismantling of staterooms began.

Frank A. Garnsey of Bangor was the freight clerk.

> *I never expected to see land again. I was going down to the engine room and met Captain Pierce. I asked him how long we'd stay up and he said: "The old* Katahdin *won't last another hour." When we began to fill, a list of the passengers and crew was made out and placed in a bottle. I was pulling down stateroom doors when land was sighted; everything else had been consumed.*

The *Katahdin* had sighted Portsmouth harbor; a short time later, visibly battered and bruised, her houses wrecked, her cargo burned, and her bulkheads smashed in, she limped into a safe harbor. Captain Pierce said that it had been a dreadful experience. "I never expected to see shore again. The only thing that saved us was a shift in the wind which beat down the seas and gave us a chance to get into Portsmouth."

THE OLIVER DYER

At 1:30 in the morning of November 25, 1888, the schooner *Oliver Dyer* anchored in the harbor at Portsmouth, New Hampshire. The wind began to breeze up at sunrise, continued throughout the day, and by evening a howling gale from the northeast had set in, bringing thick snow and tremendous surf.

At sunset Keeper Silas H. Harding of the Jerry's Point Life-Saving

Station displayed the international code signal M T, informing the *Dyer* that a lookout would be on the beach all night. When the *Dyer* began to drag anchor at 5:45 the morning of November 26, Surfman Robinson, then on the beach, fired his Coston signal, giving the alarm. Keeper Harding called out the crew and went over opposite the ledge east of the station. A tremendous sea caught the *Dyer*, throwing her fifty feet nearer shore. The seas now made breaches over the schooner, washing a man from the rigging forty feet up.

One of the vessel's crew jumped into the water and swam for the rocks. Surfman Hall dashed into the surf to save him and, although both were terribly cut by the rocky ledges, they managed to climb up on the beach. The schooner's cook then leaped into the sea, and Surfman Randall grabbed him just as the undertow was pulling him down. The last two men aboard were saved by a heaving line. Keeper Harding and his brave men received medals for their outstanding heroism.

THE PLYMOUTH PINNACE The name of the pinnace wrecked in 1624 was the *Little James*, and it had arrived at Plymouth from England in the summer of 1623, a few weeks after the *Anne*. The two ships had left at the same time but were separated during a storm. Besides new settlers, the passengers on the two vessels included the wives and children of some of the men who had arrived on the *Mayflower* in 1620. Among the passengers on the *Anne* was Edward Rowe Snow's own ancestor, Nicholas Snow.

THE INDUSTRY In his 1960 book *New England Sea Tragedies*, Snow wrote that the wreckage from the *Industry* washed ashore not only at Cape Ann, but as far north as Cape Porpoise in Maine. He continued, "In March 1960 . . . I was asked by Managing Editor J. N. Cole of the *Kennebunk Star* to visit and appraise a wreck whose ribs were beginning to appear out of the receding sands at a Kennebunk beach. I journeyed there at once . . . only to find that an easterly gale which has scoured away the sand from the wreck had covered it over again."

Snow and interested local people dug out the remains of the vessel on the beach. It was agreed that the wreck was probably the *Industry*, but as Snow said, "The evidence is not conclusive."

THE ALBANY In his 1963 book *True Tales of Terrible Shipwrecks*, Snow wrote that his cousin Willis Snow had been keeper of the Goose Rocks Lighthouse in the Fox Islands Thoroughfare, that he had made visits to the site of the *Albany* wreck, and that he was able to see the ship's guns when the seas were calm.

THE ADAMS Before the incidents described by Snow, Captain Charles Morris had taken the *John Adams* to the coast of Ireland, where he did great damage to British shipping. Earlier, he had been commanding officer of the U.S.S. *Constitution*. Morris later served as Navy commissioner and for many years supervised the Naval Academy at Annapolis, Maryland.

THE BOHEMIAN The wreck of the *Bohemian* was a contributing factor to improvements made at Portland Head Lighthouse in Cape Elizabeth. The tower was subsequently raised twenty feet and a new, more powerful second-order lens was installed.

Many of the bodies were recovered by men who had been attending a Washington's Birthday party at the Ocean House. The dead were laid out

The Bohemian *memorial in Calvary Cemetery, South Portland, Maine (photo by Jeremy D'Entremont)*

under sails in the blacksmith house next to the hotel. It has been reported that despite an armed guard sent to protect the cargo of the *Bohemian*, a good deal of clothing and other materials was pilfered in the weeks following the wreck.

The official death toll in this disaster was forty passengers and two crew members. A large 1939 painting of the *Bohemian* disaster by Maine artist Alzira Peirce hangs today in the South Portland Post Office, and the previously unmarked grave of twelve of the Irish shipwreck victims is now marked by a large granite Celtic cross in South Portland's Calvary Cemetery. The memorial was dedicated in 1985.

THE ANNIE C. MAGUIRE The *Annie C. Maguire* was originally a clipper ship in the China trade named the *Golden State*. She was sold, reconfigured, and renamed in 1883. The true name of the vessel was the *Anne C. Maguire*.

Rescuer Joseph Strout was the son of Keeper Joshua Strout, who was keeper from 1869 to 1904. Joseph became keeper in 1904 and left Portland Head in 1928. The tradition of painting the rocks near Portland Head as a memorial to the *Annie C. Maguire* is now nearly a century old. According to an article by John Strout in *Lighthouse Digest*, "My father John A. Strout was first to paint the legend on his twenty-first birthday; the day he became assistant keeper under his father, Joseph. He had to chip off much of the rock to make a flat surface, then make a mix of mortar, sand, and some paint, using a boatswain's sling. The job was completed on Jan. 14, 1912." The ship's name was further misspelled on the rocks—"McQuire" instead of "Maguire."

GALE OF 1888 This storm is not to be confused with the great blizzard of March 11–14, 1888, which blanketed much of the eastern United States and did much damage in New York Harbor. That storm is sometimes called the "Great White Hurricane."

THE CATAWAMTEAK After the *Catawamteak* (after an Indian word for "Great Landing Place," their name for an area that is now part of the waterfront of Rockland, Maine) was wrecked at Peaked Hill Bars on Cape Cod, the owners were unable to pay the bills for the vessel's recovery, and the schooner was sold at auction.

THE FLORA D. THOMPSON The Hunniwells Beach Life-Saving Station is now the Popham Beach Bed and Breakfast. It was seen in the movie *Message in a Bottle*.

THE WANDBY According to William P. Quinn's book *Shipwrecks Around Maine*, the master of the *Wandby* mistook the Kennebunk River for the Kennebec River. He wasn't even close. Legend has it that the grounding of the steamer on March 9, 1921, shook the entire town of Kennebunkport. Some of the hull was salvaged for scrap, but portions of the wreck remain underwater, not far from the Bush estate at Walker's Point.

THE CITY OF ROCKLAND The steamer *City of Rockland*, built in Boston in 1900, had a troubled career marked by several collisions and groundings. In 1904 the 274-foot vessel struck a ledge in the Muscle Ridge Channel in thick fog. After it was repaired in Boston, the steamer's next misadventure was a 1906 collision with its sister ship, the *City of Bangor*.

Today you can see the remains of the steamship on the beach at Little Misery Island near Salem. In his book *Shipwrecks North of Boston, Volume One: Salem Bay* (2000), Raymond H. Bates, Jr., reports that there is little left of the steamer, but at low tide "one can still walk along portions of its beams, and parts of its boilers remain at one end."

In notes to his 1946 edition of this book, Snow noted that he'd been presented with a section of the ship's timber (by Thomas Harrison Eames of Belmont, Massachusetts).

THE CASTINE Treasure Island is a nickname for Cedar Island, also known as Baker's Island after its private owners. Charles McLane wrote in his book *Islands of the Mid-Maine Coast: Penobscot Bay* that the owners' log cabin had doors from a Civil War frigate and running lights from the ship *Maggie Mulvey*, and that the forward quarter hull of the *Castine* was turned upside down and served as a guesthouse.

According to Roy Heisler of the Vinalhaven Historical Society, "A first-hand story of the 'summer camp' fashioned from the wreck of the *Castine* was recently related by a retired carpenter who repaired it many years ago. He said the owner of the island kept it open in the winter, stocked with canned goods and with heat in case it was needed in any emergency, possibly meaning other wrecks."

The "cottage" is still on Cedar (Treasure) Island but is said to be in deteriorating condition.

THE ISLES OF SHOALS Samuel Adams Drake wrote in *A Book of New England Legends and Folklore* that the account of the shipwreck in the Gosport town records is in error, as the *Sagunto* made port safely. But he did believe that a large Spanish or Portuguese vessel was wrecked on the ledges at Smuttynose.

Writer J. Dennis Robinson, editor of the SeacoastNH.com Web site, says that he isn't convinced that Spanish sailors are buried on Smuttynose, but he does say that "early records indicate that something happened—and poets James Kennard Jr. and Celia Thaxter have turned the legend to poetry." Robinson believes that Thaxter may have based her poem on Kennard's earlier poem called "The Wreck of the Seguntum." As Robinson points out, "Archeological studies on the site have turned up no evidence of human remains in the area of the proposed graves. Although Smuttynose is the most verdant of the rocky Isles of Shoals, the topsoil is still only inches thick. An early visitor mentioned seeing the stones, but no evidence of bodies has ever been discussed or seen."

Maritime writer Robert Ellis Cahill offered an interesting angle on the wreck in his book *Finding New England's Shipwrecks and Treasures*, saying it might have been a vessel called the *Conception* that was the true basis of the story. He wrote that both the *Sagunto* and the *Conception* "had traveled up the coast from the West Indies to Portsmouth, New Hampshire to add dried fish to their cargos, and both had slipped out of port heading for Spain on the night of January 14. The *Sagunto* apparently made it by the Isles and put into Newport, Rhode Island, rather than sailing out the storm, so says historian Samuel Adams Drake, but the *Conception* disappeared, and it is thought to be this vessel that had crashed into Cedar Island Ledge."

THE KATAHDIN The *Katahdin*, built in 1863, remained in service after this incident for another eight years.

THE OLIVER DYER Fortunately for the men on board the *Dyer*, Jerry's Point Life-Saving Station had been built just a year before this incident. The station was replaced by a new one offshore at Wood Island in 1908.

CHAPTER 26

Southern New England

THE METIS

At twenty minutes of four on the morning of August 30, 1872, the schooner *Nettie Cushing* collided with the steamer *Metis* off Watch Hill, Rhode Island. The captain of the *Metis*, Charles L. Burton, sailing the steamer from New York City to Providence, had encountered rough seas while passing through Long Island Sound. When the vessels came together, the schooner hit the steamer about forty feet abaft the bow abeam of the pilothouse. (The *Metis* was of 1,359 tons.)

It was believed at first that the damage was slight, and many passengers who came crowding out on deck were told to go back to bed as there was nothing to worry about. Shortly after this the engineer discovered that the ship was leaking badly, and so all persons were told to get up and dress. Before the *Metis* could be beached, however, she sank in the waters of Long Island Sound. The hurricane deck, crowded with passengers, soon floated free. A lifeboat and a life raft were quickly filled to capacity and pushed off from the wreck. As daylight came, the superstructure of the *Metis* was drifting toward the shores of Watch Hill.

Back on the [Rhode Island] shore, the residents of Watch Hill had heard of the tragedy. Some of them rushed down to the shore scantily clad, others hastily donned more suitable garments, while still others waited to dress in their usual manner. As dawn lighted up the sea, the beach was thronged with people all shouting in their excitement. The deck of the steamer was less than a mile away by seven o'clock, while the lifeboat and the life raft were just off the beach. The boat soon entered the breakers, and all except three passengers who perished in the undertow were saved. Then the life raft caught itself in the relentless surging of the waves and dashed against the shore. All but one or two on the raft were quickly grabbed by the people of Watch Hill.

Now the superstructure of the *Metis* was just off the beach. Those on shore, preparing for the inevitable, formed two chain gangs of a dozen or so each, the end man securely anchored high and dry above the pull of the undertow, and the lower man waist deep in the dangerous surf. With a great shout from those on shore, the hurricane deck caught in a giant comber and started for the beach. Smashing and grinding itself into the sands of Watch Hill, the deck rapidly went to pieces, but not before the human chain had done its duty well. Most of the men were pulled out of the foam, although several of the women who were not so fortunate perished in the breakers.

Some of the personal experiences of the survivors have been recorded. Colonel A. S. Gallop, awakened by the crash, later went back to bed, and then was told to dress. He jumped into a lifeboat, which capsized and was righted again. After rowing for a short time he had to bail the boat with his shoe. Before long his craft was picked up by a fishing smack. Mr. P. F. Brown, who was also awakened by the collision, was sent back to his room where he stayed a short time. According to Brown the captain ordered all hands to don life belts and jump into the raging sea. Many jumped and were lost. Several women on the upper deck were washed off. Two, however, clung to Brown, all three being saved when the deck hit the beach.

After the deck went to pieces, a man wrapped in a blanket was seen sitting on a rock gazing intently at the breakers. He and his wife had clung to a cotton bale until within a few feet of the shore, but a great wave separated them just off the beach, and she disappeared. He was unhurt, but he sat there watching each returning wave hoping it would reveal the body of the woman he loved.

At first it was feared that over 100 lives had been lost, but one by one the missing persons were located alive and well, so that the final total of victims was around twenty-five. Many of these were in the lower part of the *Metis* and their names were never known.

THE NARRAGANSETT

By the spring of 1880 the competition for passengers had become so great among Long Island Sound steamers that the price of tickets between Boston and New York had been reduced to one dollar. This ridiculously low fare brought hundreds of people daily to board the Sound steamers. Bitter races sometimes resulted from the efforts of rival ship captains to better their opponents, with chances being taken in the heat of the contest which, in saner moments, would never have been attempted.

Running at a twelve-knot speed through a dense fog the steamer *Narragansett* collided with the steamer *Stonington* near midnight on July 11, 1880. Efforts had been made to avoid the crash, but it was too late. The helm of the *Narragansett* was thrown sharply around when the other steamer came out of the fog at her, so that the *Narragansett* was broadside when the *Stonington* smashed into her forward of the wheel on the starboard side. It was a terrific shock, throwing all the sleeping passengers out of their berths. There was an immense hole ripped in the steamer's bow, all the lights aboard the *Narragansett* went out, and she caught fire. The *Stonington* had veered off into the night after the collision, and did not return, evidently becoming lost in the fog again.

The captain ran the *Narragansett* into shallow water, where she settled until she rested on the bottom. The flames gained rapidly, forcing many people to leap into the sea. All the lifeboats to leeward were caught by the flames, but windward boats were launched with one exception. Two life rafts saved many of those forced to jump overboard. About this time the steamer *City of New York* arrived on the scene in time to rescue many from the water. Afire from stem to stern, the *Narragansett* half an hour later had burned to the water's edge.

Miss Elizabeth Peall of Philadelphia had left New York for Boston on the *Narragansett*. Sick nearly all that day, she retired early. When the crash came, she quickly dressed. Her story follows:

> *Most of the ladies had time to slip on their skirts. Oh! Such scream-ing. Mrs. Branyan of Boston Highlands was with me and her little girl. We stood on the main deck and screamed as loud as we could. . . . I asked a man to save me. He pushed me away, and said he had enough to do to save himself. By this time the boat was sinking. The water was up to my knees on the main deck.*

Reaching a lifeboat, Miss Peall was placed in it by the *Narragansett's* captain himself, and the lifeboat was pushed away from the ship.

> *A lady and her baby, not more than eight months old, were left on the deck. She begged us to let her in, but the boat had floated away from the steamer, and we had no oars. . . . The last I saw of her she had her hands raised crying for us to come. . . . There was only one little spot left, where the fire had not reached, and she was standing there, crying out. Another lifeboat came up and gave us oars. We rowed up to the* City of New York *and she took us in. . . . I found on the* City of New York *a good many rescued persons. . . . A lady said she had lost three children. She was weeping so hard!*

No accurate list of the *Narragansett's* dead was ever made, but the writer believes, after comparing various estimates and accounts, that from fifty-five to seventy met their death as a result of the collision. Captain Nye of the other steamer, the *Stonington*, continued his trip to the mainland, where he reported the accident on his arrival. (Captain Nye afterwards admitted he had not learned the correct fog signal.)

BLOCK ISLAND

Block Island is known as "the island of a thousand shipwrecks" for good reason. Probably far more than that number of vessels have been wrecked around or off the shores of this beautiful land, but of course no accurate survey is possible. Only the most outstanding disasters can be included in this volume.

The ship *Princess Augusta*, commanded by Captain Andrew Brook, sailed from Rotterdam for Philadelphia with a cargo of Palatinate prisoners about the year 1720. (Palatinate lands were located in Germany on the Rhine and in Bavaria.) The stories told of this ship and the people aboard appear in so many versions that it seems doubtful if the truth can ever be separated from the myths and legends which time has woven about the *Augusta*.

That the ship "ill used by the sea, weakened by the death of half her hands was blown off her course, and forced ashore in a December snowstorm on Block Island" seems clear enough. But the record in the notarial protests that it is possible "only one side of the story" was told, adds a touch of mystery that has not been cleared.

[William P.] Sheffield writes that the vessel is known as the Phantom Ship of Block Island. He says further that the Block Islanders rushed down to the shore when the ship grounded there, and murdered the crew and passengers. The murderers took the most valuable cargo and then burned the ship. She became a phantom ship and appeared every year until all the murderers were killed or died natural deaths. In 1876, when Sheffield wrote, there was a Mr. Benjamin Congdon, then aged eighty-nine, who had seen the phantom ship six or seven times. Benjamin S. Knowles of Point Judith, aged ninety-two, had also observed it. According to Sheffield there were at least two survivors of the wreck.

Another version is that the officers took the treasure from the vessel and abandoned her, while the islanders, far from killing the passengers, befriended them. Two of the survivors on the island were women, "Tall" Kattern and "Short" Kattern. Tall Kattern married a Negro and had many descendants; Short Kattern lived among families on the island, later dying there. There are still many graves of the shipwrecked victims on the island. Richard Henry Dana's poem about the buccaneers is based on this story. Whittier's poem "The Palatine" also concerns the ship.

One of the women passengers, Mary Vanderline, is said to have preferred to keep her cabin on the *Princess Augusta*, as she did not wish to leave her possessions aboard the vessel and go to the homes of the

Mohegan Bluffs and Block Island Southeast Lighthouse (photo by Jeremy D'Entremont)

natives ashore. A great storm and a high wind floated the ship off the rocks, and it started out to sea. Block Islanders went aboard to reason with the woman, but she remained adamant, staying on the ship. As the vessel drifted away, one of the men set fire to it, hoping to compel her to leave. Mary Vanderline was stubbornly resolved not to go, however, and soon the flames forced the men to take to their boats. The burning ship with the woman standing dramatically by her possessions amid the flames disappeared over the horizon as the men rowed away.

According to the Reverend Mr. Livermore's account, which quotes the letter of Willey, "the light actually is seen, sometimes one-half mile from shore, where it lights up the walls of a gentleman's rooms through the windows." Strangers suppose it to be a vessel on fire. Willey saw it December 20, 1810. [S. T.] Livermore handles the whole matter rather roughly:

> *From this time, it is said, the* Palatinate *light appeared, and there are many who firmly believe it to be a ship of fire, to which their fantastic and distempered imaginations figure masts, ropes, and flowing sails.*

THE HESSIAN GALE

In the year 1778, on the 12th of December, Newport was swept by a blinding snowstorm still remembered as the "Hessian Gale." The grave Hessian sentries of the British army remained at their posts, faithfully carrying out their orders.

When they failed to come in from their posts, it was believed that some had deserted, but because of the storm no hunt was made; neither could the relieving sentries reach them because of the deep drifts. After the storm went down the changing guard found the missing sentries, still standing at their posts, frozen to death.

THE ANN AND HOPE AND OTHER VESSELS

An interesting incident of the *Ann and Hope* has survived the years. Laden with spice and merchandise, the *Ann and Hope* hit around 1806 during a bitter snowstorm on the south end of Block Island. One of the men washed ashore but he appeared more dead than alive. His body was placed above the tide, and after a short time spent in an effort to bring him back to life, one of the rescuers noticed another sailor in the surf.

"Let us try to save that one out there in the water, for this man is as good as dead," said the Block Islander.

"Na! Indade, I'm as good as half a dozen dead men!" was the astonishing rejoinder from the apparent corpse on the ground. The *Ann and Hope* and her cargo proved a total loss, with the exception of a few bags of coffee, which were salvaged and used by the islanders.

In 1831 Benjamin T. Coe witnessed the unfortunate disaster of the two-masted schooner *Warrior*, which Captain Scudder ran between Boston and New York. The Sound was white with foam in the heavy gale, with the two seas meeting at Sandy Point in great fury. Coe wrote that it was "impossible to describe the awful situation of that vessel when she first came on shore, the seas breaking over her masts, and seven souls hanging to the rigging, not more than 150 yards from us, and completely out of the power of man to render them any assistance."

Bottom up, her masts unstepped, her cargo of cotton and calico coming ashore, the ship was helpless. Sometimes the long bar on which the ship grounded would be nearly naked as the huge billows receded. One giant in the crew, larger and more resolute than the others, realizing that there would be no help from shore, decided to run the gauntlet. Choosing a moment when two large waves were pulling away from the thin skip of stones and sand, he jumped from the *Warrior* and ran for his life. Sprinting along the bar, he had reached a point nearly half way to shore when a towering billow began to form just ahead. Too far from the ship, he could not return. The great wave balanced itself for a moment, then it thundered and crashed on the bar, sweeping with terrific speed at the poor man, until it caught the sailor, knocked him over, and engulfed him. Swept off the bar, the man was not seen again until later, when his body was found on the beach.

Although they had lashed themselves to the deck, the others finally were swept into the sea as the vessel broke up and all perished. The seven graves of the victims may still be seen in the northwest corner of the island cemetery. There had probably been twenty-one on board— eighteen men and three women, all of whom perished.

In 1839 the schooner *Jasper* bound from Boston to New York hit the east side of the island and was badly damaged. Her cargo of cut stone was thrown over, and the schooner got off. It was not a bad wreck, but the islanders had cause to remember the incident, for many of them took the cut stones to their homes to be made into steps. Spring House,

Central House, and the home of Lorenzo Littlefield were among those so adorned.

The first large steamer wrecked at Block Island was the *Palmetto*, which struck Black Rock in 1876. [It was in 1858—*Ed.*]. Captain Baker tried to run her into an inlet, but she filled rapidly and went down. The crew and passengers left the ship, rowing to the south end of the island. Sinking to the bottom in seven fathoms of water, the *Palmetto* soon smashed to pieces. For weeks afterwards the merchandise came ashore. One native of Block Island was said to have much more of the leather goods from the cargo than he would ever wear out.

NO MAN'S LAND

During the Revolution a British man-of-war struck on the rocks of East Point and was lost, with many of her crew perishing. A quantity of gold specie in canvas bags went to the bottom. Years later, according to Mrs. Annie M. Wood in her delightful *No Man's Land*, a fisherman was sailing close to shore. On his way to sea, he saw down through the clear water to the bottom, where two bags heavily encrusted with moss and barnacles could be made out. Saying nothing to his companions on board, he planned to return later to the location. Time and time again he passed what he believed to be the spot, but he never again saw the gold bags from the British vessel.

In 1813 the *Amazon*, from Portugal, was wrecked thirty days from Lisbon while carrying a load of salt. A tublike craft was sent out to the vessel by means of a line, and the captain and crew were brought ashore. The second mate, who was carrying the ship's papers and valuables, was lost, but the others all landed safely.

THE METIS In 1873 ten volunteer lifesavers "who so gallantly volunteered to man the lifeboat and a fishing boat and saved the lives of thirty-two persons from the wreck of the steamer *Metis*" were awarded congressional gold medals.

Parts of the hull of the *Metis* are now buried in sand under 130 feet of water off Watch Hill, and the wreck is a popular dive site. The steam engine still stands twenty feet high at the bottom of the ocean.

THE NARRAGANSETT Both the *Narragansett* and the *Stonington* were repaired and returned to service.

BLOCK ISLAND The legend of the flaming ghost ship off Block Island is one of New England's enduring maritime myths. Edward Rowe Snow loved Whittier's poetry and enjoyed reciting his poem "The Palatine," with its memorable lines:

> *Behold! again, with shimmer and shine,*
> *Over the rocks and the seething brine,*
> *The flaming wreck of the Palatine!*

The *Ann and Hope* was a fast China trader that had been built in Portsmouth, New Hampshire. When it was wrecked at Block Island, it was on its sixth voyage and was said to be carrying a cargo worth $300,000.

The 1858 wreck of the *Palmetto* led to a push for improved navigational aids around Block Island, including Block Island Southeast Lighthouse in 1875. The lighthouse, moved away from the edge of eroding Mohegan Bluff in 1993, is now designated a National Historic Landmark.

NO MAN'S LAND No Man's Land is a small island almost three miles south of Gay Head (Aquinnah) on Martha's Vineyard, and is believed to be the first land in the area touched by explorer Bartholomew Gosnold in 1602. It is often spelled "Noman's Land."

CHAPTER 27

Nantucket and Martha's Vineyard Shipwrecks

NANTUCKET

Because of its exposed location in the path of American coastal traffic as well as almost all shipping to and from the old world, Nantucket has been the scene of hundreds of marine disasters.* The first wreck, hidden in the mist of Indian folklore, is that of a French treasure ship which was driven into the gulch west of Siasconset and entirely destroyed. Survivors of the catastrophe broke their way through the dense forest to reach an Indian settlement, where they were given shelter and food. The story is part tradition and part legend, but within the last fifty years treasure seekers have dug in the vicinity for the gold, which allegedly was never found.

The first recorded disaster of importance was in 1664, when a vessel bound from the Vineyard to Boston was lost at Nantucket with all on board drowned or later killed by the Nantucket Indians. Murdered by his heathen brothers, a Christian Indian named Joel was the first to die. No other details of this early shipwreck are known.

Five years later the aunt of Benjamin Franklin, Bethiah Folger Barnard, was drowned with three others as the canoe in which they were traveling to Nantucket from the Vineyard overturned. (A canoe in earlier

---

*Arthur H. Gardner's fine volume [*Wrecks around Nantucket*] lists over 700 wrecks.

times was a substantial lapstrake dory.) The only survivor was Eleazer Folger, who clung to the bottom of the canoe, righted it when the canoe grounded on a shoal, and later reached Morris Island, Cape Cod.

Tristam Coffin appears prominently in the next few wrecks, because of his position as military governor at the island. In the summer of 1673 a Dutch ship, the *Exportation*, commanded by Isaac Mellyne, hit abreast of Siasconset with a cargo of whale oil, tobacco, and cowhide. Coffin was appointed agent for the vessel, which proved a total loss.

Five years later the shoals off Nantucket caught a French ship in their grasp. Tristam Coffin became involved in the settlement of the ship's cargo. He was charged with abandoning the ship "to others, with the very best of intentions, but she was soon taken possession of by the people," so Tristam Coffin was fined £343 10s for his negligence in letting the people take over the ship. When he appealed to New York's governor, Sir Edmund Andros, under whose jurisdiction Nantucket operated, the fine was reduced to £150, "Boston money." (Coffin was placed under courtmartial.)

A wreck remembered for many years by those who saw it was that of the English sloop *Paoli*, bound for Philadelphia from Halifax. On December 6, 1771, the ship foundered on Great Point in a violent gale and snowstorm. Captain Dewlap [reported elsewhere as "Duilap"] and his entire crew reached shore, wet and freezing in the intense cold. The captain and his mate soon perished of exposure, however. Two sailors, attempting to reach a settlement, froze to death at Castine Point. Two other men, together with a boy named Weiderhold, crawled and fought their way to a barn at Squam, where they burrowed in the warm hay. Placing the youth between them, the men covered themselves with several feet of hay and fell asleep. The next day they were discovered by townsmen. Young Weiderhold became a permanent resident of Nantucket, and it is said that his descendants still live there. If those who perished had stayed on the sloop, they would have lived, for the vessel was discovered the next day by the residents of Nantucket, high and dry on the beach.

Three years later the sloop *Rochester*, bound for the African coast, struck on Great Rip, fifteen miles from Sankaty Head. A small boat reached Nantucket from the wreck. The quarterdeck washed off the vessel with thirteen of the crew aboard. Not knowing what their fate would be, the shipwrecked sailors had put aboard the quarterdeck a barrel of flour and a jug of rum, but before they could try this varied diet, the quarterdeck grounded on the southeast part of the island, and all were saved.

The keeper of Great Point Light had an unusual experience in October 1804, when the schooner *Republican* came ashore on the outside of Great Point, close to his lighthouse. After the vessel struck, the captain jumped into the water with his wife in his arms. Swimming ashore with her, he reached land, as also did the crew. So grateful was the master of the ship to Keeper George Swain for his hospitality and friendliness that he sold the schooner just as it lay on the shore to the keeper for the bargain price of fifty dollars. Swain later broke up the schooner for salvage.

Captain John Barnard of the American privateer *General Armstrong*, successful captor of many English prizes during the War of 1812, saw two of them wrecked around Nantucket Island. On December 21, 1812, the *Sir Sidney Smith* struck on Bass Rip off Siasconset with all on board perishing. A volunteer crew started from Nantucket to help them but turned back because of the weather. Although she had on board a very valuable cargo, nothing was ever recovered from the *Sir Sidney Smith*. The following month another prize to the *General Armstrong*, the ship *Queen*, went ashore at Nobadeer and broke in two. Soon a very rich cargo began to come up on the beach. Hundreds of people lined the shore, fighting and scrambling for each valuable item as it was sighted in the breakers. Several hundred hogsheads of bottled porter, sauerkraut, cheese, hams, clothing, and various other products smashed their way into the sand. Day after day, night after night, the people paced the beaches, awaiting the offering of the breakers. Estimates as high as $40,000 were made as to the value of the spoils secreted by the residents of Nantucket, but when John Barnard's agents visited the island to recover the cargo, little could be found. Still in existence on the island today are relics of the wreck of the *Queen*. An expert Owyhee swimmer was hired to dive to the bottom and place a sling around the heavier articles from the wreck, after which a capstan on the beach heaved them ashore. (This man is believed to have come from Oahu, one of the Hawaiian islands.) Without question John Barnard would have become a rich man had he landed the two prizes, the *Sir Sidney Smith* and the *Queen*, at a New York pier.

Another prize was wrecked at Nantucket during the War of 1812. After the fight between the British frigate *Endymion* and the *Prince of Neafchatel*, American privateer, in which the *Endymion*'s efforts to recapture the *Neafchatel*'s prize, the *Douglas*, failed completely, the prize floated off

Miacomet Shoal and went ashore at Sesachacha. The inhabitants of Nantucket assisted in the handling of the cargo, which consisted of 400 barrels of sugar, 190 puncheons of rum, 400 bags of coffee, 250 bales of cotton, and 22 mahogany logs. Many Nantucket people profited from the cargo, as there were no wreck agents in those days, or rather as Gardner says, "Everyone appears to have been a self-constituted agent." From the mariner's point of view, an interesting aftermath developed from a shipwreck on the south side of Nantucket in 1828. The brig *Sarah Ann*, bound for Boston from Savannah under Captain Phillips, struck on the 23rd of March near Hummock Pond. Her cargo was eventually discharged, and P. H. Folger bought her at public auction for $550. Her owners thought it was a very low sum for such a fine brig. When the *Sarah Ann* was floated off and brought into Nantucket Harbor, the original owners claimed the vessel. In court they lost out, for the chance had been very small that Folger would get the *Sarah Ann* floated free. What had happened after the transaction should not influence conditions at the time of the auction, according to the decision of the court. The case excited considerable attention up and down the coast at the time, the majority of mariners agreeing that the verdict was a fair one.

On December 14, 1828, the brig *Packet* from Saint Petersburg was carrying hemp and iron when she crashed against the south side of the island near Miacomet Pond. The brig began to break up at once. The crew took to the masts, all except the second mate, who left the vessel in a small boat. As he rowed away, the masts went by the board, carrying the other ten members of the crew to their death. Reaching the shore, the mate hunted for shelter from the bitter night, finally noticing a light far in the distance. It was a house in Newton, where a woman who had just passed away was being prepared for burial. As there were no men in the bereaved household, the frightened women would not admit him. When the door shut in his face he started out again, soon finding shelter in another residence a short distance away.

Eight years later a bolt of cloth from the wreck of the *Packet* was found embedded in the sand, and one of the Nantucket residents folded a fragment of the cloth into a napkin, writing the account of the shipwreck and placing it inside the cloth. The shipwreck expert of Nantucket, Arthur H. Gardner, read the account of the wreck from this paper preserved for many years in the folds of the cloth from the *Packet*.

On March 22, 1829, the schooner *Ranger*, commanded by Captain Wasgate of Salem, hit the island near Squam Pond during a snowstorm.

The captain and mate made shore, and stumbled in the dense snow into a rail fence, which they followed until they came to a barn. The floor was covered with hay, and there they stayed until the storm ended. Back on the schooner three crew members froze to death, unable to reach the forecastle. The same day another schooner, the *Ann*, commanded by Captain Reuben Mossman of Thomaston, Maine, drove ashore near the *Ranger*. Captain Mossman and two men were saved, but three others perished. Two of these were the captain's little sons, whom Mossman carried in his arms for more than a mile, but both died before a house was reached. Six bodies were brought to town from the two vessels and buried from the Methodist Episcopal church, where all the clergymen on the island assisted in the sad ritual.

The sugar ship *Nathaniel Hooper*, piloted by Captain Bogardus, hit on South Shoal, Nantucket, July 8, 1838. After throwing over her sugar cargo, the crew abandoned the vessel at midnight with all sails set. An hour later a heavy northwest squall freed the *Hooper*, and she drifted off. Her helm sent the ship toward Boston, and a smack which sighted her put two sailors aboard. The men sailed the *Hooper* safely all the way to Boston. A day after the incident the *Massachusetts* and the sloop *Cony* went out from Nantucket to look for the *Hooper*, but all that could be found were empty sugar boxes floating on the surface of the sea. Captain John Bogardus left for Boston, where he was going to report the loss of his vessel, but on his arrival was amazed to find her tied up at a pier in the Massachusetts capital.

On the evening of October 2, 1841, a furious gale began, which lasted for two days and did not end until twenty-five vessels were wrecked on or around Nantucket, with considerable loss of life. The storm is still spoken of as the October Gale. On the morning after the storm there were nineteen vessels wrecked or stranded around the island, while within sight of shore the masts of two others protruded out of water. It was the most unusual sight ever witnessed by the inhabitants of Nantucket.*

The strange trip of the fishing schooner *Minnie* in this gale is of interest. With foremast cut away, she was stranded on Brant Point. The crew

---

*This October gale brought great devastation to Cape Cod. Truro lost fifty-seven men; Yarmouth, ten; and Dennis, twenty. Captain Knowles' fight against this storm is described in Henry C. Kittredge's *Cape Cod*.

left the vessel in safety, and the schooner drove high on the beach, so far up that later it was decided to launch the vessel inside the point. The *Minnie* is often spoken of as the only vessel which ever entered Nantucket Harbor without coming around Brant Point.

Another curious shipwreck was that of the ship *Joseph Starbuck* which left Nantucket for Edgartown, where she was to be fitted for a whaling voyage. A number of ladies went aboard to take the trip to Edgartown. On the morning of November 27,1842, the steamer *Telegraph* towed the *Starbuck* out of the harbor and the trip began. A wind sprang up, forcing the ship to lose headway, until finally the *Telegraph* returned to Nantucket after leaving the *Starbuck* at anchor near Tuckernuck Shoal Lightship. As the gale increased the chain cables parted, allowing the ship to drift to the east. The mizzenmast was cut away, the foresail set, and every effort made to get into Nantucket Harbor, but in vain. The *Starbuck* hit the bar, going over on her beam ends. It was an awkward and dangerous situation which the crew faced. The ladies were placed in as sheltered a position as is possible on a ship over on her beam ends. The weather began to get colder, and ice formed whenever the surf hit the vessel.

It was not until morning that the people of Nantucket noticed the *Starbuck* heeled over. The steamer *Massachusetts* was dispatched at once to the scene, and by careful maneuvering reached the lee side of the vessel. A long warp was put in place, and a whaleboat began the perilous journey from steamer to ship. One by one the ladies were passed down, until they were all on the whaleboat; then the difficult trip back began. Ice formed over the crew and passengers as the whaleboat fought its way through mountainous waves, but the journey was successful. Four more trips were made, and an hour later all the shipwrecked victims were safe and sound ashore. The *Starbuck* soon went to pieces. This beautiful ship, built at Brant Point in 1838, had made only one voyage.

Early in the year 1846 a Scottish ship, the *Earl of Eglington*, under Captain Niven, left Liverpool for Boston with a heavy cargo of salt, coal, copper, and dry goods. On the 14th of March the ship struck on the South Shoal and drifted toward Nantucket, where she grounded on the Old Man Shoal. Again drifting forward, she hit near Nobadeer Pond. Eight of the crew left the ship in two boats, just as the seas made a complete breach over the vessel. One of the boats capsized, drowning two sailors, the others being rescued by men ashore who rushed into the surf for them. The second lifeboat capsized far from shore, and all four aboard were lost. By pantomime the sailors on shore signaled to the men still on the *Eglington* to throw over an oar with a line attached. This was done and the oar secured when near shore by a bluefish drail. A larger line was then carefully attached with a paper of instructions tied on. As soon as the signal was given to haul away, the shipwrecked sailors pulled the oar back to the doomed vessel. A sort of sling, capable of holding one man, was soon arranged, and by this sling the remainder of the crew was landed. When the captain came ashore the noose gave away, and he dropped into the sea, close enough to the beach to be rescued, however. The ship itself proved a total loss, for no appreciable part of the cargo was ever recovered.

In the year 1847 the schooner *Silivae* was wrecked on the west end of Nantucket. After strenuous work, the schooner was got off by one of Nantucket's greatest wreckers, Frederick F. Swain. Swain had lost a leg many years before, but in spite of this handicap floated most of Nantucket's wrecks while he was active. (The *Silivae* was his last wreck, however, for he died shortly afterwards.)

The winter of 1857 brought severe below-zero weather all over New England, and Nantucket suffered with the rest. Several vessels froze up in the ice. On January 23 the schooner *Conanchet* from Plymouth, in command of Captain Burgess, was caught in the ice and swept against Tuckernuck Shoals. Leaking badly, the *Conanchet* was abandoned. With no boat available, the sailors armed themselves with long planks and oars, crawling and pushing their way across the dangerous ice until Great Point was reached. They arrived in Nantucket when it was eleven degrees below zero, and not one of them was frostbitten. For days afterwards the *Conanchet* drifted about, finally disappearing in the vicinity of the South Shoals Lightship.

The King of Prussia figured in the aftermath of a Great Point Rip shipwreck of 1863. During that year the Prussian bark *Elwine Fredericke*, loaded with coal, struck the rip during a fog. Captain David Patterson and Captain Aaron Coffin reached the scene of the wreck shortly afterwards and saved the fourteen sailors aboard. Almost at once the bark went to pieces. So impressed was the King of Prussia when he heard the story that he sent the one in charge of the rescue boat, Captain David Patterson, a handsome silver chronometer.

One of the most amazing feats of rescue work was performed by Frederick W. Ramsdell of Nantucket on the occasion of the wreck of the schooner *Eveline Treat*, October 21, 1865. For his unusual display of heroism, he was awarded the highest medal of the Massachusetts Humane Society. The *Treat* was on her way from Philadelphia to Gloucester, loaded with coal, when she struck on Miacomet Rip. Discovered at daybreak by the people ashore, she was then 300 feet off the beach. Five of the sailors were lashed in the rigging, the captain, his two sons, and two other men. The schooner's house went by the board shortly afterwards, and the waves swept across her decks. After the mortar and apparatus of the Humane Society were brought to the beach, a small line was shot across and secured by one of the captain's sons. The boys forced their father to step into a sling, but at the last minute he lost his nerve and climbed back into the shrouds. The mate started ashore, but the rope sparked and stuck when the sling neared the beach. A line was thrown out, which he caught and fastened around his neck, whereupon the mate leaped into the breakers and was pulled up on the beach. One of the captain's sons followed, making the trip successfully.

Three men were left in the rigging of the *Treat* as the afternoon advanced. They agreed that the captain should be sent along next, as he was slowly weakening. A life car which was fastened to the hawser failed to work and was taken down. Finally the young men persuaded

Ramsdell's daring rescue saving the captain of the schooner Treat *(based on Folger's painting)*

the captain to get into the sling, and he started for the beach. When he was midway between ship and shore the line again sparked, and there the poor captain hung bareheaded and in his stocking feet for an hour and a half. As night began to fall, the men in the rigging worked feverishly at the snark, but made little progress.

A young Nantucket man named Frederick Ramsdell volunteered in an effort to save the captain. Fastening a light rope about his waist, Ramsdell started out arm over arm on the hawser until he reached the captain. Cutting the lines on each side of the sling, he retied them and fastened the light rope to the sling. Ramsdell then worked his way back to the beach, and the captain was finally hauled to safety. The other two sailors were soon brought ashore. It was a miraculous feat which Ramsdell had performed. (For this feat of bravery, Ramsdell was presented with the silver medal of the Massachusetts Humane Society.)

A notable battle with the treacherous ice floes was fought on February 5, 1871, off the Cliff Shore, when the five members of the coal schooner *Mary Anna*, were saved by the men of Nantucket. Captain Lennan had sailed from South Amboy, anchoring the *Mary Anna* off Chatham. The ice became so thick that she broke from her moorings and started drifting toward the Nantucket Inner Bar. So heavily encased in ice that she was in danger of sinking, the *Mary Anna* finally stranded on February 4. The next day her distress flag was sighted from Nantucket, and the steamer *Island Home* was made ready. After reaching Brant Point, the rescue steamer was unable to make further progress as she also became imprisoned in the ice.

Several attempts made during the day to reach the schooner failed because the ice was too dangerous to walk on and boats were soon caught in the enormous floes. At 10:00 in the evening a plan was formed to reach the vessel. Eight men started out over the ice, dragging and pulling two dories, carrying with them several long planks and plenty of lines. Whenever the ice would not bear the weight of the dories, the rescue party would lay the planks out and slide the boats over them. When the open sea was encountered, the men rowed the dories across the water. In this way, two miles of firm ice, rubber ice, and water were traversed by half an hour after midnight. The night was clear, but the cold stung through the men's heavy garments. They saw the schooner over on her beam ends, sheathed in ice several inches thick, in ten feet of water.

When they arrived at the *Mary Anna*, the men found the crew almost frozen to death. The steward, with both feet frozen, had already bade farewell to his comrades, who had covered him over with a sail and left him to die. All the men were soon placed in the two dories, and the long, dangerous journey back to shore began. The entire party reached Nantucket at 3:00 in the morning, safe and sound. The heroic Nantucket men were each awarded a silver medal by the Massachusetts Humane Society.

An Italian bark, named *Papa Luigi C.*, loaded with wine and brimstone, hit the south side of Nantucket, March 21, 1877. Having a small boat, the crew arrived safely near shore, but the lifeboat went broadside as the breakers caught it. All were saved. The vessel did not go to pieces for over a year, finally breaking up in October 1878.

Captain Roberts of Salem was wrecked aboard the bark *Hazard* with a cargo of hides from Africa on the Old Man Shoal at midnight, February 14, 1881. Leaving the crew to pump, the captain and three men rowed for help. When the vessel began to settle in the water, the second mate and one man went aboard a small raft which was moored astern, but the others decided to stay on the bark. As the float drifted away, the bark settled lower and lower into the water until the others changed their minds and began to swim toward the comparative safety of the raft. It was too late, however, and only one man reached the float, the others drowning.

Later in the afternoon the captain's boat reached Nantucket, but the sailors told such a confusing story that few townspeople believed that a raft was floating off the coast. The next morning the steamer *Island Home* searched the vicinity in vain, so the men were given up for lost. Two months went by when one day the supply ship *Verbena* brought two survivors into Nantucket, the second mate of the *Hazard* and one sailor. When the raft, almost entirely submerged, drifted out to sea, the *Island Home* had steamed close by without noticing it. The shipwrecked men then drifted by the South Shoal Lightship, where the lookout spotted them. The three men were soon taken aboard, one of them dead from exhaustion. The two survivors left Nantucket after a brief rest, returning to their homes, where they had long been given up for lost.

An unusual story of the sea is the tale of the schooner *French Van Gilder*, the six-master *Alice M. Lawrence,* and the *Unique*. On March 29, 1885, the three-master *French Van Gilder* struck on Tuckernuck Shoal, and her crew landed safely. The schooner, loaded with paving blocks, stayed where she struck. Years went by. In 1914, twenty-nine years later, the *Van Gilder* again figured in the news.

On the 5th of December, 1914, the great six-masted schooner *Alice M. Lawrence* stranded on Tuckernuck Shoal in the early morning hours, but it was not discovered until later that the *Lawrence* had broken her back by striking the hulk of the *Van Gilder*, wrecked back in 1885. Because of the heavy cargo of paving stones, the two schooners could not be separated or taken off the shoal in any way, so after all movable material had been taken off, the 305-foot six-master was abandoned. On November 27, 1915, the wreck was set afire, burning to the water's edge. The *Alice M. Lawrence* was one of the largest vessels ever wrecked in the vicinity. (Built in Bath, Maine, in 1906, her gross tonnage was 3,132.)

The third part of this strange story took place on July 17, 1917, when the British schooner *Unique* struck squarely on top of the hulk of the *Van Gilder* and the *Lawrence*. The crew of the Muskeget Coast Guard Station rescued every sailor aboard the *Unique*, which soon became a total loss.

One of the most valiant fights ever put up by a volunteer life-saving crew was that enacted on Sunday, January 10, 1886, when the three-

The remains of the schooner Alice M. Lawrence, *which struck a schooner that had been wrecked off Nantucket nearly thirty years earlier.*

master *T. B. Witherspoon* hit on the south side of Nantucket. Captain Alfred H. Anderson, bound from Surinam to Boston, mistook Sankaty Head Light for the flash from Montauk Point, Long Island, in the blinding snowstorm, bringing his schooner up in the breakers near Little Mioxes Pond. News of the disaster reached town, and large groups of people were soon on the shore, watching with that strange fascination which holds crowds at fires, disasters, and shipwrecks. One by one the sailors dropped to their death in the raging sea, which was so rough that a lifeboat could not possibly be launched.

The Surfside Life-Saving crew shot several lines over the schooner, but the survivors still on the vessel were powerless to move, having frozen into the rigging. A life raft was launched into the breakers, the men aboard hauling themselves off by a line shot out to the schooner. A huge wave towered over them for a second, then broke with devastating force on the raft, knocking two of the men overboard, but they grabbed the raft and regained its deck. The shock, however, had snapped the hawser, and the lifesavers were pulled ashore by a second line paid out from the beach. Time after time the mortar sent out its line to the schooner, until at the sixth effort a line struck squarely across the vessel's bow, and was made fast to the forerigging by the two sailors still alive on the *Witherspoon*. A running block with the lines rove through was sent out. By dusk the breeches buoy had been rigged and the men were able to crawl into it.

It was after dark when the two men reached the shore, more dead than alive. One of them, the first mate, had watched his wife and little boy perish when the sea broke into their cabin. It is said that this shipwreck, which cost the lives of seven persons, was the most sorrowful in Nantucket history. The loss of life in many other cases had been greater, but the victims of the *Witherspoon* wreck lingered for many hours a short distance from safety, only to perish in the waves in full view of hundreds of people on the Nantucket shoreline.

Bound from Manila to Boston with a load of hemp, the ship *Asia* struck on Round Shoal in a severe northeast storm February 20, 1898. Captain Dakin had taken his wife and daughter on the long voyage, and must have suffered terribly with his family before they perished. When the *Asia* began to break up, the captain is believed to have given the care of his daughter to the mate. The first news of the disaster was on February 22, when a tug steamed into Wood's Hole with the bodies of the mate and the captain's daughter, the little girl fast in the arms of the mate. It is not known what became of the captain and his wife, but some time later news came that three of the crew had been picked up by the sailors on the Handkerchief Lightship. They had been floating in the wintry sea for twenty-four hours. The vessel broke up, her $100,000 cargo coming ashore at Cape Cod, Nantucket, and Martha's Vineyard.

The schooner *Saint Elmo*, built at Rockland, Maine, sailed from that port with a load of lime early in 1898, commanded by Captain Hall. While on the way to New York she struck on the shoals east of Nantucket Island. Two days later Keeper Remsen of Sankaty Light saw the rigging and masts of the sunken vessel, and the Humane Society's boat at Siasconset was sent out to the wreck. As the surfboat approached the wreck a nearby fishing smack signaled to the men, who found the only survivor of the *Saint Elmo* aboard the fishing vessel. The captain, his wife, and three seamen had all been washed overboard, the lone sailor clinging to the rigging while the vessel went through a strange series of maneuvers. As the schooner was hove down, the deckload shifted. When she rolled over, the compressed air inside burst out her stern, and she righted and sank until her decks were awash.

In this condition the *Saint Elmo* drifted around the shoals, grounding at low tide and floating at high. Two days and two nights went by before the vessel finally hit the Rose and Crown Shoal, where Keeper Remsen sighted her. The mate later left for home, after a rest from his experience.

The schooner *Stephen Morris* was abandoned early in June 1898, later becoming the object of an unusual chase between the steamer *Petrel* and the underwriter's boat from Nantucket. When the *Morris* was first sighted near Bass Rip off Siasconset on June 5, a tug was sent out after her but failed to find the schooner. The next day off Great Neck Station the steamer *Petrel* spoke a vessel which had fallen in with the schooner a day before. The entire 7th of December was spent cruising around, looking in vain for the derelict. At last it was decided that she had broken up and gone to pieces on the rips.

But the elusive *Morris* had not finished her strange game. A short time later she again appeared, and the *Petrel* started in pursuit immediately. Meanwhile a crew from Nantucket was mustered and soon launched the underwriter's boat from Surfside. The *Petrel* arrived at the wreck first and started to tow her to Vineyard Haven just as the underwriter's boat appeared on the scene. The lifeboat crew caught up with the slow-moving tug and tow, going aboard the *Morris* to claim her, but it was no use. The *Petrel* received the $500 salvage money for the schooner, and the Nantucket lifeboat crew, although protesting vigorously, had done all their work for nothing.

The steam collier *Middlesex* crashed into the five-master *George P. Hudson* on July 11, 1914. Because of the crash, the *Hudson's* gasoline tanks exploded, killing one man. Except for another sailor killed by a falling mast, the remainder of the crew were rescued by boats from the *Middlesex.* Captain John Thomas, however, in keeping with one of the sea's traditions, went down with his ship. During a severe northeast gale the same fall, a large section of the *Hudson* washed ashore at Quidnet.

The disappearance of the Cross Rip Lightship in 1918 is one of the unexplained mysteries of the sea. Torn from her moorings February 1 by the heavy ice packs in the vicinity, the lightship was last seen from Great Point Light on February 5. At the time it vanished the vessel was without power, had no sail, and was helpless against the elements. Tugs and cutters sent out to find her never located a trace of the ship, and her disappearance became one of the unsolved mysteries of Nantucket's maritime history. Not a trace has ever been seen of either the vessel or her crew of eight men.*

The last of that great fleet of Palmer-owned schooners, the *Dorothy Palmer,* was sailing off Nantucket on March 29, 1923. Perhaps her captain was thinking of the days when so many of the schooners, all with the last name Palmer, sailed the seven seas. There had been the Davis, wrecked at the entrance to Boston Harbor, the *Prescott* and the *Fuller,* lost off the Georges, and many others, including the *Fanny,* the *Marie,* the *Harwood,* and the *Singleton.* The *Dorothy* alone was still afloat. Suddenly the keel of the *Dorothy Palmer* grounded on the edge of Stone Horse Shoal, and the schooner settled into the sand. The days of the Palmer fleet had ended. Although her crew were all saved, the schooner soon became a total loss.†

A terrific blizzard swept the coast on the night of March 11, 1924, sending the great six-masted schooner *Wyoming* to her doom, with

---

*There were six aboard when the lightship was lost. The commanding officer was not aboard at the time.—Ed.

†Others in the Palmer fleet include *Baker, Elizabeth,* the second *Fanny, Maud,* and *Paul.* With the exception of *Fanny,* they were all lost in 1915.

The Wyoming, *lost with all hands near Nantucket in 1924*

all the members of her crew, thirteen in number, going down with the vessel. The *Wyoming* had last been seen at anchor that afternoon near Pollock Rip lightship. The next day her quarterboard came ashore, followed by much wreckage from the 305-foot schooner, and it was feared that she had pounded to pieces during the night. No additional information about the *Wyoming* was ever revealed by the sea.

Closing our remarks on Nantucket, we can conclude by saying that although the shoals around Nantucket have probably caught enough ships and vessels since the beginning of history to make it a greatly feared location, the men of Nantucket have proved themselves of sterling worth in going to the aid of seamen when tossed by the tempest against the shores of "the faraway island."

MARTHA'S VINEYARD

During the same storm of 1778 which wrecked the *General Arnold*, a privateer sloop came ashore at the east end of Martha's Vineyard Island, with seventeen men perishing. Although a fearful gale, it proved a blessing to the islanders, whose food and supplies had been removed by the British.

Shortly after the gale, one of the residents walking near the Lagoon Pond found an immense quantity of striped bass buried in the ice and snow on the beach. Packed closely together, there were actually thousands of fish piled up on the beach, evidently washed ashore there from the wrecked privateer.

The news of the discovery spread rapidly around Martha's Vineyard and soon the inhabitants were carting the fish away. As there was little salt on the island the people packed the bass in the snow. The fish lasted all that winter, and together with eels, clams, and wild fowl the fish kept the Vineyard residents from starvation.

At sundown on November 26, 1898, the *Amelia G. Ireland* anchored near Menemsha Bight in company with the *Clara Leavitt*. At about 10 that night Surfman Manning of the Gay Head Life-Saving Station reached Lobsterville on his regular patrol along the Martha's Vineyard shore. In the vicinity of Dogfish Bar he saw the flash of a torch and realized that a ship must be in trouble. It was a three-masted schooner, the *Amelia G. Ireland*. Surfman Manning lighted a Coston signal to indicate to those aboard that the wreck had been sighted, and hurried back to the station at Gay Head, where Keeper Hayman organized a rescue party. The surfmen rushed down to the boathouse and decided to transport the surfboat overland because the stranded schooner lay directly to windward and the gale was momentarily increasing. The going became so difficult, however, that the keeper sent for the oxen of Simon Devine, a farmer living a short distance away, and with the help of these beasts of burden, the Gay Head lifeboat was pulled around to the other side of Menemsha Bight, which they reached at midnight.

The lights of the schooner could now be seen a third of a mile out into the ocean. The shoal broke the heavier seas. So violent was the wind that repeated attempts to launch the boat failed. As the lifesavers struggled on the shore, another schooner loomed up in the night and crashed against the same Dogfish Bar, settling into the water less than a hundred yards from the *Ireland*. At 2:00 A.M., desperate in the face of adversity, the keeper sent for the beach apparatus. Fearing the schooners were too far away, he determined to exhaust every possible effort. As the surfmen went for the ox team, the second schooner started to break up before their eyes. Wreckage soon covered the shore. The surfmen, searching anxiously for bodies of the sailors, found nothing. The second schooner had disappeared completely.

The wind now reached such a pitch that the heavy surfboat was picked up and blown the entire length of the beach, falling into a pool of water almost 300 feet away. As soon as the beach apparatus arrived at daylight, Keeper Hayman made ready to fire the smallest possible line, a number 4, but the wind, now at its peak, upset the faking box. A larger line, number 7, was fired with a six-ounce powder charge, but failed to reach its objective.

Daybreak revealed the figures of men still clinging to the shrouds of the *Ireland*. The other schooner had entirely disintegrated, not even her wreckage remaining where she had struck the night before. The sailors were all believed drowned, but unknown to the surfmen, sailor Philo G. Sparrow had actually made shore in safety, although quite a distance away from the place where the lifesavers had gathered. When the foremast went, he had grabbed a stanchion, and a gigantic wave threw him high on the beach. Crawling on his hands and knees, he reached the bank, laboriously fighting his way up to the road, where he found the home of Charles H. Ryan. Here he aroused the family and told his experience. If he had not been saved, the fate of the three-masted *Clara Leavitt* of Portland, Maine, would have remained in complete oblivion, sharing the unknown with the *Addie E. Snow* and the *Pentagoet*.

Back on the shore Keeper Hayman watched with failing hope the growing intensity of the gale. By this time the wind had veered to the north, so that another attempt in the surfboat could be made from a more favorable point. Time and again the picked crew of the station, with three volunteers, charged against the force of the wind, each time thrown back in confusion. Again Keeper Hayman shot the projectile out toward the vessel, but in vain. Sunset was approaching, with a hard night ahead, so Keeper Hayman announced a rest period.

At midnight, when the tide was down again, the wind relented a trifle, and Keeper Hayman made his final effort. One of the best volunteers now decided against going in the surfboat, simply because he felt there was no possible hope of reaching their objective. Successfully, however, the crew launched the boat and slowly but surely shortened the distance to the schooner until the lifeboat reached its goal! Since the port bow of the wreck was found to be encumbered with wreckage, a new attempt was made to get to the schooner at the martingale. As the surfboat hovered underneath, the exhausted sailors dropped one by one into the craft from the schooner. Leaving one man frozen to death in the rigging, the men made for shore.

It was a feat that high praise could not overestimate. For twenty-nine hours the men of Martha's Vineyard had fought for the lives of the sailors on the *Ireland*, and had finally delivered the six then alive to the safety of the shore. The names of the members of this heroic crew follow: N. C. Hayman, Keeper; Francis Manning, Ben Attaquin, Timothy Mayhew, Jesse Smalley, and Samuel Anthony, surfmen; with two volunteers, Abram Cooper and Linus Jeffers. The *Amelia G. Ireland* was commanded by Captain Oscar Knapp, and carried a cargo of oil in tanks. Westly Mark, who perished in the rigging, was later brought ashore, where his body was buried in the Gay Head graveyard.

The *Port Hunter*, an English steamer sailing for Gravesend Bay, collided with the tug *Covington* on the night of November 2, 1918. Those on board thought that the shock was a torpedo. The *Port Hunter* grounded on the Hedge and Fence Shoal nearby, and a large hole was found in her hull.

A few weeks later material from the steamer showed up in Boston, where it was placed on sale. There had been a $9 million cargo, which eventually was disposed of for $1 million. Part of the cargo drifted ashore at Martha's Vineyard, where scores of paper cartons were washed up on the beach.

NANTUCKET The 1664 wreck mentioned by Snow happened at Coatue. The Wampanoag Joel and his father Hiacoomes, who was the first native Christian minister on Martha's Vineyard, were on their way past Nantucket bound for Joel's commencement at Harvard. Hiacoomes survived the incident and lived until about 1690.

When Bethiah Folger Barnard drowned in 1669, she had been married about three months. Her husband, John Barnard, also died in the canoe accident. Lone survivor Eleazer Folger was Bethiah's brother.

The October Gale of 1841 remains one the worst on record for Nantucket and Cape Cod. Much of the Cape Cod fishing fleet was caught at sea, and more than fifty men died from the town of Truro alone. Up to a foot and a half of snow fell inland.

The names of the crew of the Cross Rip Lightship, lost in 1918, are inscribed on the Lightship Memorial on the waterfront of New Bedford, Massachusetts. The memorial includes the bell of the Vineyard Sound Lightship, lost with all hands in 1944. The location of the Cross Rip Lightship (LV6) is still not known, although in July 1933 a government dredge in Vineyard Sound area brought up pieces of oak planking and other materials that may have been from the lost lightship.

The *Wyoming*, built at the Percy and Small shipyard in Bath, Maine, was the last of the ten six-masted schooners built in the 1900–1909 period. According to *Shipwrecks Around Maine* by William P. Quinn, the *Wyoming* was the largest wooden sailing vessel to carry a cargo. A land-locked "evocation" of the

The Lightship Memorial in New Bedford, Massachusetts, showing the bell of the Vineyard Sound Lightship, which was lost in 1944 (photo by Jeremy D'Entremont)

329-foot schooner is being constructed at Bath's Maine Maritime Museum at this writing. Tom Wilcox, executive director of the museum, says the work will have a stem and jibboom, a section of the hull at each mast, and a stern post and transom. It will exceed 400 feet in length and is expected to be completed by late summer 2003.

MARTHA'S VINEYARD A significant portion of the *Port Hunter* cargo, including rubber boots and leather vests, washed ashore and was scooped up by enterprising residents of Martha's Vineyard. In her book, *Shipwrecks on Martha's Vineyard*, Dorothy Scoville writes that the *Port Hunter* wreck was among the most productive wrecks the Vineyard ever had known. "For a time it was 'finders keepers' in the salvage work and there was a brisk business in selling salt damp articles."

A salvage company attempted to remove steel rails and billets from the vessel's hold in 1962; storms hampered the operation but some material was recovered. Still largely intact, the 380-foot wreck is a popular dive site. Some items that were brought up by divers in 1960 are now at the Martha's Vineyard Historical Society.

CHAPTER 28

Massachusetts Bay

From earliest times until the late eighteenth century, Boston had far more shipping than either New York or Philadelphia, and because of the great number of vessels going to and from the port which was called for over a century "the Mistress of North America," there were many shipping disasters in times of storms and gales. To the more famous storms and wrecks we have devoted individual chapters. Those found here achieved local importance. Literally hundreds had to be omitted in full.

THE 1740 GALE

The December 1740 storm was of outstanding violence around Boston Harbor. Captain Underwood's craft hit the rocks at Rainsford's Island and bilged, Captain Tilden's vessel ran aground at Scituate, while two Newburyport sloops went ashore at Lynn Beach. There were twenty vessels wrecked at Marblehead. Captain McCloud and his entire crew of ten perished when their ship hit the rocks off Scituate. At Nantucket Captain Griffith's ship was wrecked. A sloop belonging to Captain Lowell was wrecked down Massachusetts Bay, but all were saved. Five ships were ashore at Cape Cod, three from the Vineyard, one from North Carolina, and Captain Higgins' vessel bound for Connecticut, which came ashore near the Highland. (In this period the vessels were listed by the names of the captains.)

THE MAGNIFIQUE

On a cool spring morning shortly after the First World War had ended, Captain Charles H. Jennings of the Lovell's Island Range Lights in Boston Harbor (keeper of Boston Light from 1916 until 1919) was industriously digging in the garden near his house when his spade brought up an object which resembled a coin. Working in the same location, he uncovered several of the round, flat disks, and later brought them into the kitchen of his home, where he and his wife scrubbed one of the objects until the deposit of dirt had been removed. There revealed to them was a gold coin, later found to have a market value of twenty-nine dollars. The other coins yielded under the rubbing and scraping to reveal that they were valuable gold and silver pieces of a period between 1650 and 1775.

Although he did not know it at the time, Keeper Jennings had actually uncovered coins from the treasure of the great French man-of-war *Magnifique*, which had been wrecked on Lovell's Island during the Revolutionary War.

Keeper of the Lovell's Island Range Lights, Charles Jennings, and Edward Rowe Snow, January 1, 1937 (from the collection of Edward Rowe Snow)

Keeper Charles Jennings next to one of the Lovell's Island Range Lights in Boston Harbor (photo by Edward Rowe Snow)

In August 1782, the French Fleet was entering Boston Harbor, and David Darling, the pilot of the seventy-four-gun man-of-war *Magnifique*, missed stays in the Narrows. The frigate crashed on the rocks off Lovell's Island, ripped her bottom out, slid over the ledge, and sank in deep water between the ledge and the island. Her career was over.

Pilot Darling lost his position because of the accident, and became the sexton of the Old North Church. His record was known, however, for one day he found written in chalk on the meetinghouse door:

Don't you run this ship ashore
As you did the seventy-four.

Attempts were made from time to time to recover the treasure which sank with the ship, but failures were recorded as late as 1869. By this time the entire contour of the island was changing because of the position of the wreck.

The currents of the Narrows created a bar over the skeleton of the *Magnifique*, which in turn connected itself to the island. The bar built up during the storms until even at high water it was visible. When Mayor Shurtleff of Boston visited the island around 1870, he found that the spot where the *Magnifique* sank was dry land, part of the island itself.

Evidently when the Lighthouse Department erected the keeper's dwelling, they built near the skeleton of the *Magnifique*, and at the time Keeper Jennings dug at the rear of his home, he was actually digging in the soil over the old wreck. Nevertheless Jennings did not become wealthy from the treasure, for later another keeper, in Jennings' opinion, probably obtained coins worth more than $7000 of it. That, however, is another story.

THE ELIZABETH AND ANN

Late in the afternoon of March 6, 1829, Captain William Tewksbury, the famous lifesaver, arrived in Boston from Deer Island with the news that Captain Savage and his entire crew had been lost on the *Elizabeth and Ann*, which was then coming ashore a shattered wreck after hitting the rocks off Nahant. Her cargo of oranges and cigars was strewn all along the waterfront from what is now Winthrop Highlands to the end of Deer Island. The captain's watch was found still hanging on a hook in the cabin, when it came up with other wreckage on the Point Shirley beach. The quarterdeck came ashore at Cedar Island at the entrance to Shirley Gut. (The Minot's Light storm destroyed all vestiges of this island.)

The day after the storm the inmates of the poor house in Chelsea, along with several laborers, were gathering kelp and seaweed on the rocks at what is now Fort Heath, Winthrop. One young Negro lad, more active than the others, saw a partially submerged plank floating in waist-deep water. There seemed to be a white cloth attached to the wood, so the young Negro lad waded out into the water to get the plank.

To his astonishment, the boy found the cloth was actually a large canvas bag, torn at one end. He could not easily lift it, but managed to bring it ashore. Pulling it upon the rocks, he opened the sack and found it filled with gold pieces! The others naturally crowded around him, but the overseer was firm, and allowed the boy to keep his discovery, taking him at once to the local Chelsea bank. The money totaled a handsome fortune. Needless to say, the Negro's days as a laborer were over, but it would be interesting to know how much money he recovered and his subsequent life history.

Incidentally, the hole in the canvas bag had allowed many of the gold coins to escape into the ocean. Search was made at the time, but nothing was found. Years later, around 1880, the son of the Reverend Mr. Duffield was playing in the sand off Grover's Cliff, Winthrop, when he dug up a coin with his shovel. Taking it to his father, the boy found that he was the happy owner of a gold piece. Word quickly traveled around, as news of that sort does, and soon the entire shoreline was crowded with people searching for gold. Many of them were lucky, as the local papers of the period reported the finding of around $300. Whether more money is still buried from the wreck of the *Elizabeth and Ann* lost back in 1829 is an interesting question. (Only rocks remain today where the sandy area was.)

THE TEDESCO

The American bark *Tedesco*, hailing from Portland, Maine, homeward bound with a cargo of sherry wine, salt, and raisins, went ashore on Long Rock, about 300 feet east-northeast of Galloupe's Point, Swampscott, Sunday night, January 18, 1857. It had been a furious blizzard that swept the coast late in the evening after an unusually calm day. The sea had been so smooth when the fishermen came in that afternoon that they had left their dories just a little above the highwater mark. In the morning nothing but splintered remains could be found.

Captain Peterson of the *Tedesco* had been sailing between Pig Rock and Egg Rock Light in a moderate northwest wind late that afternoon. The wind hauled to the northeast and a furious gale began shortly afterwards.* The residents on shore had the impression that the *Tedesco* sailed on up the bay.

The storm was so severe that few people knew of the shipwreck until late in the afternoon, when residents discovered the shore strewn with wreckage, including many casks of wine. Every person on the *Tedesco* perished in the surf. Later the bodies of the sailors came ashore on Whale Beach, where townsmen brought them to the Methodist Church. After an impressive funeral, the men were buried in the Swampscott Cemetery.

Two locations in Swampscott are named for the *Tedesco*, whose men perished off the town's shore. The boulder where the bark hit is still called Tedesco Rock, while one of New England's prominent social organizations along the North Shore of Massachusetts is the Tedesco Country Club.

THE VERNON

The British bark *Vernon*, loaded with oranges and lemons, sailed for Boston from Messina, Sicily, during the winter of 1859. Running into heavy seas off the coast, she crashed on Lynn Beach near Little Nahant, February 3. Residents near the shore quickly noticed the shipwreck, and soon hundreds of persons from nearby Lynn and Nahant lined the beach.

A boat which was manned by the mate and two sailors put out for land, but swamped immediately. The craft washed ashore while two of the men were pulled back to the bark by rope. The third sailor, William Bond, drifted to a point near the beach where, just as he was about to sink, he was taken out of the water by Otis Newhall, who had courageously launched a dory into the waves.

---

*Egg Rock Light was first lighted September 14, 1856, and discontinued in 1922. The brig *Judge Hathaway* and the schooner *Geneva* both came ashore in the same gale.

The *Vernon* began to break up and the passengers and crew seemed doomed. Zebedee Small manned a lifeboat, but failed after two attempts to get it through the heavy surf. By this time the shore was littered with oranges and lemons, which the people quickly gathered as the breakers washed them in.

Captain Miles Blanchard then organized a small group of men and boys who successfully launched their dory and made their way to the doomed *Vernon*. About the same time a group of Swampscott fishermen arrived on the scene with a dory, which they had dragged through the snow. The natural rivalry between the two groups of men, representing two sections of the North Shore, stimulated the rescuers to almost superhuman efforts. Soon everyone on the *Vernon* was taken ashore to safety through waves which at times stood the dories on end. For many years afterwards the people of Lynn, Nahant, and Swampscott dated events in relation to the time of the wreck of the British bark *Vernon*.

BOSTON HARBOR'S WORST SHIPWRECK

The *Maritana*, a ship of 991 tons, was built in Quincy, Massachusetts, in 1857, and owned in Providence by Suchet Mauran, 2nd. When the question of a figurehead was discussed, Mauran decided upon a graceful French carving which had been salvaged from the French warship

Figurehead from the Maritana, *which was wrecked in Boston harbor in 1861. This figurehead was said to bring bad luck. It had previously been on the* Caroline, *which was wrecked; later it was placed on Lincoln Wharf, which caught fire. (Courtesy of the Bostonian Society)*

Berceau after her capture by the American frigate *Boston* back in the quasi-war with France at the turn of the century. Some years later the figurehead was placed on the ship *Caroline*, which was soon wrecked in a storm. The figurehead was again preserved, this time being placed on the new *Maritana*. The ship's career was fairly uneventful until she sailed from Liverpool, September 25, 1861, with a great cargo of coal, wool, potash, steel, and iron, headed for Boston.

The *Maritana* sighted Highland Light at Cape Cod, November 2 at 4:30 in the afternoon. Four hours later she took a bearing on Race Point Light, which was then fifteen miles away to the east-southeast. Keeping on her course for Boston Light, the *Maritana* ran into a southeasterly gale while far out in the bay. Shortly after midnight Captain Williams obtained a brief glimpse of Boston Light's welcome flash before snow came down so thick that the light was obscured. Captain Williams ordered the crew to tack ship, but before she could be brought to the wind, breakers were discovered. With a grinding crash, the *Maritana* struck on Egg Rock or Shag Rocks, half a mile to the eastward of Boston Light.

Although the ship was seaworthy, its position on Shag Rocks was almost hopeless. The writer has visited this ugly ledge on several occasions, and believes that there is very little chance for any vessel unfortunate enough to hit here in a storm. Six other disasters to shipping are known to have occurred at Shag Rocks.

Courageous Captain Williams made plans to reach the rocky ledge. A heavy sea was smashing against the hard, unyielding pinnacles which jut out from the water, so that his plans were foredoomed to failure. The ship's longboat was got over, but it was stove in almost at once, while the other ship's boats were crushed to pieces in the davits. At 3:00 in the morning the masts were cut away.

A brave seaman named Thomas Haney now swam ashore with a line. Since he could not climb high enough on the ledges to escape the direct force of the mighty billows, he signaled to be hauled back to the boat where he was hoisted over the side, bleeding from scores of jagged cuts. The captain now realized that there was little hope for most of the crew and passengers.

The *Maritana* was new and strong, however, and there was no water below decks at all, hours after the crash. Grinding and chafing on the ledge, the vessel dropped lower and lower as the tide receded. The strain was too great even for a new vessel. Suddenly the captain noticed the ship was beginning to break in two.

"Look out for yourselves!" shouted Captain Williams, and fell to his death in the crevice of the break. The scenes which followed were terrible to witness. With the guiding spirit of the vessel gone, the passengers and crew struggled for their lives. Five seamen were able to swim over to Shag Rocks, while seven persons on the ship's poop deck floated against the ledge when the poop came free. All the others, twenty-six in number, were drowned. (This is the largest number lost in Boston Harbor. The Thompson's Island disaster of 1842 cost the lives of twenty-five, while the *Mary E. O'Hara* tragedy of 1941 totaled twenty deaths.)

Meanwhile, over at Boston Light, Keeper Moses Barrett had noticed the lights of the vessel shortly before midnight. He saw her bearing east-northeast when she suddenly changed her course and seemed to be running for the light. At 12:20 she burned her torch lights, enabling him to recognize her as a square-rigger. The snow now came so fast that the ship's lights faded out. Barrett hoped that she had slipped by safely to make her way into the calmer waters of the inner harbor. The gale increased at a fearful rate, with the visibility at daybreak less than one hundred yards. The lighthouse keeper climbed down to the edge of

Shag Rocks in Boston Harbor, where the Maritana *struck in 1861. Snow called them "the ledges which have cost the lives of over 100 sailors."*

the ocean, where he found the standard of a ship, and decided, correctly, that a large vessel had been wrecked nearby.

When the storm lifted a little, the anxious inhabitants of Lighthouse Island were able to see the *Maritana* fast ashore on Shag Rocks. Keeper Barrett knew a lifeboat would not last in the gale. He could do nothing to help. Across Lighthouse Channel lies Hull, and Barrett set the signal for a ship in distress. The wind blew the signal flag to shreds.

By afternoon the wind and the seas had fallen, and Captain Barrett's new signal flag was acknowledged. At 2:00 pilot boat *William Sharkey* sent a dory manned by the lifesavers of Hull ashore at Shag Rocks, where the survivors of the tragedy were rescued. The rescue boat was in charge of Captain Samuel James, a member of the famous life-saving family at Hull. (He was a son of the William James who helped save the crew of the *Tremont* in 1844, and a brother of Joshua James.) The shores of Boston Light received the battered bodies of Captain Williams and five others. Barrett removed the watch and other valuables from Williams' body for safekeeping.

Keeper Moses Barrett of Boston Light

A more disastrous wreck was never seen. All the outer islands were covered with supplies from the ship.

Captain Hough of the Harbor Police went down to the scene and picked up the ship's papers. The naked body of a woman was recovered from the bar near Bug Light. Across the Narrows at historic Fort Warren this scene was observed by a small group of Confederate prisoners of war. One of them, Lawrence Sangston, had described the storm in his diary the night before, and to give the reader a southerner's views of a New England gale we include it here:

> *Storm increasing, fearful night for ships on the coast; at times the wind would whistle through the casemate windows equal to the shrill whistle of a locomotive engine, and after listening an hour to the howling of the storm, and the waves breaking over the rocks, went to sleep.*

The storm was a severe one in Massachusetts Bay. Several other vessels were wrecked, including the bark *Nathaniel Coggswell* at Scituate. All hands were saved from this disaster. The schooner *Emma Wadsworth* went ashore on Spectacle Island in Boston's inner harbor, while the tide swept across Broad Street and Commercial Street in the city itself. Mountainous waves at Revere Beach swept ashore the schooner *Canton* of Newburyport with 20,000 feet of lumber. Hull became an island at the height of the storm. Chimneys, waterspouts, and awnings were blown down everywhere by the gale.

A few days later the figurehead of the ill-fated *Maritana* was brought up to Boston, where it was placed on Lincoln Wharf. The pier later caught fire, and some of the superstitious blamed the figurehead. The graceful wooden figure is now on exhibition at the Marine Room in the Old State House.

The following March part of the body of one of the sailors came up on the beach at Boston Light and was buried on the island. Later in the year the wife of Captain Williams visited Keeper Barrett there, and sat in the shadow of the lighthouse looking out at the merciless ledge which had separated her happy family forever. Keeper Barrett gave the widow the watch and other keepsakes which he had been saving for her. At the time he remarked that it was the worst shipwreck in the history of the harbor, and although over three-quarters of a century have gone by since his remark, it is still true today.

THE 1869 SEPTEMBER GALE

September is, without question, the month of gales. In 1676, 1815, 1821, 1869, 1879, and 1938 gales hit New England with devastating force, just to mention a few of the many September occasions when the winds have penetrated with telling effect our coastal areas.

On the afternoon of September 8, 1869, a hurricane raged over a narrow fifty-mile-wide strip across Massachusetts and Maine. In Boston the Coliseum Building was wrecked, and with it the great organ and drum located there. Granville M. Clark, standing nearby, was hit when a portion of the wooden sidewalk was torn up and struck him on the skull. He died shortly afterwards.

The Hanover Street Methodist Church lost its steeple, an entire tenement block was leveled in Chelsea, Massachusetts, while the spire of the First Baptist Church in Lynn crashed into the left wing of the edifice. Up and down the coast similar damage was reported.

In Maine the gale was known as the Saxby Gale, as it had been predicted by Saxby. The schooner *Helen Eliza* struck on Peak's Island, Maine, during the gale, and all except one man perished. The survivor, Charles Jordan, floated ashore on a barrel. He drifted near two of his companions, who were clinging to a plank, but they never made the beach.

The well-known steamer *Cambridge* was out in the tempest. Off Monhegan Island at the time, Captain Otis Ingraham brought the two-year-old paddle-wheeler through the gale, but only after her steam pipe and rudder had broken. The *Cambridge*, according to John M. Richardson, drifted almost to the mouth of the Georges River. Captain Ingraham sounded, getting twenty-three fathoms. He ordered both anchors let go when just off the ledges, and the anchors held. Captain Ingraham had saved the *Cambridge* for a career which lasted until 1886, when the steamer broke in two after piling up on the Old Man's Ledge off Port Clyde.

THE GALE OF 1888

The south shore of Massachusetts suffered greatly during the 1888 storm, which was a terrible hurricane while it lasted. Minot's Light in particular underwent a terrific battering.

Joseph Frates, Keeper Reamy's assistant at the light, told him that one of the waves which struck the tower on Sunday, November 25, 1888, made his hair actually stand on end. The tower remained firm, however. The wave caused a strong vibration at the time, but Keeper Reamy declared that nothing but an earthquake would ever shake down the lighthouse. We quote from *The Story of Minot's Light*:

> *Keeper Reamy feared that the steamer* Allentown *with eighteen on board had gone down after striking the dangerous reef a mile to the northeast of the lighthouse. He was later asked if he had heard a whistle that fateful night when the* Allentown *was lost.*
>
> *"I did not," he answered, "and it would have been impossible to hear a whistle, if it had been within ten feet of the Light, owing to the tremendous roar of the waves as they dashed over the light."*

Fifteen ships were wrecked between Scituate Harbor and Boston in that 1888 hurricane. Life preservers and marked lifeboats soon came ashore in Cohasset to prove that the *Allentown* actually had foundered near Minot's Light, and the *Edward H. Norton* went ashore on the First Cliff, Scituate, with the loss of all fifteen of her crew. (This schooner had previously left Canada under spectacular conditions.) The schooner *Sasonoa* drifted by Minot's Light and came ashore on Pleasant Beach, after having snapped her anchor chains in Gloucester Harbor. High and dry, the craft remained a picturesque landmark for many years.

Mr. Fitz-Henry Smith, Jr., of Boston, has written an outstanding account of Boston Bay shipwrecks in which he includes deeds of valor performed by the lifesavers of Hull. He gives glowing and well-deserved praise to the heroes who rescued a great many men from death in the 1888 storm, especially singling out for commendation Captain Joshua James. One of Captain James' outstanding achievements, according to Mr. Smith, was the rescue of twenty-nine men in twenty-four hours from five different vessels during the storm.

THE VENETIAN

Heavily loaded with grain, flour, provisions, dressed beef, 645 live sheep, and 845 head of live cattle, the Furness Liner *Venetian* sailed from the Boston Hoosac Tunnel Docks shortly before 3:00 on March 2, 1895.

The weather was overcast, but visibility was good as the *Venetian* drew abeam of the Bird Island Flats and headed for buoy number 12.

Suddenly there was a violent snow squall which blanketed everything around the 423-foot steamer. The pilot was unable to locate a single identifying marker. A few minutes later the *Venetian* hit on Governor's Island Flats; her last voyage had lasted less than an hour. Captain Farthington tried desperately to back the steamer off, but it was high water and the tide slowly receded. Soon afterwards the long Furness liner snapped her back, and all thoughts of salvage were abandoned.

Though the thirst-maddened steers which had been left aboard had to be shot, most of the cargo was safely brought ashore. It is said that an enterprising Brockton shoe manufacturer purchased the rights to advertise his wares by painting a huge sign extolling the benefits of his particular brand of shoes on the side of the *Venetian*, and for the whole of the following summer until the *Venetian* was finally broken up, the passengers on the various harbor excursion boats were treated to an unusual advertisement. After various efforts to plan repairs, junkmen bought the ship and broke her up.

THE NORSEMAN

During the early morning hours of a very foggy day in March 1899, the freighter *Norseman* drove aground on Tom Moore Rocks off Marblehead. As there was a tremendous sea raging at the time and it was feared that the vessel might go to pieces, lifebelts were quickly passed around. Captain Rees ordered a rocket shot off, while at the same time he blew a distress signal on the *Norseman*'s whistle.

At daylight a crew from the Massachusetts Humane Society's station rowed a lifeboat out to the scene, 250 yards from shore. Captain John H. L. Giles, in charge of the surfboat, was unable to establish contact with those on the steamer because of the heavy surf. As soon as Captain Giles decided that he could not take off any of the 102 men aboard, he returned to shore. News of the shipwreck spread rapidly, and soon the rocks of Marblehead were covered with people.

When the sun came out to disperse the fog, a line was shot across to the stranded *Norseman*. In a short time the breeches buoy was in place, and at 8:00 that morning, less than five hours after the wreck, the first passenger rode high above the breaking waves to land safely ashore. Another gun was fired across the ship, and another breeches buoy was attached. With the rapid service of the two lines, every one of the crew and passengers was ashore within a few hours.

Two men coming ashore on the breeches buoy from the Norseman, *wrecked at Marblehead, 1899*

Plans were made to save the *Norseman*. Great crowds gathered daily on the rocks, conjecturing about the possibility of getting her off. Camera tripods were set up in every suitable location, and hundreds of pictures were made. A few days later the combined efforts of the tugs *Juno, Mercury, Pallas,* and *Confidence,* all from Boston, freed the *Norseman.* It was indeed a thrilling spectacle as the victorious tugs started for Boston with the crippled steamer in tow.

THE DAVIS PALMER

Captain Leroy K. McKown anchored the *Davis Palmer* off Finn's Ledge on Christmas Day, 1909. He had hoped to have dinner with his wife that afternoon, but it was not to be, as contrary winds had made him drop anchor three miles off the Winthrop shore. The five-masted schooner swung restlessly as the afternoon waned, while the captain grew more and more worried as the barometer dropped.

By nightfall the first indication of a severe northeast storm was in evidence, and the crew made the ship ready to weather the blow. It was

Flooding in Winthrop on December 26, 1909 (from the collection of W. E. Meryman)

no use, however, for before morning the rising seas had pushed the *Palmer* across from Finn's Ledge, capsizing the great vessel somewhere off Fawn Bar Beacon and drowning the entire crew of twelve men.

On the mainland the snowstorm brought waves and the highest tide since the Minot's Light gale, in fact less than a fraction of an inch below that famous storm and six inches higher than that of the Portland Gale. It was the highest tide yet recorded in the twentieth century.* The Winthrop seawall was washed out in many sections, houses along the lower part of Fawn Bar Avenue were undermined by the ocean, and Point Shirley was isolated by a gully five feet deep which the tide cut while sweeping across from the ocean to the harbor. One of the two remaining elms on Apple Island went over in the gale.

The people who climbed to the top of Great Head in Winthrop looked down upon a terrible scene from their vantage point atop the 105-foot cliff. The writer was among those who saw the five masts of the *Davis Palmer* as they projected at an angle out of the water a short distance off the Winthrop shore. Captain McKown's wife by this time had been noti-

---

*The Minot's Light tide averaged 15.62 feet in Boston, while the Portland tide was 14.94 in Boston. The 1909 storm was 15.60 feet. Two residents of Everett drowned when the tides flooded the area.

fied of the tragedy, but she still continued to hope that her husband had been rescued. As the days went by she reluctantly became convinced that her husband had perished in the Christmas storm of 1909.

THE MOXIE

The tragedy which befell thirteen young boys from Lynn, Massachusetts, left an impression of unusual degree on all those who were in any way associated with it. On the night of March 29, 1917, the small twenty-three-foot motor boat *Moxie* left Stone's Wharf in Lynn at about 9:00 P.M. Shortly before 11:00 Winthrop residents walking along the Crest (Winthrop's Shore Drive) heard shouts for help coming from the ocean. Telephone calls were sent to the Nahant Coast Guard Station. Unfortunately the boat there was out of order, so the Nahant Station telephoned to Hudson Robertson, the owner of the *Moxie*, asking him to go out in search of the persons in trouble. Robertson went down to the wharf, but found his boat missing. This was the first he knew that the boys had taken the boat out.

Meanwhile those on the Winthrop shore had lighted huge bonfires to guide those in trouble to shore, but their cries grew weaker and weaker, finally dying away altogether. Gus Johnson of Winthrop now launched a small dory from the beach, but there was such a heavy groundswell that the dory went over, and Johnson barely reached shore. After vainly staying up until early morning hours, the crowd on the shore dispersed.

Thirteen boys never returned to their Lynn homes, however, and the realization was soon to come that they had all probably drowned in the surf off the Winthrop shore. On the afternoon of April 6, just as this nation was declaring war on Germany, my chum Tom Johnson and I began to walk toward the beach to see if any sign might be found of the missing boat *Moxie*. To our surprise we found that the bodies of the boys were washing in on the beach. In a relatively short time the parents were notified, and pitiful scenes took place as the identifications were made.

THE NANCY

A goodly proportion of the residents now living in Greater Boston have seen the five-masted schooner *Nancy* on the beach at Nantasket.

Her story is now one of the sagas of that historic beach which has seen scores of shipwrecks in the past three centuries.

On February 19, 1927, the schooner anchored off Boston Light to ride out an anticipated gale. The next day when a sleet storm hit, the *Nancy* let go three anchors. The wind increased to fifty-five miles an hour. First the anchors dragged and then the chains parted. The schooner began to head for the dreaded Harding's Ledge but Captain E. M. Baird tried the daring maneuver of setting a staysail to clear the dangerous rocks. In this he was successful, and soon the shores of Nantasket Beach loomed ahead in the driving sleet storm. The *Nancy* brought up on the beach

The Nancy *on Nantasket Beach, stranded February 20, 1927*

about one hundred yards off shore. (In the same storm the *C.G. 238* was lost with eight men off Highland Light.)

Patrolman Ned Gleason of Hull was among the first to sight the *Nancy,* and a volunteer life-saving crew was organized. Captains O. C. Olson, Edwin Hatch, Adelbert Nickerson, and eight other volunteers quickly launched the Massachusetts Humane Society's lifeboat into the breakers and reached the lee of the *Nancy.* The surfmen held the boat fast while the entire crew, one of them holding the ice-covered ship's cat, jumped into the boat. Twenty minutes later all were safe ashore.

The *Nancy* did not break up, and stayed high and dry on the beach for many years. People came from every state in the union to see the five-masted schooner, with those who wished to go aboard paying for the privilege. Every so often, during a run of high tides, efforts were made to launch the schooner, but as the years went by, she became a fixture at Nantasket Beach. One day at high tide she slipped a short distance toward the sea, but grounded again. In another storm she came up ten feet higher than ever.

It was finally arranged that she should be broken up. Her towering masts were acquired by the Hitchcock Quarry in Quincy, and the lumber was taken by residents of Hull.

It was then believed that the people had seen the last of the *Nancy,* but during a northeast storm in the winter of 1940, the keel of the schooner was washed out of the Nantasket sands.

THE ROBERT E. LEE

On the night of March 9, 1928, at the height of a raging snowstorm, the *Robert E. Lee,* considerably off her course, hit the Mary Ann Rocks off Manomet Point, Massachusetts, while running for the Cape Cod Canal. There were 273 men, women, and children aboard.

Captain Harland W. Robinson said that the *Lee* was going at full speed when she struck. Clearing the first of the rocks, the steamer hit four others in rapid succession and then began to ship water on the starboard side. The snow coming in the open wheelhouse window had affected the compass, Robinson believed.

The discipline of the crew was good, but some of the passengers had to be quieted. A short time after the vessel hit the rocks, the lights failed and the entire ship was blacked out. As the 400-foot steamer rolled back and forth in the darkness, the passengers became uneasy and wandered nervously about the vessel. A short time later the seacocks were opened, allowing the *Robert E. Lee* to settle down on the rocks as in a cradle, and the rolling ceased. It was possible for those on the upper decks to go back to bed, but the water rose higher in the staterooms on the lower decks as the tide came in. All the officers were worried as to what might happen at 2:00 A.M. when the tide was high, but the ship held firm. At the turn of the tide the crisis was over.

The next day the Manomet Point Coast Guard Station, under Boatswain's Mate Cashman, sent its surfboat out to the *Lee*, negotiating with difficulty the giant swells on the way to Mary Ann Rocks. Arriving at the scene of the accident, Cashman went aboard the *Lee*, where he consulted with Captain Robinson about taking the passengers off the wrecked liner. It was finally agreed that rowing them all ashore would be not only a long and tedious task, but one fraught with the danger of capsizing in the breakers, and so the rescue craft then standing by were instructed to get ready to receive the passengers from small boats which could be sent over to them.

The large powerful surfboats at Sagamore and Wood End were sent for, and Boatswain's Mate Cashman finally started back for the shore

The Robert E. Lee *on Mary Anne Rocks, Manomet, 1928. The lifeboat later capsized, drowning three of the crew.*

with his men, pleased that satisfactory arrangements had been made. One load of passengers had been ferried across to the patrol boat when the Manomet lifeboat started back to the beach. It was then a little past 11:00 in the morning, and the surfboat had reached a position just off Stage Point, where she was making good headway. Suddenly the lifeboat was lifted clear by an enormous wave and hit by another before she could settle, sending her straight up into the air. She came down bottom up. Watchers on the shore saw several of the men come to the surface as they struggled in the angry sea. A. A. Proctor, one of the crew, describes the incident:

> We were nearly unable to move when we landed in the water. All of the seven men in the power dory were shocked so badly that we had all we could do to grab the boat. . . . First thing I knew I began to feel awfully numb. It was a tough fight to keep above water.

Three of the crew died as a result of the capsizing, Boatswain's Mate William H. Cashman, Frank Griswold, and Edward Stark. The others were rescued and rushed to the hospital.

Every passenger was taken safely from the *Robert E. Lee* and placed on the patrol boats *Bonham, Active,* and the *C.G. 176.* Seven others returned to Boston on the *Red Wing.* One of them, Gurden S. Worcester of Cambridge, said:

> I was in my stateroom on the saloon deck when there was a sickening, terrifying crash. I went on deck and found the other passengers wandering nervously about trying to find out what had happened. The snow was whirling thickly about the ship and I could see nothing. Suddenly, from someone, came word that a girl had thrown herself overboard and that we were stopping to pick her up. . . . The story was false. But it was typical of the dozens of rumors and speculative remarks that I heard later.

Worcester and the other six passengers were landed in Boston at 5:15 on Saturday afternoon. Perhaps the most surprised man on board was J. J. Keeley of Winthrop, Massachusetts. Sleeping through the confusion of the shipwreck and subsequent excitement, Keeley did not awaken until 7:00 Saturday morning, when he dressed and went down to the ship's barbershop for his morning shave.

The following Sunday thousands of cars jammed the highway around Plymouth to see the wreck of the *Robert E. Lee* off Manomet Point. Later in the month the steamer was pulled from the rocks.

THE NORTHERN SWORD

During a howling February blizzard in 1934, the collier *Northern Sword* came up on the Winthrop beach at a point just below the water tower situated on nearby Great Head. When the storm went down, Captain Sorenson found his craft resting comfortably in three feet of water at low tide, with no apparent danger of disaster.

The local papers soon carried the account of the stranding of the collier, and hundreds came to Winthrop to see the unusual sight. For more than a week the steamer stayed on the shoals near Winthrop. One morning during another storm she was pulled off and floated. (The writer performed an unusual duty when he delivered mail to the stranded collier, as the postman was unable to reach the ship.)

The bar inside of which she grounded has now extended itself to the great seawall on shore, and is called Northern Sword Bar, commemorating

The Northern Sword *off the Winthrop water tower, with Winthrop Bar visible in the right foreround. Edward Rowe Snow spent his childhood a few houses down from the edge of Great Head, where the water tower stands at the left.*

the stranding of the collier during the February gale of 1934. (This new bar runs parallel to and about an eighth of a mile to the northward of Winthrop Bar, erroneously called Fawn Bar.)

THE ROMANCE

During one of the severe September fogs of 1936, the Provincetown excursion steamer *Romance* and the Boston-to-New York steamer *New York* collided off Graves Light in outer Boston Harbor. The captain of the New York boat kept his bow wedged against the hole in the side of the *Romance*, allowing the passengers on the smaller craft to climb to safety aboard the *New York*. In this way the quick-wittedness of the *New York*'s captain prevented what might have become a tragedy. The *Romance* went down soon afterwards, and the next day her superstructure floated ashore at Winthrop, where souvenir hunters found many a treasure.

THE CITY OF SALISBURY

Entering Boston Harbor on April 22, 1938, in a dense fog, the heavily laden 419-foot cargo steamer *City of Salisbury* struck an uncharted pinnacle twenty-four feet below the surface, and was unable to move. Loaded with animals, rubber, jute, and many other supplies (valued at approximately $1,500,000), the *Salisbury* contained the richest cargo ever wrecked in outer Boston Harbor.

The writer made the first air photograph of the disaster later that afternoon, his plane dropping down in a rift of the fog bank. It was quite a thrill to circle above the huge vessel and to see the animal crates, the Lascars with their life belts on, and the general state of orderly excitement on the steamer as the vessel slowly settled upon the ledge.

Barges began to unload the steamer, but it was too late. Shortly after noon the next day an ominous sound was heard, and the vessel cracked in two. The many animals aboard were hurriedly brought into Boston, with the exception of two snakes and several monkeys which disappeared in the confusion. One of the monkeys appeared later in the week, five miles away on Deer Island, where he was seen by Robert Mackey of Point Shirley, while Nelson Maynard of Deer Island found the carcass of a large snake on the same beach.

All the following summer the *City of Salisbury* hung on the pinnacle, with much of the cargo removed by the last of August. Excursion steamers took thousands upon thousands of people out by the wreck, for it was a spectacular sight. The steamer was rechristened the "Zoo Ship" by those who saw it grinding away on the ledge that year. By midsummer the entire forward section had slipped off into deep water, and a crack was developing amidships in the remainder of the vessel. When the autumn winds began to blow, the stern alone was above the water. It was a weird sensation to the writer and others who went aboard the afterdeck two weeks before she sank completely. The grinding and gnashing of the iron rods and broken timbers far down under the water could plainly be heard, and the steamer would shudder and jerk as the ground swell passed alongside. Incidentally, the great September hurricane did not move the wreck at all. A northeasterly storm during October came in out of the Atlantic, and when it had cleared the *City of Salisbury* was no longer visible.

THE MARY E. O'HARA

The last great marine tragedy of Boston Harbor was enacted on January 21, 1941, when nineteen [usually reported as eighteen—*Ed.*] brave men from the fishing schooner *Mary E. O'Hara* fell to their death into the icy seas near Finn's Ledge off the shores of Winthrop. (Finn's Ledge is approximately half the distance from Winthrop's water tower to Graves Light.) Within a few minutes of the end of her voyage, the *O'Hara* smashed into the barge *Winifred Sheridan* at 3:00 in the morning, sheered off, and settled in forty feet of water.

All but three members of the crew were in their bunks when the collision took place. In an almost unbelievably short time, the schooner went to the bottom. The men were barely able to scramble up into the rigging, to which they clung as the icy waters broke over the schooner. As the hours passed, however, the men grew numbed and weakened, one by one dropping into the sea. It had been impossible to use the dories, as they were buried under tons of ice. Just before the schooner foundered Captain Fred Wilson tried to hack the gripes holding the dories down, but the ice still held them to the deck. The captain hacked away until the water reached his waist before he climbed up to the top lift.

Several boats passed the men. They cried out but could not be heard above the wind and surf. Then the trawler *North Star* came along. John Sheen cried out, "Hang on, a boat is coming," but when Captain Lars Lunde of the *North Star* arrived, Sheen had already dropped to his death

The City of Salisbury, *wrecked off Graves Light, April 22, 1938*

The last hours of the "Zoo Ship" City of Salisbury *early in October 1938*

in the freezing sea. By this time the *O'Hara* had listed so that the water was up to the foremast crosstrees. The members of the crew who were rescued were in the rigging about three hours before being taken off. They had watched their friends drop into the ocean, some with the Lord's Prayer on their lips, others without even a groan.

Captain Lars Lunde, the master of the rescue vessel *North Star*, estimated that the *O'Hara* sank about 3:00 A.M. and that he sighted the masts at about 5:40 A.M. The thermometer was 12 above zero at the time. The shouts of the men first attracted his attention; then he saw dimly the masts of the sunken ship. With his engines idling, he slid the *North Star* up alongside and took off the five survivors, Gabriel Welch, Frank Silva, Cecil Crowell, Cecil Larkin, and Stanley Conrad.

Lunde said afterwards that if one of the other three vessels which passed the wreck earlier that bitter morning had heard the cries and stopped, many others and possibly all of those who later perished would have been saved.

The tragedy of the Mary E. O'Hara, *January 21, 1941 (showing the Point Allerton Coast Guard crew securing a line to the foremast)*

THE MAGNIFIQUE Much more about the coins found by Keeper Jennings can be found in a book by his son Harold, called *A Lighthouse Family*.

Some dispute the assertion that the wreck of the *Magnifique* is now under the shore of Lovell's Island. According to Donald L. Ferris in his book *Beneath the Waters of Massachusetts Bay*, "Today, her rotted bones lie in relatively shallow water. Her hull timbers, with copper sheathing, are scattered about. Several large piles of iron cannon balls, two to four feet high, are found in the general area. . . . It lies just off the northwest corner of Lovells Island."

THE TEDESCO Near Fisherman's Beach in Swampscott, the anchor of the *Tedesco* is on display as a memorial to the twelve men who lost their lives in the wreck.

In his book *Shipwrecks North of Boston, Volume One: Salem Bay* (2000), Raymond H. Bates, Jr., reports that every January 18, local residents lay flowers at the Swampscott gravesite of the *Tedesco* sailors. Bates, who is also a diver, has found copper spikes among the rocks at Galloupe's Point, and he believes them to be from the *Tedesco*.

THE VERNON According to Raymond Bates, Captain Gott of the *Vernon* mistook the light of Egg Rock Lighthouse off Nahant for that of Boston Light a few miles away. The captain was quite amazed to find his ship suddenly grounded at Lynn Beach. The vessel remained on the beach for a few days and was eventually refloated and taken to Boston for repairs.

Anchor believed to be from the Tedesco, *on display in Swampscott, Massachusetts, near where it was found in 1968 (photo by Jeremy D'Entremont)*

THE *MARITANA* The *Boston Journal* of November 5, 1861, said of the *Maritana*, "A more complete wreck was never seen. . . . God save us all from a death like this."

THE 1869 SEPTEMBER GALE Stephen Martin Saxby (1804–1883) was a lieutenant in the Royal British Navy who based his weather predictions on the positions and phases of the moon. On Christmas Day 1868, Saxby predicted a great gale for the following October 5. His prediction came true, as an intense storm and unusually high tides that day killed over a hundred people in the Bay of Fundy region. The storm of September 8 may have also been nicknamed the Saxby Gale, or it may have been confused with the later one as time passed, but the terribly destructive storm that hit eastern Canada on October 5, 1869, is remembered as the true Saxby Gale.

The September 8 hurricane also wreaked its havoc at several New England lighthouses. It was reported at Bird Island off Marion, Massachusetts, that the lighthouse station was reduced "from a condition of perfect order to a perfect wreck." The roof of the keeper's house at Warwick Light in Rhode Island was damaged, outhouses destroyed, and a fence blown down. At Long Island Head Light in Boston Harbor, the chimney was knocked from the roof of the keeper's house, and the fog bell tower was destroyed at Pond Island Lighthouse off the mouth of the Kennebec River in Maine. And perhaps most memorably, at Maine's Portland Head Light the wind knocked the fog bell into a ravine, nearly killing Keeper Joshua Strout.

THE GALE OF 1888 In recognition of his extraordinary heroism during this storm, Joshua James was awarded gold medals by the U.S. Life-Saving Service and the Massachusetts Humane Society. The following year, at the age of 62, he became the keeper of the new Point Allerton Life-Saving Station at Hull.

THE NORSEMAN The *Norseman* was a 392-foot steamer in the Warren Line, making regular trips between Liverpool and Boston. Besides 100 passengers, at the time of this incident the ship was carrying 250 head of cattle and various other freight. According to Bates in *Shipwrecks North of Boston*, Marblehead Neck became so crowded during the salvage operations that carriage drivers were able to charge sightseers twenty-five cents for passage to the site. After being towed to Boston, the *Norseman* was fully repaired and returned to service.

THE DAVIS PALMER Edward Rowe Snow was seven years old when he witnessed the wreck of the *Davis Palmer*, and it quite possibly contributed to his growing interest in such dramatic events. In his 1952 volume *Great Gales and Dire Disasters*, he wrote, "I was among those who went up on Great Head to gaze out in horror at the five masts sticking up through the breaking waves about a mile off Fawn Bar."

The *Davis Palmer* had been launched in Bath, Maine in 1905. In 1912 it was reported in the *Notice to Mariners* that most of the remains of the schooner were removed by dredging. The ship's bell was recovered about a decade ago.

THE MOXIE Along with the Christmas 1909 wreck of the *Davis Palmer* off the shore of his hometown of Winthrop, the *Moxie* tragedy was undoubtedly a seminal event in the young life of Edward Rowe Snow. He provided more detail in his 1970 book *Great Atlantic Adventures*. It seems that Snow's brother Nicholas and some friends were among those who heard cries for help from offshore. When Gus Johnson, who was superintendent of the Winthrop Yacht Club, arrived on the scene, Nicholas Snow and his friend Lawrence Cox helped him carry his dory to the beach.

Snow wrote, "I shall never forget the terror we experienced" when he and Tom Johnson walked the beach on April 6 and came across a body that had washed ashore. On a lighter note, he remembered that there was a "special relaxing of parental discipline that night," and he and Tom were allowed to go to the movies on a school night.

Two days later the *Moxie* lay exposed on the beach, and Snow examined the boat at low tide. "As I stood there I thought of the great tragedy that had separated so many happy families," he wrote.

THE NANCY In his 1976 book *Marine Mysteries and Dramatic Disasters of New England*, Snow reported, "Only a handful of residents witnessed the beaching of the *Nancy* at Nantasket, and of those few three are alive today. However, those who saw her and read about her through the years are many. They look back at her as an old friend associated with the glamour of the days of sail."

Robert F. Sullivan's book *Shipwrecks and Nautical Lore of Boston Harbor* tells us that the *Nancy* was launched in Portland, Oregon, in 1918 and that the schooner served the French army for a time. He also mentions that sightseers were allowed to tour the wreck on Nantasket Beach for twenty-five cents.

THE ROBERT E. LEE In his 1970 book *Great Atlantic Adventures*, Snow quoted Paul Bettinger, who witnessed the tragic capsizing of the lifeboat from Manomet. Bettinger described the scene:

She pitchpoled, going stern over bow, and that was it. Every man was thrown into the icy seas, and those who could clambered up on the keel. Altough near to shore, the lifeboat was quite a distance from the station. It is probable that before the rescue craft could reach the men the three who were lost had died of shock and exposure.

In 1970 Snow also talked to Russell Anderson of Manomet. Anderson, along with his friend Earl Harper and a state trooper named Horgan, launched a small boat from the beach and helped rescue some of the men who had been thrown into the sea from the lifeboat.

A bronze tablet was dedicated on May 30, 1928, to the memory of the three coastguardsmen who lost their lives. The inscription reads in part, "Greater love hath no man than this that he lay down his life for his friends. Erected by the citizens of Plymouth, Massachusetts."

On July 30, 1942, the *Robert E. Lee* was en route from Trinidad to New Orleans with over 400 people on board, including American construction workers and survivors of U-boat attacks in the Caribbean, when it was sunk by a single torpedo fired by the German submarine *U-166*. Two crewmembers and 15 passengers were killed, but the rest were rescued by other vessels in the area. The *U-166* was subsequently sent to the bottom by a depth charge.

The remains of the *Lee* have been located in the Gulf of Mexico, about forty-five miles southeast of the mouth of the Mississippi. The *U-166* has also been located in 5,000 feet of water through the joint efforts of the Minerals Management Service and BP and Shell Oil Companies.

Memorial to the Robert E. Lee *in Plymouth, Massachusetts (photo by Bob Jannoni)*

THE NORTHERN SWORD Here Snow mentions the water tower on Great Head at Winthrop, Massachusetts. One of the rescues not mentioned in this volume is one performed by Snow himself at that location in 1937. A young boy, climbing up the steep face of Great Head with his friends, became trapped halfway, too afraid to go up or down. Snow, who at the time lived right next door to the water tower, heard the boy's cries. A neighbor lowered Snow down the side of the cliff with a rope, and the boy was raised to safety. The whole scene was reenacted for the benefit of a newspaper photographer a short time later, much to the boy's consternation. Snow later received a citation from the Massachusetts Humane Society for his efforts.

Edward Rowe Snow's wife, Anna-Myrle (Haegg) Snow, claimed that her husband was probably responsible for saving at least twenty people from drowning during his lifetime. In the early 1930s he had worked as a lifeguard in a very large indoor pool in Montana, and several times he saved boaters in trouble in the vicinity of Winthrop and the Boston Harbor islands.

THE ROMANCE The *Romance* was later dynamited as it presented a hazard to navigation. What's left of the 250-foot steamer today lies on the muddy bottom in about 85 feet of water, two and a half miles southeast of East Point in Nahant.

THE CITY OF SALISBURY Amazingly, the great hurricane of September 21,. 1938, wasn't enough to send the *City of Salisbury* to the bottom. It took the October nor'easter mentioned by Snow to sink the freighter.

The twisted remains of the *City of Salisbury* have long been a popular dive site. According to Snow's 1963 book, *True Tales of Terrible Shipwrecks*, material was salvaged from the hold as late as 1962, and just a few years ago the anchor from the freighter was recovered by divers.

In *True Tales of Terrible Shipwrecks* Snow reported, "The rock on which the *Salisbury* cracked apart was later named Salisbury Pinnacle. All coastal surveys had missed it since earliest times because the soundings had taken place all around the pinnacle, unfortunately never hitting it."

THE MARY E. O'HARA The *Mary E. O'Hara* was a haddocker out of Gloucester. Thirteen of the men on board were Nova Scotians, one was from Newfoundland, and the other nine were New Englanders.

CHAPTER 29

Cape Cod Shipwrecks

The great beach at Cape Cod has seen more than three thousand shipwrecks in its long career as guardian of Massachusetts Bay. Beginning in earliest times and extending even to the present day, ships have struck the bending arm of Cape Cod with unfortunate regularity as the years have gone by. The *Sparrowhawk* crashed near Eastham back in 1626, while the last shipwreck to be included in this book is that of the *Teresa Darr*, a two-masted schooner which ran aground during Christmas week, 1942.

THE ALMIRA

On a hillside overlooking Sandwich Harbor on the afternoon of January 16, 1827, stood an old, experienced captain watching a small schooner sail out to sea. So intent in his gaze was the old man that an acquaintance accosted him, asking what was the matter.

In response the old seaman raised his hands and said, "Gone out! He will never come in again." His friend reminded him that the wind was southerly, but the old man, totally ignoring this fact, walked away convinced that the ship was doomed.

The master of the schooner in question, the *Almira*, was Captain Josiah Ellis, a large, dignified man, who had concluded that there would be a few days of pleasant weather, and had sailed from Sandwich with a crew of two—his son and another sailor, John Smith, by name. By early evening the vessel was off Mary Ann Rocks, Manomet, with the northwest sky clear and bright. The temperature dropped so low, however, that the mariners realized that it would be necessary to make the nearest harbor or perish in the bitter cold. They tried to reach Plymouth by tacking, but the wind increased and they failed.

The men realized now that their condition was perilous indeed. The spray soon coated the mainsail with ice and down it came. The vessel was laid to the wind, the foresail braced fore and aft, but the jib, which was frozen, could not be hauled down. The wind soon cracked the ice and tore the canvas to shreds. Obeying the helm, the schooner came up to the wind, where it remained.

It was so cold that icicles formed on the bodies of the crew, forcing them all to go below and build a fire in the cabin. When they returned to the deck, they found it covered with ice. The sun rose on the coldest morning of the winter. Captain Ellis and his crew decided to sail back to Sandwich, but when the *Almira* reached a position off the harbor, the men in their frozen condition were unable to maneuver the schooner. The sailors were swept past their homes, where they could see the smoke curling from the chimneys of their houses. The last sail now went to pieces, and the vessel drifted helplessly before the wind. Sandwich, Barnstable, and Yarmouth all were passed, but when the schooner approached Dennis, a ledge of rocks loomed ahead, and the schooner crashed upon them.

From the nearby hill some of the Dennis residents saw the schooner approaching. The vessel was so close to the beach that the watchers ashore could look down on the decks, which were masses of ice. Wondering if anyone might be aboard, they shouted out to the vessel, whereupon the three men slowly emerged from the cabin. Standing like statues in their frozen condition, they indicated that they were in desperate need. A boat was put out to them, making its way with difficulty through the frozen sludge, but a wave swamped it. Those on shore then threw out a warp, which was secured by one of the lifesavers in the swamped dory, and the men were drawn back to the beach. Out on the *Almira*, the waves still broke over the doomed vessel. One sailor dropped to the deck, and was soon encased in ice. The captain sank down, dying of exposure shortly afterwards. Only the captain's son was still alive. The tide began to rise, freeing the *Almira* from the rocks, and the schooner drifted nearer the shore, where those on the beach boarded her. Young Ellis, the captain's son, eventually recovered, but the prediction of the ancient mariner came true. Captain Josiah Ellis never came in again to Sandwich Harbor.

THE LOSS OF THE FRANKLIN

> *Mr. Hopkins of Wellfleet arrived in this city last night and states that the ship* Franklin, *Capt. Smith from London, of and for Boston, went ashore at Wellfleet, Cape Cod, on Thursday morning, at nine o'clock, and Capt. Smith, with the first mate, and eight others, perished. Twenty of the passengers and crew were saved. The ship went to pieces and her cargo was scattered along the shore.*

Thus did the inhabitants of Boston and New England, through the pages of the *Boston Courier* for March 3, 1849, learn of a shipwreck which was destined to attract much attention because of the interest of Henry David Thoreau, and the recovery from the Atlantic of several documents which told the strange story of a planned wreck.

The actual number of persons aboard the *Franklin* was thirty-three, of whom eleven were drowned. The following fall Thoreau visited Cape Cod, walking along the beach where the wreck had taken place. One night he and his friend, William DeCosta, visited the home of Uncle Jack Newcomb, better known as the "Wellfleet Oysterman." Thoreau tells of Newcomb's story of the *Franklin*:

> *He told us the story of the wreck of the* Franklin, *which took place the previous spring; how a boy came to his house early in the morning to know whose boat that was by the shore, for there was a vessel in distress, and he, being an old man, first ate his breakfast, and then walked over to the top of the hill by the shore, and sat down there, having found a comfortable seat, to see the ship wrecked. She was on the bar, only a quarter of a mile from him, and still nearer to the men on the beach, who had got a boat ready. . . .*
>
> *"I saw the captain get out his boat," said he; "he had one little one, and then they jumped into it one after another, down as straight as an arrow. I counted them. There were nine. One was a woman, and she jumped as straight as any of them. Then they shoved off. The sea took them back, one wave went over them, and when they came up there*

were six still clinging to the boat; I counted them. The next wave turned the boat bottom upward, and emptied them all out. None of them ever came ashore alive."

The lady mentioned as jumping into the lifeboat was Miss Skehan, one of several members of that family aboard the *Franklin*. The little child which the captain held was an eleven-month-old girl, a sister of the Skehan woman.

The *Franklin* began to break up when the lifeboat left the vessel. It was said that the lifeboat was hit by the breakers from twelve to fifteen times as it floated toward the beach. Shortly afterwards the *Franklin* worked its way over the bar and started for the shore. This encouraged the watchers on the beach, who launched a small boat into the tremendous swell then running, and started for the survivors. They let over a line held by the crowd on shore, one of whom was a woman who, it is said, did more than her share.

When the rescue boat arrived at the *Franklin*, they found that one woman had been washed overboard, but all the rest were able to climb into the fishing boat and reach the shore in safety. By this time the *Franklin*'s wreckage was strewn up and down the beach. An inhabitant of Cape Cod, writing of the incident two days later, noticed a small boy who had been rescued from the vessel:

I took the little boy saved up in my lap, yesterday afternoon, and as I looked upon him and the little babe, his sister, also rescued, I could not help exclaiming, in admiration of the providence, without which a sparrow falleth to the ground.

Some time after the wreck Captain Isaiah Hatch of Wellfleet was walking along the beach when he came across a suitcase owned by Captain Charles Smith, the *Franklin*'s master. In the valise were incriminating documents indicating that the master was planning to wreck his vessel for the insurance, a deed in which the ship's owners, James W. Wilson and John W. Crafts, were fellow-partners. The captain had become the victim of his own nefarious plan to wreck the *Franklin*, and had not only snuffed out his own life in the attempt, but the lives of ten others. Incidentally, the Boston partners in this crime, Wilson and Crafts, were never properly punished for their share in such a terrible deed.

THE JOSEPHUS

During a heavy April fog in the year 1849, the British ship *Josephus* ran aground on the outer bar off Highland Light. Carrying a cargo of heavy iron rails, the *Josephus* struck during a strong northeasterly gale and soon began to go to pieces. When the fog opened up momentarily, the lighthouse keeper saw the vessel and spread the alarm. A large crowd gathered on the beach within the hour, and efforts were made at once to save the men on the ship.

The masts soon went by the board, scattering the members of the crew to various parts of the *Josephus*. Some could then be seen clinging to the broken ship, their screams echoing even above the roar of the gigantic breakers. Although anxious to help the sailors, the watchers on shore did not dare to risk going out to them in the mountainous seas then pounding the Cape Cod beach.

Suddenly two men were seen running down the side of the Highland Cliff, Jonathan Collins and his friend Daniel Cassidy. Having just returned from a long fishing voyage, the men did not even stop to greet their families, but on hearing of the shipwreck rushed across the town and up to Highland Light. On their arrival at the beach, they found a fisherman's dory, which they carried to the water and launched into the high waves. When urged to give up the dangerous attempt, they replied: "We cannot stand it longer to see these poor fellows being swept into the sea, and we are going to reach them."

They had hardly gained a point two hundred feet from shore when a mighty billow loomed over them, poised its tremendous bulk for a moment, and then engulfed the two heroic fishermen. They were not seen again.

Night came, and the cries of the sailors aboard the ship *Josephus* became fainter and fainter, finally stopping completely as the surf continued its ceaseless pounding on the white sands. The powerful beacon in the tower was lighted, and the keeper sat down for a moment, his thoughts on the men who might still be alive off the Highland Cliffs.

About midnight Keeper Hamilton came down from the tower, strangely troubled in his thoughts. He realized that only by a miracle could anyone have reached the shore, but in spite of this he was uneasy. Finally deciding that only a walk along the beach would quiet his nerves, he threw on his overcoat and made his way out to the edge of the cliff. As he descended to the great beach, the Highland light keeper noticed that considerable wreckage from the *Josephus* was being buffeted by the waves. In the distance he saw what seemed to be a part of the ship's cabin. As he walked closer, Keeper Hamilton heard a groaning noise coming from the wreckage, and then made out the form of a man clinging desperately to the timbers. Another wave washed the wreckage nearer to the beach. The keeper rushed into the water, grabbed the sailor, threw him over his shoulder, and brought him ashore.

Half an hour later the survivor was carried into the keeper's home, and a doctor sent for. Within a few days the man had completely recovered. Twenty-three of his shipmates and the two heroic fishermen had perished. He alone could tell the story.

A silent watcher of the tragedy was Isaac Morton Small, who later in life spent over half a century reporting shipping for the Boston Chamber of Commerce. Although he witnessed scores of other disasters in his career, Morton Small always carried with him the memory of that April day in 1849 when his mother held him by the hand at the edge of the Highland Cliff, and they watched with dreadful fascination the disaster which befell the *Josephus*.

THE CALEDONIA

A dispatch received at the Merchants Exchange Room in Boston on January 2, 1863, stated that the "British steamer *Caledonia*, Captain Weston, via Portland for N. Y., ran on Peaked Hill during thick weather Wednesday night [December 31, 1862]. She lies about six hundred feet from the beach."

The *Caledonia* had mistaken Race Point Light for Highland Light. It was hoped that she would be got off, but the tide swept out the sand from under her, and when the steam tug *Walpole* reached the scene, the *Caledonia* had broken her back. Most of the cargo, railroad iron and linen, was removed from the ship, which was the same size and model as the famous southern raider *Alabama*. It was also in this storm that the *Monitor*, which fought the *Merrimac*, went down off Cape Hatteras, with the loss of thirty-three lives.

THE SHIP PERUVIAN

On the night after Christmas, 1873, a terrific gale swept along Cape Cod, sending mountainous waves high against the cliffs of the Highland there. The ship *Peruvian*, captained by Charles H. Vannah, had sailed from Calcutta several weeks before with a load of tin and sugar. The captain had a special reason for a speedy voyage. His sweetheart, for whom he had been planning a home for several years, was awaiting his return in a New Hampshire town, as this was to be his last voyage.

All had gone well with the *Peruvian* until Christmas Day, when the weather shut in, making any observation impossible. Nevertheless the captain was sure he was off Cape Cod. Keeping the ship sailing northward, he hoped to beat around into calmer waters; but this was not to be.

The seas grew more mountainous, the wind increased in violence, and it was impossible to make headway. Just before midnight the vessel struck on the dreaded shoals of Peaked Hill, a mile from shore, and ground its weight into the sands.

All was now chaos in the blackness of the gale. The ship gradually went to pieces, the crew one by one giving up their hopeless fight and dropping off to their death. At daylight the watchers on the beach found the shore littered with wreckage, but only three bodies of the sailors ever reached shore. The disaster had taken place too far out at sea. (Twenty-eight perished in the disaster.)

Meanwhile Captain Vannah's fiance had made all arrangements to visit Boston just as soon as the ship had been reported as passing the signal station at Cape Cod. Finally, some days after Christmas, word reached Boston of the disaster, and the next day the girl read the overwhelming news that the *Peruvian* had foundered, carrying the man she loved to his death.

THE FRANCIS

Out in the same wild gale which conquered the *Peruvian*, but several miles to the southward, the bark *Francis* was thrown against Cape Cod within five hundred feet of the beach. Settling quickly into the sand, she was observed by watchers along the shore, who located a double-ender whaleboat on the bay side of the Cape several miles away. Twenty men dragged the boat to the edge of the pond at North Truro and then slid it across the ice to the Post Office, where a pair of horses and wheels facilitated matters. Great drifts blocked their way to the beach, however, and it was 10:00 in the morning before the scene of the wreck was reached. (Captain E. P. Worthen of Highland Station was in charge of the rescue.)

With the double-ender launched into the waves, the most difficult part of the journey to the wreck was begun. Out on the *Francis* Captain Kortling, the master, who had been ill for many days in his cabin, was the first to be lowered from the deck into the pitching and tossing whaleboat. The other twenty crewmen were also rescued, but the captain lived only four days after he was brought ashore, as the sickness and exposure proved too much for his weakened body.

Several days later the work of salvage began. The sugar, packed in great straw mats, was hoisted out of the hold day after day, and occasionally one of the packages would break and scatter sugar on the deck. The kind-hearted foreman suggested to the twenty-five workmen from nearby Cape towns that it would be all right if they filled their empty dinner pails and baskets with sugar to take home. Gradually the foreman noticed that the size of the dinner containers in which the laborers were transporting their lunches was growing almost daily. At first holding two or three quarts, in a comparatively short time the receptacles which the men were using for their lunches could have accommodated the family laundry. When the shore boat left after work at night, the craft was in danger of swamping, with each of the twenty-five men carrying twenty, thirty, and forty pounds of sugar in what they alleged were lunch baskets. On the day the overseer visited the wreck, the free sugar ended, but not before several of the workmen had obtained enough sugar for nearly a year's supply.

The *Francis*, an iron bark, seemed an attractive proposition for a wrecking company, which attempted to raise and float the vessel. The moment came for the floating of the bark, the water was pumped out, and the ship started to rise. The *Francis* came to the surface for a moment, shuddered, and sank at once to the bottom. The waves had worn holes in the bark's iron bottom, through which water poured when she lifted off the sand, quickly sending the *Francis* to the bottom again. The wrecking company accepted the inevitable, and left the bark to her fate. Year after year the great storms would expose the iron bark to view, but not since around 1928 has she been seen by watchers from the shore.

THE ITALIAN BARK GIOVANNI

In the winter of the year 1875 the Italian bark *Giovanni* sailed from Palermo with a cargo of sumac, nuts, and brimstone. On March 4, running into a northeast storm off Cape Cod, she drove upon the outer sandbar three miles north of the Highland Life-Saving Station. The crew from the Life-Saving Station, unable to launch their boat into the mountainous breakers, set up their mortar gun on the beach.

Few thought that the gun could carry to the vessel in the face of that terrific gale, but several attempts were made before the project was abandoned. The bark was seen to be breaking up. Two men jumped from the wheelhouse to wreckage which was beginning to float ashore, and one of them soon disappeared from view. The other slowly drifted ashore, where the lifesavers rushed into the sea, joining hands until they formed a living rope. Soon the breakers forced him near the beach, and the foremost man in the chain pulled him from the raging surf. This Italian sailor was the only man rescued from the fifteen on board the *Giovanni.**

All that long night huge bonfires burned on the beach to give hope and encouragement to the survivors on the wreck, but no other person, dead or alive, ever came ashore from the bark. The next day a man was seen to jump from the bow of the vessel and swim to the deckhouse, there to join three of his companions. Soon afterwards the *Giovanni* went to pieces. Although two of the men clung to wreckage until they were halfway ashore, their strength then failed, and they sank beneath the waves. The drama of the *Giovanni* was over.

THE SLOOP TRUMBULL

On the morning of November 30, 1880, the patrol from the Peaked Hill Bars Station discovered a shipwreck on the outer sandbar a half mile south of the station. It was the stone sloop *Trumbull*, carrying a deck load of granite from Rockport, Massachusetts, to New York. When she left Rockport the previous afternoon, the *Trumbull* carried a crew of five men.

Captain David H. Atkins, in charge at the station, launched the lifeboat into the surf and six men soon were rowing out to the wreck. Reaching the scene, Captain Atkins found that he could not approach too near for fear of swamping his craft and so he shouted to the *Trumbull*'s crew to jump into the water where they would be picked up. Three of the sailors leaped into the water, but the captain and mate refused to take the chance, remaining on the sloop.

---

*J. W. Dalton, in his *Life Savers of Cape Cod*, says that no one was saved.

The lifeboat returned to the beach with the three sailors, although the captain was troubled by the thought of the two men still out on the sloop. Finally he announced that he was going to make another attempt to rescue the mariners, and began his second trip. All went well until the sloop was reached, when the boom and loosened main sheet of the *Trumbull* caught the lifeboat and overturned it. The surfmen clung desperately to the bottom of the boat, but Captain Atkins, weakened by his efforts earlier in the day, gave up and sank to his death. Elisha Taylor and Stephen Mayo followed him shortly afterwards.* The other three men began the long swim to shore, where they were hauled out of the water by the man on patrol, John Cole.

With the ocean always performing the unexpected, the incoming tide brought a moderating wind, allowing the stone sloop *Trumbull* to free herself from the dangerous Peaked Hill Bars and continue on her journey down the coast. But the captain and mate of the *Trumbull* must have carried to their dying day the realization that had they obeyed the captain of the lifesavers and jumped for the lifeboat, the second trip of the surfmen would not have been necessary.

Later the same afternoon Captain Atkins' own son helped to recover the bodies of the three drowned men. As he carried his father's remains along the beach, it was a proud son who knew that his parent had died carrying out the stern code of the Life-Saving Service.

THE MONTE TABOR

An unsolved mystery of the sea was the fate of the Italians aboard the bark *Monte Tabor*, wrecked on the Peaked Hill Bars of Cape Cod, September 14, 1896. Although the loss of life was comparatively small, the shipwreck was never completely explained to the satisfaction of men of the Cape.

The *Monte Tabor*, hailing from Genoa, was loaded with salt from Trapani, Sicily. Struck by a hurricane on September 9, she was trying to make Provincetown Harbor at the time she hit. Patrolman Silvey of the Peaked Hill Station discovered the wreck, but it was impossible

---

*Elisha Taylor, just before he sank, said to Isaiah Young, father of Cy Young, "Isaiah, have you got a chew?" Isaiah, struggling in the water, finally got his tobacco out. Elisha took a big bite, smiled in satisfaction, and slipped beneath the waves to his death.

The Monte Tabor, *wrecked on Peaked Hill Bars off Cape Cod, September 14, 1896*

to launch the lifeboat. The bark's cabin broke away from the vessel and carried six of the crew ashore to safety. Another young Italian, who reached land by swimming, hid in the beach plum bushes until taken by the lifeguards. He explained that he expected to be killed if shipwrecked at Cape Cod, which was what the others aboard had told him.

Of those who did not reach land, three committed suicide, according to survivors from the bark, while the remainder of the crew disappeared in the storm. Some say that the captain was so humiliated at the loss of his fine vessel that he killed himself, and two of the other officers followed his example. (An investigation later proved that the captain had taken his own life.) At the time the survivors claimed it was an Italian custom for the captain of a wrecked craft to take his own life, but this seems to have no basis in fact.

THE COLERAINE

The barge *Coleraine* was one of three which left Bangor, Maine, in April 1915, bound for Philadelphia. Towed out of Bangor Harbor, by the tug *Mars* (owned by the Reading Railroad Company), the barges encountered heavy weather as the four vessels approached Cape Cod. The following day it began to snow, with the wind setting in from the northeast. At 6:00 that afternoon the captain noticed white water ahead, and realized that he was nearing the Cape. He ordered the cables cut, changed the tug's course, and a few hours later anchored in Provincetown Harbor, where his propeller dropped off.

The three barges, the *Coleraine*, the *Tunnel Ridge*, and the *Manheim*, now began to drift against the shores of Cape Cod. One by one they grounded in the sands, but the *Tunnel Ridge* and the *Coleraine* were badly damaged before they hit the beach. The other vessel, in command of Captain George Israel, let go both her anchors, delaying the action of the sea in pushing her up on the beach. By the time she joined the other barges on the shore, the storm had begun to abate, so that the *Manheim* was still in good condition.

The action of the sea soon built up a great breakwater of sand around the *Tunnel Ridge* and the *Coleraine*, which were lying stranded one on each side of the *Manheim*. Thus it was impossible to try to float off the uninjured *Manheim* until the two badly wrecked barges were disposed of. It was finally decided to set fire to the wrecked vessels after Captain Israel had allowed the men of Cape Cod to take off the deckhouses from the *Coleraine*. The houses were landed on the beach, cut into smaller sections, and pulled up the steep sides of the Highland Cliff by four horses. Made into a three-room building, it soon bore the name of the Highland House Golf Links. (The building was later used as a summer cottage.)

On the fourth day of April, 1916, the barge *Manheim* was towed off the beach at Cape Cod. Just a year had elapsed since the wreck of the vessel.

THE 1927 SHIPWRECKS

Two serious shipwrecks occurred on Cape Cod during the year 1927. On February 2, 1927, the three-masted lumber schooner *Montclair* hit the beach at Cape Cod a quarter mile from the Orleans Coast Guard Station. Two men washed ashore on wreckage, but five others were drowned in the great surf. Henry Beston, in his *Outermost House*, gives a fine description of the shipwreck.

Another great storm broke out later in the month. On February 18, the Coast Guard cruiser *238* broke down a mile from the Peaked Hill Bars during the height of the storm, and radioed for help. Navy craft starting down from Boston to help the *238* were unable to reach the doomed cruiser in time. Around midnight the last distress signals were received on the mainland from the *238*, and it is believed that she foundered around 5:00 the next morning. All eight men aboard were lost.

THE TERESA DAN

The last important shipwreck on Cape Cod was that of the fishing schooner *Teresa Dan*, wrecked one mile north of Highland Coast Guard Station on December 21, 1942. Her master was Captain John Hall. After several unsuccessful attempts to free the beam trawler from the sands, the *Teresa Dan* was sold to Captain Ben Pine, famous Gloucester fisherman and international racer, who salvaged her on the beach.

A substantial portion of the original timbers of the *Sparrowhawk* are on display at Plymouth's Pilgrim Hall Museum.

THE ALMIRA The lone survivor of the *Almira*, the captain's son, was found with his hands frozen to the ropes and his feet encased in ice. He lost both hands and both feet to frostbite, and it was reported at the time, "The memory of that fearful night and day is fresh in his mind."

THE FRANKLIN In *Cape Cod*, Thoreau also describes encountering a wrecker sometime after the *Franklin* disaster. The man was attempting to salvage tow cloth from the remains of the vessel using a grapple and a rope. Thoreau also described a bed of beets "flourishing vigorously" at the high-tide mark on the beach, which he believed to be the result of seeds washed from the *Franklin*.

According to other accounts, Benjamin Swett Rich of Wellfleet, twenty-one years old at the time, was the one who found the papers incriminating Captain Smith. Rich went on to become the Superintendent of the Sixth Life-Saving District. His obituary stated that his father, Captain Mulford Rich, led the heroic rescue efforts described by Snow.

THE JOSEPHUS In his 1928 book *Shipwrecks on Cape Cod*, Isaac. M. Small wrote of the *Josephus*, "The terrible circumstances attending the destruction of this ship were so vividly impressed upon my childish mind (I was four years old at the time) that they are as plain in memory as thought they had occurred but yesterday." Small stood on shore holding his mother's hand as he watched the two brave fishermen, attempting to save those on the *Josephus*, vanish in the seething sea.

THE CALEDONIA In 2002 a team from NOAA and the Mariners' Museum of Virginia raised the gun turret of the *Monitor* to the surface, twenty miles off the North Carolina coast.

THE FRANCIS The *Peruvian* and the *Francis* had left Calcutta a few days apart and they had been practically within sight of each other on the voyage, and they met their ends in the same storm three miles apart on the sands of Cape Cod.

THE GIOVANNI There was some criticism leveled at the Life-Saving Service for the crew's failure to save more of the crew of the *Giovanni*, but there's little doubt that everything humanly possible was attempted. As Isaac M. Small wrote in *Shipwrecks on Cape Cod*, "It was one of those terrible marine disasters, of which there are many, where man is a plaything in the grip of the sea when the storm king is abroad in his might."

THE TRUMBULL In *Shipwrecks on Cape Cod*, Isaac M. Small wrote, "This tragedy could have been averted had not the requirements of the service and the sense of duty urged the Coast Guardsmen to attempt the rescue."

THE MONTE TABOR In his 1946 book *A Pilgrim Returns to Cape Cod* (reissued by Commonwealth Editions in 2003), Snow related the contents of a note put into a bottle and cast adrift by Captain Genero of the *Monte Tabor*. After describing the hurricane and the desperate situation of the crew, the note concluded, "The captain and crew, all resigned to the will of Providence, gave their souls to God, thanking him for the destiny assigned to them. Our prayer from the finder for their souls."

It appears that the vessel wasn't wrecked so much by the storm but by the captain's misreading of his position. Thinking he had already cleared Race Point, he steered the *Tabor* to the west directly into the Peaked Hill Bars. The rescue of six of the crewmen was credited to Surfman Fish of the Peaked Hill Bars Life-Saving Station and Edwin B. Tyler of the Race Point station.

THE COLERAINE Five men lived aboard the *Manheim* for about a year, waiting for suitable conditions for the barge's refloating. In preparation they rigged hawsers to three large anchors in deep water, hooking them to winches on the barge. When the barge floated during a storm, the men used the winches to pull the barge safely into deep water.

The deckhouse from the *Coleraine* was used as a bar until the 1950s. Highland Golf Links is the oldest golf course on Cape Cod, and in 1996 Highland Lighthouse was relocated to the seventh fairway.

CHAPTER 30

The Portland Gale

When the first chilling winds of a piercing November gale come swirling into the harbors and inlets along the New England Coast, there are gray, aging mariners who recall a night in 1898 when the steamer *Portland* sailed from Boston never to return. The loss of this side-wheeler was the worst marine tragedy of the nineteenth century in New England waters. (The *Saint John*, with 143, was second in the number drowned.) And although the passing years have brought many controversial theories regarding the fate of this handsome steamer, it is probable that the complete story of the *Portland* will never be known.

The gale which caused the loss of the Maine side-wheeler was one of truly cyclonic proportions. It began November 26, 1898, lasting twenty-four hours in violent intensity, and then tapered off to its end. So quickly did it rise that by the time the *Portland* had reached a point off Gloucester, Massachusetts, on her journey from Boston, almost 200 vessels were hurrying for shelter up and down the coast, trying desperately to reach a haven. Gloucester, Vineyard Haven, Provincetown, and Boston were the main objectives of vessels caught in the storm in New England waters. At Martha's Vineyard over twenty ships were damaged or wrecked by the gale, while in Gloucester and Provincetown the shores were strewn with wreckage. Boston Harbor took a severe lashing from the elements, around twenty-five vessels going ashore. In all, 141 different ships were wrecked because of the Portland Gale in New England.

In such a titanic marine disturbance, we can only cover the outstanding shipwrecks or disasters. The loss of the *Calvin F. Baker*, the *Mertis H. Perry*, the *Albert L. Butler*, and the pilot boat *Columbia* will be considered in detail; the vessels which some claim may have crashed into the *Portland*, the *King Philip*, the *Addie E. Snow*, and the *Pentagoet* will be discussed. The *Portland* itself will be considered at the close of the chapter.

Seven individuals out in the gale have left statements as to the severity of the tempest. Captain Joseph I. Kemp, probably Boston's best-known sailing master, who has piloted more than $2 billion worth of shipping from the Fore River yards, was coming into the harbor on that night of 1898. Aboard the tug *Elsie*, Captain Kemp was on the way from Lynn:

> *It was the greasiest evening you ever saw, quite similar to the day of the great 1938 hurricane. About seven o'clock it started to spit snow, and a light easterly was blowing. We had towed the barge* Woodside *from Lynn to Quarantine anchorage. Around 7:15 P.M. the* Portland *came down the harbor and passed fairly close to us near Deer Island Light. We landed at Lewis Wharf, and by the next morning they were rowing dories up and down Atlantic Avenue.*

Lieutenant Worth G. Ross, assistant inspector of life-saving stations in Boston, recorded his impressions of the storm:

> *There were at sunset marked indications of approaching bad weather in the vicinity. By midnight it was blowing heavily from the northeast, accompanied by thick snow. Throughout the night the wind and sea increased, and by sunrise of Sunday, November 27, a tremendous gale was raging. Such a violent outburst of the elements had not occurred in this vicinity within the memory of the oldest inhabitant. The wild fury of the wind and driving snow continued without abatement until late in the afternoon. At times the force and roar of the tempest were so appalling as to be indescribable.*

Keeper Joshua James, lifesaver of Hull, Massachusetts, known from Boston to Baltimore for his unsurpassed bravery and rescue work, made some of his most spectacular rescues during that November gale. His comments follow:

Snow began falling early, and the wind increased until by 10 o'clock it was blowing a gale from the northeast with sleet and snow so thick that we could not see one hundred yards at most. At midnight it was a hurricane.

On the other side of the harbor Keeper Wesley Pingree, well known around Boston Bay, was marooned at Deer Island Light during the storm. He spent the night in the tower on watch. Some years before his death he signed a statement for the writer about the storm:

At two o'clock in the afternoon the ocean was as smooth as glass. At five P.M. it had started snowing and the wind was coming up. A little later the Bangor boat went by but returned to the harbor, as the sea was rapidly getting worse. At 7 P.M. the Portland *came down the channel, and the other boat, anchored in President Road, whistled a warning to her. At this time the waves were hitting so high that I was lashing my dory fast to the light.*

Farther out to sea, on Bug Light at the entrance to Boston Harbor's Narrows, Mrs. Frank Tenney, who kept house for Captain Gershom Freeman, says that she had been digging clams on the bar that afternoon, for there were no signs of the gale then on the way. Later that night the stones thrown up by the waves played strange tunes as they

A giant wave hits Minot's Light, which Snow often called "America's most dangerous lighthouse."

hit the iron supports holding up Bug Light.

Captain William Abbott, who was aboard the steamer *Ohio* when she ran aground at Spectacle Island, said that it had been a terrific experience. "I could hardly see across the ship," were his words. (The *Ohio* was later got off the Spectacle Island beach.)

Keeper Milton H. Reamy of Minot's Light had so often felt the great waves as they crept up the sides of America's most dangerous lighthouse, that he made no particular preparations for the blow when he saw it coming. He took his regular watch in the usual manner, and thought nothing more about it. In the morning, however, when he stepped out on the lower turret of the 114-foot tower, he swept the ocean with his glass, locating many wrecks along the beach. It was only then, said Reamy, that he realized the storm must have been of unusual severity.

The Boston Weather Bureau states definitely that it began snowing at 7:37 on that Saturday night. At the hour the *Portland* sailed, 7:00 P.M., the barometer in Boston was 29.70, the wind was blowing from the northeast at a rate of thirteen miles an hour, and the weather was cloudy.

A vessel did not have a chance in most cases when caught off a lee shore in such a terrific effort of wind and storm which developed before sunrise the next morning. As a result the entire shore from Casco Bay to Cape Cod was littered with wreckage and disabled ships, with Martha's Vineyard and Nantucket experiencing their share of the tempest. No one out in the Portland Gale ever believed anything else equaled it in intensity. On the 141 vessels wrecked along the New England coast in the hurricane, the loss of life amounted to over 456 persons. The suddenness and intensity of the storm were probably due to the rapid increase in energy which took place when two cyclones, one from the Gulf of Mexico, and one from the Great Lakes, came together.

THE COLUMBIA

The first of the many wrecks caused by the Portland Gale which we shall discuss was that of the pilot boat *Columbia*. The *Columbia*'s last known act was to discharge her pilot Captain William Abbott aboard the steamer *Ohio*, which later pushed ashore on Spectacle Island. The storm grew worse as the evening wore on, and it is believed that the *Columbia* was then in the vicinity of the Boston Lightship. No one escaped the wreck, so conjecture alone must dictate the story of the loss of the *Columbia*.

The following morning Surfman Richard Tobin of the North Scituate Life-Saving Station had the south patrol along Sand Hills from 8:00 to 12:00. His report says:

> I went down the beach to the key post about three miles from the station. . . . The seas were coming over with such force that I was washed into the pond back of the ridge. It was blowing so hard that that I was obliged to kneel down to get my breath.

At 9:30 Surfman Tobin was on the veranda of the very cottage into which the *Columbia* crashed later in the day. When he returned to the station it was 3:00 in the afternoon. The storm was now so intense that no patrol was permitted to leave; in fact not until midnight did the next patrol go out. Surfman John Curran set out on the south patrol this time, and at quarter of two in the morning he sighted a schooner right in the line of his patrol, lying on the beach where she had crashed into a cottage. The wreckage from the shattered building was lying in heaped confusion on the decks of the careened vessel. Since Surfman

The pilot boat Columbia, *wrecked during the Portland Gale at Scituate. All on board were drowned. When W. Sidney Davey made this picture, the boat had been a museum for many years.*

Tobin had stood on the veranda of that very cottage at 9:30 Sunday morning, the *Columbia* had washed up on the beach between then and 1:45 a.m. on Monday. No one witnessed the disaster and no one ever knew what took place.

By 3:20 that morning Curran had returned to the station and notified the keeper, who visited the scene with three surfmen. On the way they found the body of the *Columbia's* first boatkeeper. The other four men were later found in the vicinity. The wreck of the *Columbia* was complete. The starboard side of the pilot boat had split near the garboard, the planking was torn where she had hung and ground on the rocks, and the sternpost was broken to pieces. The foremast was gone, two anchor chains hung from the hawsepipes, and the anchors were missing. Probably the five men on the pilot boat were dead before the *Columbia* struck the beach, and the fact that both anchors were gone showed that the vessel had attempted unsuccessfully to weather the storm. This opinion was shared by a majority of seafaring men who visited the scene.

The pilot boat *Columbia* was left where she hit on the beach, high above the reach of the normal tides of the years. Made over into a museum, the wreck stayed on the Scituate Beach for about forty years. Thousands visited this vessel during the first quarter of the present century, but about the year 1935 the elements began to make inroads on the wreck, so the Scituate officials ordered the pilot boat burned. Thus ended the career of the Boston pilot boat *Columbia*, the schooner on which five brave men tried unsuccessfully to ride out the Portland Gale.

THE CALVIN F. BAKER

The schooner *Calvin F. Baker* encountered heavy weather on the night of November 26, and ran for the safety of Boston Harbor. About 3:00 in the morning of the 27th, when the storm had reached terrific proportions, the captain saw Boston Light loom up on the port bow, and the schooner crashed almost instantly against a submerged ledge in back of Lighthouse Island [Little Brewster Island]. Everyone aboard made for the rigging as the breakers swept over the ship, and the schooner careened to and fro in her rocky cradle on the ledge.

Keeper Henry L. Pingree of Boston Light (keeper from 1894 until 1909) saw the schooner but the waves at that time were sweeping the entire island, preventing him from helping the unfortunate sailors. All that Sunday the *Baker* rocked in her cradle, the helpless men calling for aid from their precarious positions in the rigging of the ship. The mother of one of the assistant keepers was so affected by the shock of hearing the frozen men calling for aid throughout that day and the following night that she died shortly afterwards.

At dusk during the evening of the Portland Gale there was a momentary lull in the storm, which gave Keeper Joshua James of the Point Allerton Coast Guard Station an opportunity to look out on the ocean with his telescope. James sighted the spars and masts of the Baker showing behind Lighthouse Island, but, since he and his men were nearly exhausted, having already that day saved the crew of the *Henry R. Tilton* and coal barge No. 1, they reluctantly decided against attempting any more rescues so late in the day.

When the first glimmer of dawn appeared the next morning, Keeper James anxiously focused his glass on Lighthouse Island. He saw that the

Keeper Joshua James of the Point Allerton Coast Guard Station, a renowned lifesaver

wreck was still there and that the distress signal flag at Boston Light was flying. Engaging the services of the tug *Ariel* to tow him across the harbor in his surfboat, he let go the towline when reaching the lee of Boston Light. Keeper James now steered his craft across the bar between the lighthouse and Great Brewster Island, finally reaching the *Calvin F. Baker.*

With the arrival of the surfboat, the men who were still alive took heart. First Mate Burgess S. Howland had fallen to his death the day before, while Second Mate Isaacs disappeared during the night. Just before the surfboat arrived, the master of the *Calvin F. Baker* noticed Willis Studley, the steward, standing with his hand against the taffrail. When a shout failed to arouse him, the captain hit the man heavily on the shoulder to wake him up, but Studley fell over to the deck. He had frozen to death while leaning against the rail, and the captain's blow had keeled his body over. When Keeper James boarded the *Baker* he found the five sailors huddled on a remnant of the forward deck of the schooner. They were all taken into the surfboat, the four living and the one dead man. A short time later they were inside the life-saving station, their experiences in the Portland Gale at an end.

THE MERTIS H. PERRY

With 15,000 pounds of fish in her holds, the fishing schooner *Mertis H. Perry* was coming into Boston Bay when the gale hit. Snow and sleet shut in around 9:30 that Saturday evening, and at 11:00 the captain wore ship to edge offshore. At midnight the jib split, the main gaff snapped, and the vessel could make no further headway, so the crew lowered the foresail and let go the port anchor. The snow descended in such quantities that visibility was entirely blocked out. When the port anchor failed to hold, the starboard anchor was let go. The *Perry* now fetched up, but with the storm increasing the crew of fourteen knew the vessel would soon start to drag anchor again.

Sometime early that Sunday morning the dreaded event happened—all on board felt the anchors begin to drag. Gradually the *Perry* worked her way into shallow water. The captain ordered the masts cut away. Soon afterwards the port anchor cable parted, and the starboard chain separated around 7:00 in the morning. Their only chance was to run before the wind toward shore, trusting that they would strike a sandy beach.

Now in the heavy breakers, the *Perry* hit bottom. The tide was coming in, carrying the *Perry* along with it. The sailors had no idea where they might be. When about 200 yards off the beach, sailor William Bagnell of Cape Breton Island died of exposure. Captain Joshua Pike decided to try to reach shore, so he jumped over the side with a part of a broken dory. He was never seen again.

A few minutes later a gigantic breaker seized the schooner and pushed her high up on the beach so that the jib boom actually hung over the banking above the shore. They had hit at Brant Rock, Massachusetts. Four of the sailors dropped from the schooner's jib boom down on the bank, but then another wave pulled the *Perry* around broadside. The remaining fishermen threw a line to the men on shore, but before it could be used the schooner again swung around into her former position, with the jib boom over the bank. Six men jumped to safety. Joseph Veader, however, leaped just as another billow swept around the bow, and fell into the surf. He lost his life.

The survivors were now all ashore. George Bagnall soon died from exposure as he lay on the sandbank, and when the others started to look for shelter Charles Forbes could not keep up with them. Near death from exhaustion, Forbes begged the others to go on without him. After walking some distance, they found a farmhouse. Knocking at the door, they met the owner, Mr. Ames, who took them in and also sent

The Mertis H. Perry *on the beach at Brant Rock (from Snow's* Great Atlantic Adventures, *courtesy of W. Torrey Little)*

two of his men back to the wreck to bring back Forbes. But the unfortunate fisherman had died there on the bank. Nine of the sailors were saved aboard the *Perry*, while five perished because of the wreck.

At nearby Brant Rock Life-Saving Station the surfmen were energetically attempting to save their wave-battered building, which was filled with many residents who had sought safety from the high tides there. As wave after wave smashed against the edifice and the tide rose even higher, the women and children were ordered upstairs. A few minutes later the surf crashed open the boatroom doors and swept through the dining-room windows. Fearing that the entire structure would be carried away, the men threw open the rear doors, allowing the tide to sweep through the lower floor of the station while the second floor remained intact. The tide finally began to go down, and as soon as the area around the station was bare, all the women and children were taken over to the Union Chapel, a stone church nearby, which was considered safe. That night the surfmen joined the townspeople in the church, and the night went by without further trouble.

THE ALBERT L. BUTLER

When the Portland gale hit the *Albert L. Butler*, the schooner was forty miles east-southeast of Highland Light. By midnight the wind was blowing from the northeast, and at 7:00 the next morning the captain wore ship under bare poles. No sooner had the schooner gotten around than a tremendous sea boarded her, drove portions of her deck load of logwood through the rigging, carried away booms and gaffs, and smashed into hatches, leaving the *Butler* a helpless wreck. Oil bags proved of no value when put over. At about 10:00 that morning shore breakers were under her forefoot. The sea was frightful by this time—greater than the captain had ever seen before. A short time later the *Butler* swung broadside high on the Cape Cod sands.

Surfman B. F. Henderson from the Peaked Hill Bars Life-Saving Station and Surfman Benjamin Kelly from the High Head Station had just met and parted near the halfway house, over which the surf was breaking, when the *Albert L. Butler* loomed up before them out of the storm within the limits of the Peaked Hill Bars Station. Within a half hour Henderson had returned to the station. Soon the beach wagon was manned and on the way down the beach toward the wreck. As they made their way through the swirling snow, a flash of lightning came, followed by a clap of thunder. Captain Michael F. Hogan of the *Ruth M. Martin*, out in the same wild storm, believed the flash to be from the *Portland*, which he thought might have blown up at the time. As scores of residents in the vicinity of Cape Cod heard the thunder during the Portland Gale, the captain must have mistaken the lightning for an explosion.

Reaching the scene of the wreck, the rescuers found a man on the bank. Since he was not seriously injured, they left him there to save those still on the *Butler*. Four sailors were seen in the rigging, only fifty yards away. The lifesavers fired a Lyle gun, dropping a number seven line between the mainmast and the mizzenmast, but the sailors ignored the lifeline completely. Another shot was fired, this time right across the deck. One of the sailors, instead of reading the tally board of instructions sent out with the whip line, merely made the tail-block fast to the mizzen rigging, and without waiting for the hawser or breeches buoy, tried to reach shore by the whip block. Of course the slender line sagged until it was in the surf, but the men on shore hauled him as rapidly as possible through the breakers. He was lucky to reach shore alive, but he did make it. Shortly afterwards the mizzenmast gave way and crashed forward. If the sailors had only waited a few minutes, another line

The Albert L. Butler *on the beach on Cape Cod, wrecked during the Portland Gale*

would have been sent out, but evidently they became panic stricken by the crashing mast and tried to get ashore by the whip line, as the other sailor had done. The falling mast fouled the line, and though the surf-men pulled hard, the sparked rope would not run freely through the tail-block. Just as a gigantic wave formed on the other side of the vessel, the line jammed. As the wave struck, it buried the ship under tons of water. The tragedy is mentioned in the official report of Captain Cook: "I had hold of the whip line, and could feel when the sailors lost their grasp. They were washed off, and that is the last we know of them." A moment later a surfman heard a moan coming from under the bank and rushed over to find a man crying for help. He had been cast up on the shore some time before.

There was now no sign of life on the *Butler*. After the surfman had taken the survivors back to the station, an unexpected incident took place. As the tide went out, more and more of the beach was exposed until the vessel was at the water's edge. Just as the surfmen were about to climb aboard the wreck, they heard a scramble, and two men, who had been in the cabin all the time without the knowledge of their shipmates, jumped to the beach. They were taken to the life-saving station, where the five members of the crew were brought together again.

After the storm the *Albert L. Butler* remained on the beach for many weeks a picturesque wreck, its masts and fittings gradually stripped by the wreckers of the Cape. It was here on the beach near the *Butler* that much of the material from the *Portland* later washed up.

THE PORTLAND

Regardless of the number of other vessels sunk or wrecked during the terrific hurricane of November 1898, mention of this gale usually brings back one outstanding event in the minds of New England inhabitants—the loss of the steamer *Portland*. Although nearly half a century has elapsed since the momentous night when she steamed out to meet the gale which proved her doom, there are many who still vividly recall the famous vessel which gave her name to that devastating cyclone.

The 291-foot steamer *Portland*, designed by William P. Pattee, was built at the Bath, Maine, shipyards in 1890. (Amos E. Haggett, of New England Shipbuilding Company, was in charge of building the *Portland*, which took fifteen months and ended in May 1890.) She was one of the outstanding paddle-wheelers of the time. Seaworthy and of great

Last known picture of the Portland, *fall 1898.*

strength, the *Portland* was unusually spacious and comfortable. When photographed on her trial run by N. L. Stebbins,* the greatest marine cameraman of his day, the white-and-gold–trimmed steamer appeared as a vessel of beautiful lines on her way down Boston Harbor. Drawing eleven feet of water, the *Portland* could navigate Broad Sound Channel in Boston's outer harbor, and with her beam of forty-two feet she was considered an ideal craft for the trip to Portland.

Since November 26, 1898, was the Saturday after Thanksgiving, there were more passengers than usual who wished to make the journey to Portland that night. Many were returning to Maine from Philadelphia, New York, or farther south, where they had been with their folks on the holiday. That morning the weather was pleasantly fair, with a light breeze. As the day wore on, however, the clouds above Boston grew heavier, giving first evidences of an advancing condition of grave danger. A tremendous cyclone from the Gulf of Mexico was about to join forces with a storm of only slightly lesser proportions roaring across from the Great Lakes.

Meanwhile, the loading of the steamer's freight continued at India Wharf in Boston. The passengers who had made reservations for the journey began to come aboard. Some of them later cancelled their accommodations, but the majority, more than 100 people, sailed with the ship.

---

*Stebbins published his *Coast Pilot* from scores of pictures which he took up and down the New England coast in 1890.

The crew of the Portland, *some of whom did not sail on November 26, 1898. The names of the two men in the back and of the bootblack (in front, on the capstan) are unknown. The remainder are James A. Philbrook, Apt, Deering, Verrill, Wells, Saunders, Dyer, Anderson (in derby), William Craig, James Hunt (freight clerk), Swett, and J. McKay. (Courtesy of R. W. Phillbrook)*

Together with the crew, there were 176 persons (108 passengers and 68 crew members) aboard the *Portland* by sailing time.*

The general manager of the Portland Steam Packet Company, John F. Liscomb, on receiving warning of the approaching storm from New York, tried to communicate by phone from Portland with the steamer's captain, Hollis H. Blanchard. Failing in this, he left word that the *Portland's* companion ship, the newer *Bay State*, would not leave Portland until 9:00, when the size of the storm could be better gauged. When he returned at 5:30, Blanchard talked over the phone to the *Bay State's* captain, Alexander Dennison, called because of his comparative youthfulness the "Kid Pilot."

Captain Dennison told Blanchard of manager Liscomb's suggestion to hold the *Portland* until 9:00. Captain Blanchard replied that the *Portland* would sail on schedule at 7:00, giving as his reason the direction of the storm, which he predicted would not reach the city of Portland until

---

*According to the most recent estimates, 192 people died on board.—*Ed.*

after the steamer had safely docked. Dennison, said Blanchard, would be proceeding southward, and would run into the storm before he reached Boston.

The fact that the two captains talked over the phone that day has given rise to the popular legend that Captain Blanchard sailed contrary to the advice of the general manager because he was anxious to prove his sailing abilities superior to those of Captain Dennison by steaming into Portland Harbor, where the *Bay State* would still be at the wharf. There seems to be no foundation in fact for this tale, to which many still cling.

Captains of passenger vessels invariably feel the responsibility for so many lives which depend upon their skill and judgment. Those who really knew Captain Blanchard were convinced that he was no exception. His decision was based upon his best judgment, and at least twelve other sea captains have admitted that under similar conditions they would have reasoned and acted as he did. (Seven of them were under oath at the time of their statements.)

Throughout the day special bulletins from the weather bureau arrived. At 10:33 A.M. the bureau informed C. F. Williams, the line's Boston agent, that a storm of considerable intensity was on the way. At 3:15 P.M. a special report from New York stated that a northeast snowstorm had already begun there. At 6:07, fifty-three minutes before sailing time, the final notice arrived with the information that it was still snowing in New York, but that the wind had backed around to northwest. This news gave Captain Blanchard confidence that he could reach Portland ahead of the storm as he had done many times before. Agent Williams then left India Wharf for his home. (The exact time was 6:15 P.M.) At precisely 7:00 that November evening, the final departing whistle from the *Portland* split the chill night air of Boston's Atlantic Avenue, and Captain Hollis Blanchard sailed into the unknown.

Many claim that it was snowing when the *Portland* left her pier at 7:00. Wesley Pingree, down at Deer Island Light, later mistakenly remembered that it had begun to snow around 5:00 that afternoon. The official report of the Boston Weather Bureau, which can hardly be wrong, stated that the snow began to fall at 7:37, two and one-half hours later than Pingree's recollection claims. While the fact that the lighthouse is five miles down the harbor from the city would account for some discrepancy in time, the difference could hardly be so great. Besides, Captain Kemp, who was near Deer Island Light, stated positively that the snow did not start there until about 7:00.

It is commonly believed that the *Portland* was never seen again after leaving Boston. Nothing could be further from the facts. The records tell a remarkable story.

The Bangor boat *Kennebec* dropped anchor in President Road just before the *Portland* proceeded down the harbor. Although Captain Collins had started for Bangor, the threatening storm caused him to return to safety. As the *Portland* steamed by, he whistled what seemed by others to be a warning to Captain Blanchard, but the latter, unheeding, continued out to sea. (Keeper Pingree believed the warning was definitely given.)

A short time later the incoming *Mount Desert*, piloted by Captain William A. Roix, passed the *Portland* just as both vessels drew abeam of Graves Ledge in Boston's outer bay. According to Thomas Harrison Eames, those in the wheelhouse of the *Mount Desert* expected to see the *Portland* come about and return to port, but she followed her regular course until the lights faded in the distance.

Captain William Thomas of Bailey's Island, Maine, master of the fisherman *Maud S.*, saw the lights of the *Portland* when he was 3 ¾ miles southwest of Thacher's Island. Believing that his wife was on the steamer, Thomas naturally was watching for the *Portland* with unusual attention. Less than two miles away from the side-wheeler at the time, Thomas thought that the steamer was closer to shore than usual. He said to his crew, "There goes the *Portland*. She will probably run close to Thacher's." It was then two and a half hours after Blanchard had sailed from Boston. Nothing at that time led Thomas to believe that the captain of the *Portland* was foolhardy in continuing her journey. Incidentally, Thomas' wife was not on the *Portland*, having made fortunate use of the privilege of changing her mind.

Captain A. A. Tarr of Thacher's Island Twin Lights off Gloucester agreed with Thomas about weather conditions at the time the *Portland* passed that point. He said that it seemed so nearly normal weather at the time the ship was scheduled to pass the island that he did not even bother to look for the sparkle of the lights of the side-wheeler. There seemed to him to be no reason why the *Portland* should not have reached that point at the usual time as the wind and sea were not boisterous. Moreover, we have the evidence of another man stationed at Thacher's Island. Captain Lynes B. Hathaway of Brockton, master workman of the Lighthouse Department, at about 9:30 or shortly afterwards was in the smoking room which the workmen used on the island when he saw the *Portland's* lights as the steamer passed within 500 feet of the shore, between Thacher's and the Londoner Ledge. The *Portland*, then on schedule, continued up the coast.

Around 11:00, less than ninety minutes after Captain Hathaway saw the steamer, Captain Reuben Cameron of the schooner *Grayling* sighted the *Portland* twelve miles south by east of Thacher's Island. Thus, without question, the vessel had changed her course. The *Portland* came so near to the *Grayling* that Captain Cameron burned a Coston flare to warn the steamer away. The paddle-wheeler at this time seemed rolling and pitching badly, although her superstructure appeared intact.

Also in the vicinity was the schooner *Florence E. Stearns*. At approximately 11:15 P.M. her master Frank Stearns passed a paddle-wheel steamer, doubtless the *Portland*, as there was no other vessel of her type in the area. Half an hour later Captain D. J. Pellier of the schooner *Edgar Randall*, then fourteen miles southeast by east of Eastern Point, Gloucester, noticed a large vessel bearing down upon him out of the night.* Pellier swung the *Randall* away and escaped a collision, but had time to see that the ship was a paddle-wheel steamer. At the time, he believed that the steamer's superstructure had been damaged, but how accurately he could see from the lurching deck of a small schooner is a matter of conjecture.

Meanwhile the storm had increased in intensity. In Portland at noon there had been a north wind blowing at nineteen miles per hour, which increased at 2:00 P.M. to twenty-six, changing to northeast at 3:00, then increasing to thirty-six miles per hour at 7:00 that evening. Having swung around to north at 6:00 P.M., the wind shifted to northeast an hour later. There were spells of wind which blew during this period at almost a mile a minute. The official Weather Bureau records at Boston indicate that the wind velocity increased from fourteen miles per hour at 7:00 to thirty-one miles per hour at midnight. Occasionally the wind reached almost unbelievable intensity, many gusts of at least seventy-two miles per hour were experienced. The barometer at Boston dropped from 29:70 at 7:00 to 29:44 at 12:00.

Shipping all along the coast scurried for shelter. Vessel after vessel, failing to reach a safe harbor, was tossed ashore along Nantasket Beach

---

*The writer talked with Captain Pellier at Ten Pound Island in 1936, and Captain Pellier believed the superstructure of the *Portland* badly damaged when he saw it that night.

and the North Shore of Massachusetts, while every coastal town and city in the path of the storm was fearfully battered. Giant breakers swept through many main thoroughfares, and the tide, as measured at Cohasset, rose even higher than it had during the record Minot's Light gale which toppled over the lighthouse. (The high-tide marks are still visible from the two storms of 1851 and 1898 on the rocks near the keeper's residence on Government Island, Cohasset.)

When we left the *Portland*, she had changed her course off Thacher's Island and, probably damaged, seemed not to be making progress toward her destination but rather to be engaged in tactics designed to enable her to weather the storm.

Just how far on her scheduled journey did the *Portland* go? There were those, including the late yachting enthusiast and newsman, William U. Swan, who believed that the *Portland* reached a point north of Boon Island (about sixty-five miles in a northeasterly direction from Boston) off Portsmouth on her voyage up the coast. This belief is hard to reconcile with the known facts. If the side-wheeler passed the Londoner Ledge off Thacher's Island around or shortly after 9:30, she could not have attained a position near Boon Island, many miles to the north, and at the same time have changed her course and still be twelve miles southeast of Thacher's Island ninety minutes later at 11:00 P.M. Logically it would seem that the *Portland* never attained a position more than five miles north of Thacher's Island.

Captain Albert Bragg, master of the steamer *Horatio Hall*, sailed out of Portland Harbor approximately an hour after Captain Blanchard steamed from Boston that Saturday night. The wind and sea were light when the *Hall* left her dock. Bragg's course took him sixteen miles east of Boon Island and forty miles east of Thacher's Island, but the storm hit with such unprecedented fury that he hove to about 1:00 in the morning, staying in that position until 8:00 A.M. "I never saw such a storm in my life," was his statement.

Captain Frank Scripture of Rockport, Massachusetts, described how the gale seemed to travel in veins, as indicated on shore by the track it made through forests. Not within his memory had there been such a hurricane as that which hit Cape Ann shortly before midnight. Nevertheless, said Scripture, when the *Portland* sailed there was no reason why a prudent captain should not leave Boston. The storm came on more rapidly than any other he ever experienced on Cape Ann. Probably when the cyclone surprised Captain Blanchard somewhere north of

Thacher's Island Lights, the *Portland*'s master headed her out to sea to ride out the gale, as he had done before.

Exactly six hours after the *Portland* was sighted by Captain Pellier of the *Edgar Randall*, off Eastern Point, Gloucester, Captain Samuel O. Fisher of the Race Point Life-Saving Station on Cape Cod, standing at the foot of his bed at the station, heard, he says, four sharp blasts from a steamer's whistle. It was 5:45 A.M. Sunday, November 27.

"I went out," said Fisher, "and glanced at the clock and rang the gong for the boat." He then telephoned to the Peaked Hill Bars Station and afterwards sent a man down the beach to look for the wreck. The sea and tide were then combining to make conditions the worst Fisher had ever seen.

The storm continued in violence until about 9:00 that Sunday morning when a surprising event took place. Cape Cod's Life-Saving District Superintendent Benjamin C. Sparrow tells us about it:

> *Between 9 and 10:30 o'clock A.M. on Sunday Nov. 27 there was a partial breaking up of the gale, the wind became moderate, the sun shone for a short time, and the atmosphere cleared to an extent which disclosed two coastwise steamers passing southward, also a fishing schooner lying to under short sail. . . . About eleven o'clock A.M. the gale again increased and vision was obscure from the offing until after daylight on Monday morning.*

As the *Portland* and the *Pentagoet* were the only two steamers of their type in the vicinity, it is reasonable to assume that they were the vessels sighted during the partial breakup in the storm.

Miss Lillian Small, daughter of the Boston Chamber of Commerce ship observer Isaac Morton Small, also saw the *Portland* during the lull in the gale from her home near the Highland Light.

The fishing schooner mentioned in Superintendent Sparrow's report was the *Ruth M. Martin*. Aboard the schooner was Captain Michael Francis Hogan, with a crew of twenty-six men. Making Chatham Light at 10:00 that Saturday night, he tried to anchor but failed. The next morning he had reached a point off Highland Light, where around the middle of the morning, during the lull in the storm, Hogan noticed a large white steamer which appeared to be underway. The superstructure did not seem to be damaged noticeably. Captain Hogan, anxious to save his schooner, put a distress flag in his rigging to attract the attention of the vessel, which he later believed to be the *Portland*, as it was the only steamer of its type anywhere in the vicinity. (There was no other paddle-wheel steamer within 100 miles.) Patrick Droohan, the man in the crew who placed the distress flag in the rigging, said that the *Portland* was visible for two hours that morning, until the storm set in again. As it turned out, the *Ruth M. Martin* escaped while the *Portland* foundered. Hogan worked the *Martin* around Cape Cod's Race Point and into Province-town Harbor safely.

On the basis of the evidence of Hogan and Droohan, if the *Portland* was first seen in midmorning, about half past 9:00, and was visible for two hours, it must have been at least 11:30 when she faded from sight. This point should be remembered in order to estimate the approximate time of the *Portland*'s sinking.

The people on the *Portland* must have seen Hogan's schooner and the cliffs of the Highlands. They probably were congratulating themselves on escaping from the terrific gale, when the weather began to shut in again. First the cliffs faded from view in the gathering snowstorm, then the fishing boat was lost to sight. Whether the *Portland* and the *Penta-goet* ever sighted each other will probably never be known, although they were both seen from the Cape. Sometime during the evening the *Portland* came to her end. Imagination must describe her last hours. We cannot do better than quote from the pen of Thomas Harrison Eames:

> *It seems probable that the intense smashing she received through the night had weakened her, and finally the pounding of the sea under her guards opened her up and allowed tons of water to rush into the hull, flooding engine and boiler rooms, drowning the men working there, and depriving the ship of her power. The passengers above must have experienced a sense of horrified dismay as the vibration of the engines stopped and the ship swung around broad-side to the oncoming seas, lurching sickeningly and settling deeper each moment. The water crashing into the helpless vessel would smash any lifeboats which may have remained, tear off doors, and burst through windows and ports, ripping away the sheathing of the superstructure and washing helpless occupants of staterooms to death in a churning sea.*

As she took her final plunge, the superstructure was probably torn away at the main deck and was smashed to kindling wood. Those inside were thrown into the icy water as the wooden deckhouse disintegrated, some being killed outright by falling beams and other debris, others being caught in the wreckage and carried under the surface to drown, while many who had equipped themselves with life belts or who succeeded in grasping floating wreckage were benumbed by the frigid water and hammered so unmercifully by the gigantic waves that they soon died.

On the Cape Cod shore, the afternoon came to an end. The bitter wind continued to fill the air with snow and sand, making it nearly unbearable for Surfman Johnson of the Peaked Hill Bars Station, who was plodding his lonely way through the gale along the beach. He knew that another lifesaver was pushing toward him from the Race Point Coast Guard Station several miles away, and that ahead was the halfway house where the two were to meet. The gale increased and the waves, swept in by the tides, rose higher and higher.

Finally arriving at the halfway house, Johnson met his fellow watchman, Surfman Bickers, exchanged a story or two, spoke of the gale, and started back along the windswept beach. The darkness increased. At 7:20, Johnson thought he saw something thrown up by the incoming tide. Keeping his eye on the object, he fought his way down to the shore, ran the last few steps to avoid an oncoming breaker, reached down, picked up his find, and hastily retreated to the bank above the surf. In the dim light of his lantern he examined the object. It was a life belt, and on it he read the words *Steamer Portland of Portland*. (All the life belts were not marked alike.) Even then he had no reason to suppose anything but that the boat had lost a life preserver.

Here is his statement:

> *I was bound west toward the station, when I found the first thing that landed from the steamer. It was a lifebelt and it was one-half mile east of the station. At 7:45 o'clock that evening I found the next seen wreckage, a creamery can, 40-quart, I guess. It was right below our station, and nine or ten more of them, all empty and stoppered tightly came on there closely together.*
>
> *Jim Kelly succeeded me on the eastern beat, leaving the station at 8:20 P.M. and at 9:30 he found doors and other light woodwork from the* Portland *on the shore. When I found the lifebelt the wind was north northeast.*

Only two months ago, Surfman George Henry Bickers, who after his service at the Race Point Station became Keeper of the Wood End Life-Saving Station, told the writer of his meeting with Johnson that night.

> *I had the dog watch with Johnnie; he started walking eastward toward me from Race Point and I began the long hike westward from Peaked Hill. We met as usual at the Half Way House. Neither of us had noticed anything on the beach at that time. After he left me around seven he picked up a life belt, and later a large, empty milk can.*

It was not until dead high tide, around 11:00 Sunday night, that the real flood of wreckage started to come ashore. Edwin B. Tyler of the Race Point crew found doors, electric lightbulbs, washstand tops, and other wreckage, but his most important discovery was the upper part of a steamer's cabin, about ten feet square, painted yellow and red. The colors were not those of the *Portland*, but of another steamer, the *Pentagoet*, thus piling mystery upon mystery.

When the midnight watch returned, the beach was buried with wreckage and debris from the *Portland*. Mattresses, chairs, upholstery, windows, doors, and paneling all came ashore in a great mass shortly before midnight. Jot Small, former Provincetown lifesaver, comments as follows:

> *In my opinion, the* Portland *hit on Peaked Hill Bars and went all to pieces. That is the only way one can explain the mass of wreckage in one place. To prove my statement, no bodies could have come ashore as fast as they did unless the* Portland *was fairly near shore. The bodies do not float as woodwork does, but the tide and waves push and roll them along the bottom until they reached shallow water, when they get into the undertow and are tossed up on the beach.*

There are other theories of the *Portland*'s last hours besides those of Thomas Harrison Eames and Jonathan Small, already quoted. The finding of the *Pentagoet*'s cabin with the wreckage of the *Portland* has given rise to the theory that the two steamers were in collision. The *Pentagoet* was on a voyage from New York to Rockland, Maine, with a Rockland master, Captain Orris R. Ingraham (twin brother of Otis Ingraham, also a sea captain from Rockland), and fifteen men, and she carried a great load of Christmas toys and holiday gifts for Rockland stores. She was sighted off Highland Light the night the storm began. It is improbable to assume that a collision occurred, as no bodies from the *Pentagoet* were ever found. Had the two steamers met their doom together, bodies from both vessels instead of from the *Portland* alone would have washed ashore.

Very few mariners at the time considered the possibility of a collision between the *Portland* and the 162-ton schooner *Addie E. Snow*,* but later the brother of the schooner's captain examined some of the *Portland*'s wreckage on the beach. To his surprise, Captain Brown's brother found the *Addie E. Snow*'s medicine chest in the Portland litter, and afterwards found several other articles which had been on the schooner. The crew all perished with their captain, and none of their bodies was ever found.

Others believe that the schooner *King Philip*, heavily loaded with coal, collided with the *Portland* during the storm. The *King Philip* was last seen by the schooner *Alicia B. Crosby*. Her master, George W. Bunker, said later that she was a mile and a half on his lee near the Hue and Cry Ledge off Cape Elizabeth at 8:00 P.M. Saturday night. The two vessels had been following a similar course since Friday, November 25, and were together when they made Cape Elizabeth Light. Entering Portland Harbor, where she dropped anchor at 1:45 A.M., the *Crosby* rode out the storm safely. The *King Philip* was never seen afloat again.

Wreckage from the *King Philip* as it came up on the beach at Brewster, Cape Cod, was first identified by William U. Swan, covering the story for the Associated Press:

> *On the Wednesday after the* Portland *went down I helped pull the bodies of two poor Negro waiters from the surf. It was blowing like the very devil at the time, for another northeaster had set in. I later drove across to the beach at Brewster where I heard that some wreckage had come ashore on the inside of the Cape. I stopped at the home of a fisherman who was having a quarrel with his wife, and he directed me down to the beach where the wreckage had come in. There were some pieces of a schooner's deck timbers, with a steam pump three feet high attached, painted green. I found a metal tag with a serial number on the pump, which had been sold by a Boston firm.*

---

*Named for Addie E. Snow, granddaughter of Israel Snow, who founded the Snow shipyards in Rockland, Maine.

> *Anxious to find the name of the schooner, I returned to Orleans, where all lines to Boston were down. I cabled a message to Boston by way of France, Ireland, Newfoundland, New York City, and Albany. The message finally reached Boston and was delivered. I received my reply the next day. The steam pump was from the schooner* King Philip. *If the* Portland *had collided with the* King Philip *wreckage from both vessels would have come in together.*

Wreckage from the *Portland* came ashore Sunday night, while no wreckage from the *King Philip* washed up until the following Wednesday, far inside the arm of the Cape. Thus we must assume that the two vessels foundered many miles from each other, and any belief in a collision between them can have no foundation considering what we know to be true.

Recalling Keeper A. C. Fisher's belief that he heard four blasts from a steamer's whistle at 5:45 A.M. Sunday, we offer a statement made by one of the surfmen then at the Race Point Life-Saving Station. This Cape Cod man, who later became captain at the Wood End Station, told the writer a few months ago that in his opinion Keeper Fisher never heard any whistles:

> *We told him what he really heard was the wind whistling through the steel guy rods holding the chimney on the roof, but he did not like us to say that. All of the rest of us knew that was what he really heard. On the day he was to take the train for Portland to testify about the shipwreck, I was standing by the door as he started out.*

"I would have taken you with me," Captain Fisher said, "but you had an opinion of your own."

These were the words spoken to my Provincetown friend, who prefers not to have his name mentioned in connection with this particular story.

Another veteran lifesaver of the Cape whose opinion must be considered was Captain W. W. Cook of the Peaked Hill Bars Station. His statement follows:

> *The steamer never got as far as the Peaked Hill Bars, but foundered. I do not think that the captain was trying to reach the lee of the Cape for shelter. If a vessel can be kept head to in a storm, she*

can, perhaps, ride it out. If she cannot be controlled, and falls into the trough of the sea, she is gone. The Portland's *whole upper works were swept off by the sea, and she went down like a sounding lead. And there she is now. She will never come ashore, she is in too deep water.*

If we accept Cook's theory that the *Portland* went down soon after the superstructure was swept away, then she foundered around 9:00 that night, as the watches were stopped at an average time of 9:15.

Souvenirs from the *Portland* are many. There are four different wheels of the *Portland* said to be in existence. That owned by Charles Ayling, of Centerville, is one of the authentic ones. (Mr. Ayling has a sworn affidavit that the crew of the High Head Station picked up the wheel with other wreckage from the *Portland*.) The *Portland*'s speaking trumpet, plainly marked *Portland*, was brought up to Boston in the summer of 1899 and sold for ten dollars, to be crated and shipped out west. A local oil dealer bought one of the life-raft cylinders and painted it red, filling the hollow metal container with fuel and selling kerosene from it on the streets of Boston.

Cy Young of Provincetown, with doors from the steamer Portland, *which he recovered the day after the gale from the beach on Cape Cod.*

Cy Young, well-known antique dealer of Provincetown, was over on Cape Cod Beach early the day after the wreck, collecting a large amount of material from the steamer's superstructure and cabins. Loading an odd assortment of bunks, cabin posts, empty coffins, bottles of rum, life belts, doors, and cabin posts on his huge cart, he drove his team across the dunes to his home in Provincetown. He later sold twelve of the large cabin posts for $100. The writer acquired two doors of the Portland from Mr. Young in 1941. (The doors in question had lain undisturbed in Mr. Young's backyard for almost forty-five years.)

In the spring of 1899 Captain Thomas of the *Maud S.*, who had seen the *Portland* near Thacher's Island the night of the storm, caught articles in his fishing trawl which were later identified as coming from the *Portland*. The location where the discovery was made was said to be 22 ³/₄ miles east of Boston Light; 24 miles north; ³/₄ mile west from Highland Light; and 14 ¹/₂ miles southeast from Thacher's Island. When the material was brought into Boston, Steward Harris, formerly on the *Portland*, and electrician Burnett, also on the same craft, identified the material. A number of small brackets actually recut by the steward to fit the *Portland*'s bunks were recognized by Harris, while Burnett was able to identify several light sockets and brackets as part of his own electrical work.

Lieutenant Nicholas J. Halpine, formerly in charge of the U.S. Hydrographic Office in Boston, contested the authenticity of the articles. None of them came from the *Portland*, in Halpine's opinion, as the ship had not gone down where the find was made.

"I am still of the opinion," he said in March 1899, "that the wreck of the *Portland* lies outside of the Peaked Hill Bars somewhere, and I am equally confident that I can locate her and bring her into harbor, and I intend to do it, too." Many summers have come and gone since this confident statement was made, but the hull of the *Portland* still eludes all efforts of those who wish to find her. (On June 29, 1934, Captain Charles Carver recovered several articles believed to be from the *Portland*. In 1936 Captain Ault brought up bathroom fixtures.)

During another gale Captain Hollis H. Blanchard had headed the *Portland* for the open sea and kept her there until the blow went down. Is it not reasonable to assume that he did the same in this storm? Would he not keep her headed into the northeast gale, carrying the rudder a point or two into the east, gradually working off the coast?

In this way he was slowly taken down toward Cape Cod, until in the morning he found himself off the fatal beach, the storm having carried him at a faster rate than he could steam against it. When he saw his position, the battle was almost won, for if the storm had then ended, he might have rounded Cape Cod's Race Point and entered Provincetown Harbor. But such a happy ending was not in store for Hollis H. Blanchard.

We do not question, as did Lieutenant Halpine, the authenticity of the material picked up by the *Maud S.* Without a doubt, during her terrible trip across the bay she lost some of her superstructure in the gale's buffeting, including stateroom panels, lifeboats, and even perhaps her pilothouse. But she continued afloat, in the writer's opinion, for about twenty-four hours after being sighted by the *Maud S.*

There are many reasons why the *Portland* did not go down on the northern edge of the Stellwagen or Middle Bank, as indicated by the find of Captain Thomas. If the *Portland* sank at any time before 10:00 P.M. Sunday night, when the wind shifted to a more northerly direction, the wreckage must by necessity have drifted to leeward. A glance at the map should convince the reader that the flotsam would have gone in a southwesterly direction, not south, and landed along the inner shores of Massachusetts Bay.

Surface tides on the night of the hurricane were dominated by the wind, and the wind was northeast. When the first object, a life belt, was driven ashore at 7:20 Sunday night, the wind as stated by the man who found the preserver was north-northeast, whereas the Stellwagen Bank's northern edge is in a northwesterly direction.

There is a much more conclusive point. The fragments of paddleboxes, life cars, door blinds, staterooms, and the like were heaped almost entirely in a half mile area between Race Point Station and the Peaked Hill Bars Station. How could this great mass of debris drift contrary to a northeast gale for twenty-four miles across as rough a stretch of water as there is? If such a heaping pile of wreckage traveled even ten miles, it would have been scattered up and down the shore.

The heavier freight came up on the beach farther east than the lighter windswept superstructure. The barrels, trunks, firkens, tubs, and boxes filled with all types of eatables and merchandise could not under any imaginative prompting have bumped, thudded, and pushed their way twenty-four miles along the bottom of the sea. All of this material actually came ashore at a point more distant from Thomas' location than the lighter, floating woodwork. Who can claim that the heavier freight would travel farther on the bottom of the sea than the woodwork

An oar from the Portland. *Left to right: Edward Rowe Snow; William Peak, who pulled bodies out of the surf the Wednesday aftr the* Portland *sank; Alton Hall Blackington, owner of the oar; and John A. Thornquist, maritime enthusiast, examining this relic from the disaster.*

floated on top? It is much more sensible to assume that the *Portland* went down at a point from three to five miles off the shore, with the wreckage masses soon washing up on the lee beach of Cape Cod.

The Provincetown lifesaver, Jot Small, is still hale and hearty, living down in Provincetown. When the writer met the well-known surfman of former days, he asked Jot why there were so many different opinions on the Cape about the loss of the *Portland.*

"Take my advice," said Jonathan Small. "Don't try to understand it, for that would be impossible. It is just a mystery, and it always will be. There is so much that can't be explained, so many things happened that just couldn't happen, that we are all mystified by the whole affair. What happened to the *Portland* will always stay a mystery from start to finish. Mark me well!"

We have tried to present as reasonable an account of the *Portland*'s last hours as could be pieced together from the evidence. The *Portland*, seen by persons at Cape Cod and on the schooner *Ruth M. Martin*, was definitely afloat after 11:00 that Sunday morning. Watches found on the bodies of victims were practically all stopped around 9:15, indicating the sinking of the steamer at about that time. As the steamer was seen afloat after that hour on Sunday morning, then the *Portland* must have foundered shortly after 9:00 that night, as evidenced by the terrific amount of wreckage which hit the beach within the next three hours. Combining all the known facts, this seems the only conclusion which can be made.

Somewhere in the swirling depths of the great beach at Cape Cod lies the answer to all our queries. Almost two generations have gone by since the *Portland* sank beneath the waves off North Truro Beach, and relatively little has been discovered during the intervening period. It is improbable that we shall ever learn much more than is now known about New England's greatest sea mystery, but if she is located, the chances are that the *Portland* will be found off the changing sands of the Peaked Hill Bars.

Edward Rowe Snow's wife, Anna-Myrle, called the *Portland* her husband's "bread and butter story." He told the saga of the lost steamer in several of his books, on radio and television, and in countless lectures around New England. For years he also met with descendants of those lost on the anniversary of the disaster for an annual memorial ceremony, and he exchanged letters with many others. In 1948, the fiftieth anniversary of the Portland Gale, Snow was responsible for the placement of a commemorative plaque at Highland (Cape Cod) Lighthouse in Truro. According to the book *Four Short Blasts: The Gale of 1898 and the Loss of the Steamer Portland* by Peter Dow Bachelder and Mason Philip Smith, Snow "actively kept alive the *Portland* story" through the mid-twentieth century.

Along with the doors from the steamer mentioned by Snow in this chapter, he was able to obtain other artifacts, including one of the ship's flags. These artifacts are now in the collection of the Peabody-Essex Museum in Salem, Massachusetts. Two doors from the *Portland* were sliced into slivers and glued inside the covers of special editions of a few of Snow's books.

For many years, Edward Rowe Snow collected information about the steamer's possible whereabouts. In 1944, a scallop dragger captained by Charles G. Carver of Rockland, Maine, brought in much debris believed to be from the *Portland*. This and other research led Snow in 1945 to commission diver Al George to explore what Snow believed to be the remains of the steamer, 7 1/2 miles from the Race Point Coast Guard Station in 144 feet of water. George described the hull as being buried almost completely in the sand. He was able to bring up a stateroom key clearly marked "Portland." For some years this expedition was believed by many people to have revealed the true location of the *Portland*.

Snow was not in favor of any attempt to recover riches that were said to be in the purser's safe, saying, "Perhaps it is just as well to let the old steamer rest for the remainder of her existence at the bottom of the sea, undisturbed by visits from the world above the surface."

John Rousmaniere, author of *After the Storm: True Stories of Disaster and Recovery at Sea*, believes that while Captain Hollis Blanchard may have behaved somewhat too aggressively, a missed weather forecast deserves some of the blame for the disaster. The Weather Bureau predicted only the arrival of the storm from the Great Lakes, with little mention of the powerful system coming up the coast. Rousmaniere speculates that Blanchard, who always consulted the weather forecasts, thought he could easily beat the single storm in the run to Portland, unaware that he would actually be up against a monumental double gale.

Rousmaniere also assigns a good deal of the blame to the steamship line, whose officials, he says, "had allowed themselves to fall into organizational

Deployment of "remotely operated vehicle" (ROV) from R/V Connecticut *by National Undersea Research Center technicians (photo by Anne Smrcina, courtesy of NOAA/Stellwagen Bank National Marine Sanctuary)*

chaos." There had been a flurry of retirements and deaths in the company, and almost everybody's job had changed in the three weeks prior to the Portland Gale. "In addition," says Rousmaniere, "all were distracted by the funeral of a senior captain. This was hardly the situation for careful risk management." Rousmaniere sums up the *Portland* disaster as "a tragic accident—the confluence of several events, not the result of any one individual's carelessness."

In *After the Storm*, Rousmaniere expresses the opinion that Snow served as a sort of therapist for many of the families of those who died on the *Portland*. "For that all should be grateful as well as for his writings," he says.

In 1989 John Perry Fish and Arnold Carr of American Underwater Search and Survey announced that they had located the hull of the *Portland* in over 400 feet of water in the Stellwagen Bank National Marine Sanctuary, about twenty miles north of Race Point. Although Fish and Carr felt certain they had found the only coastal steamer of its type ever wrecked in the area, they were not able to provide conclusive evidence.

In the summer of 2002, a team from NOAA and the National Undersea Research Center at the University of Connecticut produced side scan sonar images and video that proved the location of the intact hull, sitting upright on the ocean's bottom. Twin smokestacks, a paddle guard, and paddle-wheel hub

Side scan image of the Portland, *showing walking beam and entangling gear (courtesy of NOAA/Stellwagen Bank National Marine Sanctuary)*

were found, items that would not exist on any other wreck in the vicinity. The length of the hull is also a match. Everything above the main deck is swept clean, and there is no debris in the area surrounding the hull.

The wreck is not where Snow believed it to be in 1945. It is not that surprising that diver Al George brought up a key from the steamer, as wreckage was strewn across the area. The identity of the hull explored by George at that time is anyone's guess.

Since it is located within a marine sanctuary, the remains of the *Portland* are afforded more protection than most shipwrecks. Regulations prohibit the removing of any artifacts from the wreck, and anyone in violation of this regulation is subject to civil penalties.

According to the most recent estimates, 192 people died on board the *Portland*. Only thirty-eight bodies were ever recovered. Both the Provincetown Museum and the museum of the Truro Historical Society have displays of artifacts from the *Portland*, one of the last of our great luxury coastal steamers. The wreck led to a fresh approach to the design and construction of New England's ocean-going passenger vessels.

Underwater image of the Portland*'s anchor (courtesy of NOAA/Stellwagen Bank National Marine Sanctuary)*

CHAPTER 31

1944: A Year of Gales and Disaster

THE 1944 HURRICANE

Strangely similar in sequence to the September 1823 storm which followed the disastrous hurricane of September 1815, the September gale of 1944 followed uncomfortably close to the great New England hurricane of September 1938. Communities and counties which the 1938 blast had dealt with either kindly or not too severely were devastated by the 1944 blow, while other locations completely escaped the overwhelming disaster which befell them six years earlier.

Although the loss of life ashore was relatively small in 1944, with thirty-one deaths in the northeastern United States, there was a different story to tell at sea. A destroyer, a lightship, and two other government craft were sunk with heavy loss of life, in great contrast to the 1938 gale.

Cape Cod and Martha's Vineyard were hit heavily in 1944. Warning after warning had gone out over the radio all day September 14, and mass evacuations had been completed in many sections of New England by evening. Between 9:00 and 10:00 at night the wind increased rapidly, with 100 miles an hour a common reading before midnight.

Fortunately the hurricane held off until the tide had been going out for three hours, preventing such terrific damage as occurred in 1938, when the tremendous tidal waves swept over various sections of New England. But the wind again proved its strength by destroying thousands of trees and hundreds upon hundreds of houses. Cape Cod suffered severely from Falmouth all the way to Provincetown, which was the scene of outstanding damage. The town hall roof, the Methodist church steeple, and the town pier roof in Provincetown were all carried away. Shortly before 1:30 A.M. Chatham experienced a wind of 105 miles an hour. The Wareham railroad bridge collapsed at the height of the gale. The Methodist church steeple at West Dennis was blown over and speared its way into the roof of the edifice. Camp Edwards and nearby Otis Field were raked by the gale, while at South Sea Village in South Yarmouth a near tidal wave piled houses and cottages upon each other in hopeless confusion. There were many freak accidents. Electric light service was either curtailed or nonexistent on Cape Cod after the storm.

Southern Massachusetts again suffered heavily. Beach cottages in the area were severely damaged. The entire New Bedford section reported a disaster as great as or greater than 1938, with Mayor Arthur N. Harriman estimating that losses would reach nearly $5,000,000. Station WMBH radio tower collapsed, Dan's Pavilion was totally destroyed, and Fort Rodman was badly battered. The Fairhaven Bridge was five feet under water. Three yachts and several small boats were found high and dry on the bridge when the tide went down.

At the height of the storm, Martha's Vineyard suffered overwhelming damage, with the Edgartown waterfront torn asunder, resembling a shambles in many sections. The steamship pier at Oak Bluffs was wrecked. The southwestern section of Nantucket was severely dealt with by the hurricane as it swept along, but the losses there were not to be compared with what Martha's Vineyard suffered.

Telephone damage was severe, with 70,000 telephones out of order in New England because of the gale. The service was restored with alacrity and dispatch whenever possible, and the telephone linemen deserve much credit for the rapidity with which lines were replaced and communication again made possible.

An early visitor to the Cape after the hurricane, Alton Hall Blackington, took many remarkable pictures of the 1944 disaster. Riding along through roads made almost impassable by storm debris, he was able to photograph and record many of the unusual incidents of the hurricane.

Rhode Island escaped with minor losses, chiefly confined to Portsmouth, Newport, and Warwick, amounting to less than $500,000.

In the first gasp of relief that the storm was not as devastating as the 1938 gale, people in northern New England were inclined to minimize

This photo of the Vineyard Sound Lightship was taken by Harold Flagg, a crewman who was ashore when the vessel was lost in the 1944 hurricane. (From the collection of Douglas Bingham)

in their minds the terrific and overwhelming effects of the gale which hit the Cape, New Bedford, and Martha's Vineyard with greater intensity than its predecessor. One should not forget that many beautiful locations in these sections of Massachusetts were irreparably damaged. The hurricane on Cape Cod alone is said to have cost $50,000,000.

Located near the Sow and Pigs Ledge to the south of Cuttyhunk, the Vineyard Sound Lightship has been a well-known sea marker to the sailor and voyager. Forced to stay at its post when other ships fled to safety before the great hurricane, the Vineyard Lightship went down with all eleven of the ship's company,* probably at the height of the gale. The captain of the doomed vessel, Warrant Officer J. Edgar Sevigny, had planned to reach home on leave the day after the hurricane hit, but the skipper of the lightship went down with his vessel.

Built in Baltimore in 1901, the 129-foot lightship weathered the 1938 hurricane and scores of other storms without damage, only to disappear completely in the 1944 gale. Several of the bodies of the men were found, and it is said that the hull of the vessel was located.

---

*Actually, twelve hands were lost.—*Ed.*

John J. Stimac of Streator, Illinois, was one of the twelve crew-members lost on the Vineyard Sound Lightship when it went down in the 1944 hurricane (photo courtesy of Lisa Stimac Aukland)

The loss of life because of the 1944 hurricane aboard the destroyer *Warrington*, the Coast Guard cutters *Jackson* and *Bedloe*, the minesweeper *XMS-409*, and the Vineyard Lightship reached the unprecedented total of 344 killed or missing. While the survivor list was not made known, without question the percentage of loss was extremely heavy.

THE STORM AT CLEVELAND LEDGE LIGHT

Just as the famous Minot's Ledge Light underwent its baptism of storm in 1851 after its erection in 1850, so did the Cleveland Ledge Light experience its initial test during the hurricane of 1944. The light is located six miles west of the Cape Cod Canal. While Minot's Light fell over into the sea, the Cleveland Ledge Light, built in 1941, successfully "rode out" the gale which threatened its safety.

Lieutenant Olie P. Swenson of Bourne was commanding officer aboard the lighthouse when the hurricane hit from the southeast

Cleveland Ledge Lighthouse today (photo by Jeremy D'Entremont)

around 8:00 September 14. Four hours later the wind changed to southwest, and within half an hour a glass block skylight on the southwest side of the tower gave away, allowing tons of water to pour into the lighthouse. The entire personnel of nine men rushed to the engine room, where they bailed the water from the floor. As they worked, other waves came crashing down upon them, and only the presence of a porcelain laundry tub into which they emptied their pails saved the day. The tub drained quickly every pail of water thrown into it.

Some of the coastguardsmen tried to stop up the break in the skylight, but were thrown back by the force of the waves which swept in.

The men were only able to stop the water rising in the battery room when it had reached a point less than two inches from the top of the batteries. One by one various pieces of electrical equipment flared out a flaming warning as it was short-circuited. Finally Seaman LaMar Steed and Chief Boatswain's Mate Thomas E. Norris managed to reach the broken glass block and erect a barrier of oil drums, planking, and mat-tresses against the sea. The two men saved the lighthouse from being extinguished at a time when both the telephone and the radio were out of order.

During the gale, the launch secured to the davits thirty feet above high-water mark was badly damaged by the force of the waves. The lit-tle wire-haired terrier, the only other occupant of the tower besides the nine men, showed great fright during the ordeal. But the nine men of Cleveland Ledge Light had successfully "ridden out" the first real test of the lighthouse.

THE TRIPLE STORMS OF NOVEMBER 1944

Three gales which struck the New England coast late in November caused great damage and spectacular surf in many localities. A storm which reached its height on November 17 sent breakers entirely over the top of 114-foot Minot's Light, while it pushed tons of sand and boulders up on the great Shore Drive in Winthrop, Massachusetts. Aided by a scheduled run of high tides, the surf leaped the high seawall and came down many of the Winthrop streets, filling cellars and stalling autos everywhere along the areas near the beach.

Down at Sandwich, Massachusetts, however, a tug and the coal barge it was towing were in serious trouble. Late Thursday night the barge began to suffer from the huge billows, which were breaking entirely over her. The two men aboard, Captain Kidd of New Bedford and donkey-man Ules Hines, worked all night long on the pumps, but when Friday morning came it was seen that the barge was going down. Cap-tain Oliver Givens of the tug then started toward the sinking barge, but the craft foundered before Givens could reach the location.

Thrown into the icy waters, the two barge men stayed afloat until a rescue craft from the Sandwich Coast Guard Station reached them. Exhausted, the sailors were pulled into the Coast Guard craft and later taken ashore. Meanwhile, however, the tug became fouled from the hawser from the barge, and was even then washing ashore, her wheel hopelessly tangled by the hawser. The alert watchers from the Sand-wich Coast Guard Station soon had a breeches buoy set up and fired a line out to the tug. One sailor, a powerful swimmer, did not wait for the ride ashore, but jumped into the raging surf and swam to the beach. He was William Craig, of Decatur, Texas.

One by one the other crew members were brought ashore in the breeches buoy. Even the dog Jock arrived safely, in the arms of Chief Engineer Robert Marnell. Only Captain Givens was left on the tug. As he started ashore the tug shifted, putting a great strain on the lines, which snapped and dropped him into the raging sea. But the coastguardsmen were ready. Seaman Donald H. Ward of Portland, Maine, unhesitatingly plunged into the roaring surf and swam out to Captain Givens. After releasing him from the lines, Ward swam ashore with Captain Givens. It was a perilous undertaking, but Seaman Ward did not falter in the face of what he believed to be his duty. Another great rescue had been accomplished by members of the United States Coast Guard, able successors to the old Life-Saving Service.

The following Saturday and Sunday the waves continued to hit the New England shores with terrific force. Some as high as 115 feet were reported on Sunday from Great Brewster Island in outer Boston Harbor. The waves diminished somewhat by Monday, but that afternoon the first signs of another storm were noticed.

The second November gale of 1944 hit with tremendous force the next day. Again Winthrop, Massachusetts, received the worst damage along the coast. All Tuesday afternoon and Wednesday morning the waves made up higher and higher, until a great section of the Winthrop seawall in the vicinity of Myrtle Avenue collapsed and fell into the sea. The waves then proceeded to eat away the boulevard, and by 4:00 that Wednesday afternoon were reaching buildings across the forty-foot driveway. Water again poured down the streets, inundating the entire section, with two to three feet of water showing in several locations.

At high tide, which occurred shortly before 5:00 P.M., crowds had gathered to watch the fury of the storm at its spectacular height. Fortunate enough to climb up to the roof of a nearby house, I had my camera set hopefully waiting. A great cry from the hundreds watching the surf warned that a billow of spectacular size was even then advancing toward the beach, with a huge crest about to break. Then with a crash which could be heard for miles, jarring everyone in the vicinity, the wave struck the battered seawall. Shooting up, up, and up, until we were all spellbound by its grandeur and magnificence, the mighty ocean surge reached its peak.

The third of the November 1944 storms was the worst. Late in the night of November 29 the roar of the sea up and down the coast could be

Record-breaking waves crashing against the Winthrop seawall, November 22, 1944

heard as it ushered in another gale, and before dawn the next morning New England knew it was in for another siege of ocean battering.

The tide at Boston came in with such fury that the reading of 13.8 feet was as high as it had been in the history of the Coast and Geodetic Survey records. Office buildings as far from the waterfront as the corner of Broad and Custom House Streets were flooded. Tea Wharf, Long Wharf, and Central Wharf were among those inundated, while Atlantic Avenue was submerged in many places.

Winthrop, Massachusetts, for the third time that month, felt the tremendous force of the sea, with the ocean pouring down its streets and filling hundreds of cellars. It was truly a discouraging experience for the inhabitants. The tide was the highest for many years, allowing canoeists to paddle along Shirley Street in that town.

Vast areas were under water in Salem. Historic Derby Wharf was completely covered, while the railroad tunnel at Washington and Bridge Streets was flooded and filled with floating debris.

The storm was one of the worst ever to hit the Maine coast. Portland's waterfront experienced record tides and many disasters, one of the worst being the collapse of a grain elevator. Camden damage was high. A 10,000-gallon fuel tank there drained into the harbor when the

Winthrop's Shore Drive, showing damage caused by an ocean storm

high tide smashed a feed pipe. Rockland, famous maritime center, suffered considerably at the height of the storm. The tide, high at 11:30 A.M., caused damage which amounted to $40,000 at the Lafayette Packing Company, while a chimney in the city toppled into the street. Narrowly missing two small girls, the chimney wrecked an auto owned by Manager Tryon of the Western Union. Disaster befell the fishing vessel *Nancy*, moored off Rockland's public landing. The forty-two-foot craft, owned by Raymond Dow, dragged anchor to end her career smashing against the nearby retaining wall. The *Nancy* later sank, a total loss.

Nor was Cape Cod, already crippled by the hurricane, spared from this new storm. All along the great arm of land leading up to Provincetown the gale took its toll. In South Dartmouth twelve motorists were rescued by New Bedford firemen after they had been trapped in the swirling current at Padanavan Bridge.

Regardless of what other claim it may have to posterity, the year 1944, with three great storms, several disastrous shipwrecks, and one mighty hurricane, must go down in history as a year to be remembered in the storm and shipwreck annals of New England.

THE 1944 HURRICANE In this chapter Snow mentions his good friend
Alton Hall Blackington, who told his popular "Yankee Yarns" on Boston radio
for many years.

U.S. Coast Guard Lightship Sailors Association historian Doug Bingham says
that J. Edgar Sevigny, commanding officer of the Vineyard Sound Lightship, had
a premonition of the approaching storm. "He told his wife that although he had
survived the hurricane of '38," says Bingham, "he feared that if another such
storm should occur when he was at sea, he wouldn't make it home a second
time. Fate proved him correct in his fears."

In 1963, Professor Harold Edgerton of the Massachusetts Institute of Technology found the Vineyard Sound Lightship in eighty feet of water using an
experimental "side scan" sonar device he had recently developed. It was the
first wreck to be found using this method. Divers from the Fairhaven Whalers
Diving Club brought up the ship's bell and other artifacts.

The evidence suggests that the spare anchor, apparently dislodged by the
pounding waves, pierced the hull of the lightship in the storm. The remains of
the vessel are mostly upright on the sandy bottom and it is a popular dive site.

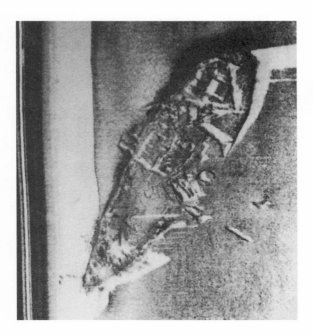

*The wreck of the Vine-
yard Sound Lightship
(sonar image courtesy
of Robert Burchstead)*

Seamond Ponsart Roberts, now of New Orleans, was a small girl living at Cuttyhunk Lighthouse at the time of the 1944 hurricane, and she spent the night in the tower with her father, Keeper Octave Ponsart. The Ponsarts were very friendly with the crewmen of the Vineyard Sound Lightship, and Seamond thought of them as her "uncles." Here is what happened that night in her words:

> I went up and down the tower with Dad all night, fetching stuf—rags, mantles, chimneys (many of these broke), coffee—I bet I made 50 trips. The height of the storm, which I think must have been about 2 A.M., was when we last saw the lights of the Vineyard Lightship. Dad had me stand on my little stool and look for the lightship. I could see its lights between clouds and blows. When the big blow came, it was so strong that the whole tower was shaking and we were holding on to the lens stand. I was really, really scared.
>
> Dad said to me, "Seamond, do you see the lightship?" And I did for a few seconds. Then, as we looked where the lights had been just seconds before, they were gone. When the next clear patch of sight came, no lights. We both knew. My father said, "The iron men in the iron ship, gone to the bottom." I knew he was thinking of days past when he too was a lightship man, and the peril they faced out there. And we were both crying because I knew all my uncles were gone.

On September 15, 1999, Seamond Ponsart Roberts attended the dedication of a lightship memorial in New Bedford, Massachusetts. The memorial incorporates the bell from the Vineyard Sound Lightship. The bell was rung for each of the twelve drowned crewmen as Harold Flagg (the last surviving crewmember, who was onshore at the time of the storm) read their names. Roberts says, "I am so thankful that the memorial was created for them and for all the lightshipmen who over the years have served in peril, but particularly for my uncles who back then in 1944 gave their all."

THE STORM AT CLEVELAND LEDGE LIGHT Cleveland Ledge Light has been automated and unoccupied since 1978, but it continues to operate as an active aid to navigation. Its Art Deco styling makes it unique among New England's lighthouses.

In his book *Exploring the Waters of Cape Cod*, Donald L. Ferris reports that "Coast Guardsmen stationed at the light for months dropped lots of interesting items into the ocean," making it a popular site for divers.

THE TRIPLE STORMS OF NOVEMBER 1944 The schooner barge and tug wrecked at Sandwich on November 17, 1944, were the *Pottstown* and the *Wathen*, respectively. The remains of the 195-foot *Pottstown*, built in Baltimore in 1917, are mostly buried in sand today in about sixty feet of water off Scusset Beach. The vessel presented a danger to navigation and was largely demolished by dynamite in 1947. The remains of the tug *Wathen* can be seen in shallow water a short distance off Sandwich Town Beach.

CHAPTER 32

The Gale of '45

Since the Minot's Light Gale of 1851 there have been only a few easterly storms in New England severe enough to deserve special mention. Most of these have taken place in November. The Gale of 1888 is still considered by many as greater than the 1898 storm which caused the *Portland* disaster just ten years later. In 1909 occurred the famous Christmas Gale, which caught the *Davis Palmer* anchored off Finn's Ledge in outer Boston Harbor and wrecked her near Fawn Bar Beacon with the loss of all on board. The storm of March 1931 was the next significant gale to attract more than passing attention. From 1931 until 1945, except for the tropical hurricane of September 21, 1938, which was not an easterly, no great gale swept New England.

The storm of November 1945, which will go down in history as the Gale of '45, caused more damage and suffering along the entire New England coast than any easterly since the *Portland* foundered. It began shortly after midnight, November 29. By daybreak a howling gale had set in, with all craft offshore running for shelter.

The wind at Logan International Airport, Boston, hit seventy miles an hour at 6:14 that morning. Wind direction at that time was east-northeast. Gusts as high as seventy five miles per hour were recorded a short time afterwards.

The state of Maine suffered a tremendous amount of damage. In Machias the storm pushed the seas across the roads. The tide reached the foot of Steele's Hill, causing the oldest inhabitants to declare that never in their memory had such a high tide inundated this attractive Maine seaport to such an extent. The gale washed out the railroad tracks at Machias, preventing trains from running for about a week.

In Rockland, Maine, the tides reached extremely high levels. The storm ten days before had given the residents a taste of what to expect. The Rockland Marine Railway suffered severely, while several craft in the harbor were damaged or sunk.

At lonely Boon Island, Keeper John H. Morris, his wife, Gertrude, and their child, Lorne, experienced a night of terror during the gale. The assistant keeper, Ted Guice, was with them. As the gale increased, the waves came up around the lighthouse itself, and even seemed to threaten the great tower. Keeper Morris took his family through the tunnel to the Second Assistant Keeper's home in the lee of the lighthouse, which, in his opinion, was the safest place on the island. There they all huddled, afraid to go to bed, listening to the storm push great rocks, weighing tons, back and forth around the island. Even above the roar of the sea came the weird noise of the grinding boulders.

"What really scared us was the sound that the rocks made as they hit against each other," Keeper Morris told me later. "Not a stone on the island was left unturned. The generator failed when a giant sea broke right into the engine room, and we had to operate for the rest of the storm with kerosene lamps. The waves actually climbed halfway up the side of the lighthouse tower itself. I shall never forget that Gale of '45."

Those two far-flung beacons of the Maine Coast, Matinicus Rock and Mount Desert Rock, experienced tremendous seas, which swept completely over the lighthouses there. At Matinicus Rock eight feet of the boat slip and twelve feet of the covered way leading to the lighthouse were washed away by the waves. The small blacksmith shop was swept completely off the island and was last seen drifting out to sea. Saddleback Ledge was another location where the storm did terrific damage. The lighthouse station there suffered the loss of the blocks, falls, platform, and even the derrick which is used to get men and supplies aboard the ledge. Part of the boat slip, the railing on the bell tower, and the base of the bell tower also washed out. At Baker Island Light thirty feet of the old boat slip disappeared in the gale. In this case the loss of the old boat slip was considered timely by the keeper. "It eliminates the necessity for the construction crew to take it out," he said.

At Halfway Rock Light in Maine, the radio beacon went off the air when the tall antenna masts were blown over, causing extensive damage at the station. Ram Island Ledge Light had 100 square feet of copper sheathing torn from the roof, while the outhouse was made useless. The boathouse planking at the Cuckolds washed away. At Manana Island Fog Station opposite Monhegan Island, the new launching slip was twisted and the anchors dislodged. Fifteen feet of the bell weight box at Ram Island went out to sea, and almost a thousand dollars' worth of damage was caused there. The boat belonging to the keeper of Seguin Island Light sank at the mooring, leaving the men without transportation to the mainland.

The storm also caused extensive losses along the New Hampshire coast. The writer talked with Lester Davis, Second Assistant Keeper at White Island Light, Isles of Shoals, where the seas swept away the three small outhouses near the lighthouse and ripped the planking off the bell tower, exposing the old building's foundation. The waves went completely over the top of the ninety-foot lighthouse tower, their full force damaging the covered way. Davis' wife, Marie, and their two girls, Sandra and Julie, bravely concealed their nervousness, thus carrying out the tradition of the lighthouse service. At the height of the storm one of the seas jumped completely over the protecting ledge to batter itself against Head Keeper Douglas Larrabee's residence, smashing open the door and flooding the kitchen waist deep, leaving a confused mass of kelp, coal, and ashes in its wake.

Down at Bridgeport, Connecticut, an oil barge became stranded half a mile off the shore. When it appeared possible that the barge would break up, word was sent to Captain Jackson E. Beighle, who flew over the location in his own helicopter, returned to the mainland, and flew back with pilot D. D. Viner in a rescue helicopter. They came down over the wreck and took off Seaman Steve Penninger, who was able to climb up the rope ladder and into the cockpit of the helicopter. After landing him safely on the beach ashore, the two airmen flew back to the oil barge and removed Captain Joseph Pawlich. Although Pawlich was unable to climb inside, he dangled just under the helicopter until he was lowered to the beach in safety. It was one of the most unusual sea rescues in New England history.

In Massachusetts the storm struck with all its fury. At Cape Ann Light Station on Thacher's Island, four sections of the trestle between the turntable and the fog whistle house were destroyed, while the radio beacon room at Eastern Point Light was damaged. Down on Nantucket the midget scout car, Number 2911, bogged down on the beach and was covered with sand for three tides. At Sankaty Head Light, Keeper Haskins reported that twenty-five feet of asbestos shingles were blown off the roof of his dwelling during the storm. It is said that the wreck of the *Herman Winter*, aground on Devil's Bridge off Gay Head, Martha's Vineyard, actually moved her position because of the gale. The *Winter*, a wartime casualty, broke in half February 1, 1946. On Cuttyhunk Island the lighthouse and the homes of the coastguardsmen were shaken by the intensity of the wind. The midget scout car was also damaged.

Cape Cod again suffered greatly, with losses reaching a quarter million dollars. At least five fishing draggers went ashore, with two of them believed damaged beyond repair. A few days after the storm we flew down along the outer beach, and from the plane it appeared that many stretches of the Cape Cod beach had been ripped out by the storm, exposing hulks which may have been buried for generations and even centuries.

Out on Graves Light in Boston Harbor, Keeper Bernard Brady reported that the storm was a terrible experience. Fifty feet of the catwalk leading to the oil house washed into the ocean, while the dory was smashed, the dory shed demolished, and the house next to the tower shattered and swept away. At the height of the storm the giant riprap blocks were moved about like pebbles. Damage of more than a thousand dollars was sustained, and it is probable that the Gale of '45 was the worst storm the lighthouse ever experienced. It was only when we flew out over the light a short time later and came down to fifty feet above the ledge to see the ruins for ourselves that we could realize why the Gale of '45 will be remembered as the worst northeaster of the twentieth century.

Boston Light Station suffered further damage to its already weakened piers, while the waves rushed across from both sides to smash together in the middle of the island. The oil tank was dragged off the station by the waves.

Minot's Light was swept time and again by waves, which shot up fifty feet above the tower. The vibration was tremendous, but the lighthouse stood firm throughout the storm, although to many anxious watchers along the shore it seemed as though the force of the mighty billows would cause the 114-foot beacon to follow its predecessor of 1850 and topple over into the sea.

Vessels in Boston Harbor were buffeted severely during the hurricane, while many craft out at sea were unreported for days afterwards. The freighter *Fordham Victory*, with fifty crew members aboard, went ashore at Spectacle Island, Boston Harbor, at the height of the gale, and it was several days before she could be floated off. Down at Nantasket, the steamer *Town of Hull* broke away from her moorings and drifted across Hingham Bay, piling up high and dry on Peddock's Island, where she remained until she floated free during a high tide on January 5, 1946.

Pemberton was cut off from the rest of Hull, and Nantasket Beach suffered heavily. Wollaston Boulevard was flooded, with residents living just off the boulevard subjected to temporary isolation and extreme discomfort when the water filled their cellars.

The entire Massachusetts shoreline was inundated by the gale. Gloucester, Salem, Nahant, Revere, Nantasket, Cohasset, and Scituate were among the locations which felt the brunt of the hurricane, but in Winthrop the storm was at its worst.

The Winthrop seawall, which protects the homes on Shore Drive, collapsed early in the gale, with scores of residences at Ocean Spray in that town damaged by the waves and water. The houses across the street from the seawall were severely affected, one of them going to pieces and washing out to sea. It was a strange sight for those of us who watched—furniture, bedding, pillows, and the electric refrigerator, all mixed in with the framework of the house and being pounded by the billows, which broke unceasingly against the wreckage. By the next morning the furniture and the timbers of the building had washed southward for miles along the coast, and the home was no more. Never before in Winthrop history had such heavy losses been sustained.

Of course, the initial trouble began back in the 1870s, when the summer homes had been erected too near the sea. Then the seawall was built to protect the homes. In the storm of 1909 the area between Beacon Street and Perkins Street was subjected to a terrific beating. Old Aphelian Hall on Fawn Bar Avenue barely escaped falling into the sea during that storm, in which several other houses were substantially damaged. Because of the seawall erected around Great Head during 1926, this section of Winthrop has since escaped damage, but when the storm of 1931 hit, another section of the old seawall was torn out and the Veterans of Foreign Wars building between Irwin and Sturgis streets undermined. Because of this particular gale a very effective breakwater was constructed off the shore directly opposite this area, and since then no serious damage has occurred in this section.

Several hundred yards to the north from the end of this breakwater,

Grover's Cliff in Winthrop juts out into the sea. Fort Heath is located at Grover's Cliff. The new breakwater, while protecting the Winthrop area to the west, created a bottleneck of water between Fort Heath and the northern end of the breakwater. Through this opening the great billows roar across to the Ocean Spray section of Winthrop during stormy weather. It would seem that the only solution would be to continue the breakwater across to Fort Heath. Otherwise, the residences in the Ocean Spray area of Winthrop are in possible danger of a catastrophe such as swept Misquamicut, Rhode Island, completely off the map in the September Gale of 1938, when more than four hundred houses disappeared into the ocean in a few hours.

The writer does not wish to be misunderstood. The present owners of the homes along the Shore Drive of Winthrop are not to blame for their close proximity to the ocean, for it was not they who planned the district back in the 1870s. However, and the following is merely a possibility, should a storm with similar wind intensity ever hit Winthrop during a high run of tides before a breakwater is extended across to Fort Heath, overwhelming losses will result. The reason is simple to understand. When one considers that the great Gale of '45, the worst northeaster of this century, came with a predicted tide of eight feet five

Snow's hometown of Winthrop, Massachusetts, has always been particularly prone to damage from storm-driven surf, as shown by these photos taken almost 100 years apart. (Above, a 1910 postcard from the collection of W. E. Meryman; opposite, 100-foot waves from a January 2003 storm, photo by Arthur Chidlovski)

inches and actually rose to more than eleven and a half feet, one can visualize what would have happened if the Gale of '45 had arrived during a full moon! Tides of thirteen, fourteen, or possibly fifteen feet would have deluged the Winthrop shore, causing almost unbelievable damage and suffering.

The tide, waves, and wind are all closely related during a storm. We read accounts of waves out on the ocean of seventy and eighty feet, but the highest recorded wave at sea has actually been little over fifty feet. Waves seem higher when viewed from aboard a craft which is coming down the side of one wave and about to reach another wave. It has been estimated that waves during a whole gale, when the wind is about sixty miles per hour, reach thirty feet in height. An eighty-mile gale might produce waves forty feet high. By height is meant the extreme vertical distance between crest and trough of regular waves. Against rocks, lighthouses, and seawalls, of course, waves go much higher. I, personally, have seen waves which were 150 feet high hitting Minot's Light; I am not referring to the spray, but to solid substantial water, capable of lifting rocks and seaweed 120 feet in the air to leave them at the top of Minot's Light!

In general, there are three factors which influence the tides: waves, wind, and barometric pressure. For every drop of one inch in the

barometer reading there is a corresponding rise of thirteen inches in the ocean. In rare cases a seiche has been known to appear—a stationary wave movement which is substantial enough to register unusual tides on the nearby beaches. The seiche, unexpected as it is, happens scores of times along the New England shores every year.

The official readings of the tide gauge in Boston during the Gale of '45, according to the statement of Commander Ray L. Schoppe of the United States Coast and Geodetic Survey, were as follows:

		High Water	Height		
November	29,1945	7:48 A.M.	10 feet	10 inches
	29	8:00 P.M.	11 feet	6 inches
	30	8:18 A.M.	11 feet	7 inches
	30	8:54 P.M.	10 feet	11 inches
December	1	9:12 A.M.	11 feet	1 inch
	1	9:36 P.M.	9 feet	11 inches

The actual prediction for the evening tide of November 29, which reached its height at 8 P.M., was only eight feet, four inches. This is the tide which caused the greatest damage. Thus we see that the hurricane caused the tide to rise over three feet higher than had been predicted. Yes, the residents along the Winthrop shore can be very thankful, in spite of their severe losses, that the Gale of '45 did not come at the time of a full moon.

The rescue of two men on an oil barge off the coast of Fairfield, Connecticut in this storm was considered the world's first helicopter hoist rescue. Pilot Dmitry "Jimmy" Viner was the nephew of aviation pioneer Igor I. Sikorsky.

Despite improvements in the seawalls protecting the town, the flooding in Winthrop, Massachusetts, from this storm was probably matched by the Blizzard of '78 (February 6–7, 1978), and the so-called Perfect Storm of October 30, 1991. This writer lived a block from Winthrop Beach in October 1991, and witnessed waves hitting the seawall and sending spray a hundred feet or more in the air. At high tide that day, water poured over the seawall, turning the side streets off Shore Drive into raging rivers.

References

Editor's note: In many of his books, Snow didn't cite sources. In Storms *and* Shipwrecks, *however, he did—though not in the final chapters about 1944 and 1945 storms.*

The original notes included both substantive and reference material, and the numbers were difficult to reconcile. For the ease of the reader, therefore, we've chosen to list here just the sources Snow cited for each chapter.

CHAPTER 1: THE SOMERSET
Samuel Adams Drake, *Old Landmarks of Boston* (1872); Captain McNeill's journal, Massachusetts Historical Society *Proceedings*, vol. 55, p. 91; Edward Rowe Snow, *Sailing Down Boston Bay* (1941); Massachusetts Archives, vol. 200, fols. 187 and 192; vol. 169, fol. 353; vol. 175, fol. 125. Interview with Coastguardsman Henrique, November 2, 1941.

CHAPTER 2: THE 1635 TEMPEST
Samuel Adams Drake, *Old Landmarks of Boston* (1872); *Bradford's History of Plimouth Plantation* (1928); J. Henry Cartland, *Twenty Years at Pemaquid* (1914); John Johnston, *A History of Bristol and Bremen* (1973); Sidney Perley, *Historic Storms of New England* (1891).

CHAPTER 3: CANNIBALISM IN ME.
John Dean, *A Narrative of the Shipwreck of the Nottingham Galley, &c.* (1730); Christopher Langman, *A True Account of the Voyage of the Nottingham Galley* (1711). William R. Dean of Boston, around 1870, questioned the authenticity of the Langman account.

CHAPTER 4: THE PIRATE SHIP WHIDAH
A Relation . . . in the Shipwreck of . . . Pirates (1717); *The Trial of Eight Persons Indited for Piracy* (1718); G. F. Dow and J. H. Edmonds, *Pirates of the New England Coast* (1923).

CHAPTER 5: THE GALE OF 1723
Fitz-Henry Smith, Jr., has an interesting discussion of the storms and high tides in Bostonian Society *Publications*, vol. II, Second Series, "Storms and Shipwrecks in Boston Bay."

CHAPTER 6: THE GRAND DESIGN
Greenleaf and Jonathan P. Cilley, *The Mount Desert Widow*; Rev. Henry White, *History of New England* (1841).

CHAPTER 7: THE GENERAL ARNOLD
Hyannis Patriot, October 21, 1937.

CHAPTER 8: THE FRIGATE ERFPRINS
J. C. De Jonge, *Geschiedenis van het Nederlandsche Zeewezen* (1845).

CHAPTER 9: THE DECEMBER STORM OF 1786
Sidney Perley, *Historic Storms of New England*; Edward Rowe Snow, *The Islands of Boston Harbor* (1935); letter from David H. Cowell, August 15, 1943.

CHAPTER 10: THE TRIPLE SHIPWRECKS
Sidney Perley, *Historic Storms of New England*; Shebnah Rich, *Truro, Cape Cod, or Land Marks and Sea Marks* (1883).

CHAPTER 11: THE STORM OF OCTOBER 1804
Boston Gazette, October 11, 1804; *The Diary of William Bentley*, D. D. (1905), vol. III.

CHAPTER 12: THE SEPTEMBER GALE OF 1815
Boston Gazette, September 25, 1815; *Columbian Centinel*, October 4, 1815. The prose on page 69 is from Holmes's *Pages from an Old Volume of Life* (1892), and the poetry is copied from Walter Channing's *New England Hurricanes*.

CHAPTER 14: THE TRIPLE HURRICANES

Fitz-Henry Smith, Jr., in Bostonian Society, *Publication*, vol. 11, Second Series, "Storms and Shipwrecks in Boston Bay"; John J. Currier, *History of Newburyport, Massachusetts*, vol. II; Sidney Perley, *Historic Storms of New England*. A complete story of the three hurricanes is contained in a pamphlet published in 1840, "Awful Calamities or the Shipwrecks of December 1839 . . . on the Coast of Massachusetts"

CHAPTER 15: THE FIRE ON THE STEAMER LEXINGTON

All quotations are from S. A. Howland, *Steamboat Disasters and Railroad Accidents in the United States* (1840).

CHAPTER 16: THE IMMIGRANT SHIP SAINT JOHN

Boston Daily Bee, October 8, 1849; the *Boston Daily Mail*, October 9, 1849; Henry David Thoreau, *Cape Cod* (1896).

CHAPTER 17: THE MINOT'S LIGHT STORM

Edward Rowe Snow, *Islands of Boston Harbor*; Sidney Perley, *Historic Storms of New England*; Edward Rowe Snow, *The Story of Minot's Light* (1940).

CHAPTER 18: THE CITY OF COLUMBUS

The Boston Post, February 9, 1884; Frank Leslie's *Illustrated Newspaper*, January 26, 1884.

CHAPTER 19: A NANTUCKET RESCUE

Boston Daily Globe, January 14, 1912; Arthur H. Gardner, *Shipwrecks around Nantucket* (1915).

CHAPTER 20: THE BAD LUCK OF THE JASON

William U. Swan is the authority for part of the story.

CHAPTER 21: THE MONOMOY DISASTER

Dr. William Flynn of Dorchester did much research for this chapter. Sources include J. W. Dalton, *The Life Savers of Cape Cod* (1902), and Henry C. Kittredge, *Cape Cod, Its People and Their History* (1930).

CHAPTER 22: THE WRECK OF THE LARCHMONT

Contemporary accounts in the *Boston Globe, Boston Post*, and *Boston Herald*, February 13–17, 1907.

CHAPTER 23: THE FAIRFAX-PINTHIS DISASTER

Contemporary accounts in the *Boston Globe, Boston Post,* and *Boston Herald,* June 12–17, 1930.

CHAPTER 24: THE NEW ENGLAND HURRICANE

The *Boston Post,* September 22, 24, 1938; *Boston Herald,* September 23, 1938; Providence Journal Company, *Hurricane and Tidal Wave—Rhode Island; New England Hurricane* (1938); Reynolds Printing, *1938 Hurricane Pictures, New Bedford and Vicinity.*

CHAPTER 25: ME. AND NEW HAMPSHIRE

Plymouth Pinnace: Bradford's History "Of Plimoth Plantation" (1928).

The Albany: Interview with Snow's cousin, Willis Snow; Charles A. E. Long, *Matinicus Isle.*

The Adams: George L. Hosmer, *An Historical Sketch of the Town of Deer Isle, Maine* (1886).

The Sarah: Interview with Captain Ernest Delesdernier Sproul.

The Bohemian: Interview with former Mayor Fitzgerald. In *Lighthouses of the Maine Coast,* Robert Thayer Sterling writes a fine account of the wreck of the *Bohemian.*

The Gale of 1888: The *Rockland Courier-Gazette,* November 27, 1888.

The Portland Gale: Interview with Will Snow, 1940; letter from Mrs. H. A. Bain.

The Pemaquid Shipwrecks: The *Boston Post,* September 18, 1903.

The Catawamteak: Letter from George M. Cook.

The Goat Island Shipwrecks: Interview with Captain John I. Snow, 1940.

The Wandby: Interview with Captain John I. Snow, 1940.

The City of Rockland: *Boston Post,* "The Observant Citizen," September 2, 1943.

The Oliver Dyer: *Annual Report of the . . . Life Saving Service* (1889).

CHAPTER 26: SOUTHERN NEW ENGLAND

Boston Daily Globe, August 31, 1872; *Boston Daily Advertiser,* July 14, 1880; Notarial Protests, vol. IV; William P. Sheffield, *Historical Sketch of Block Island;* Rev. S. T. Livermore, *A History of Block Island;* Wilfred G. Munroe, *Picturesque Rhode Island* (1881).

CHAPTER 27: NANTUCKET AND MARTHA'S VINEYARD SHIPWRECKS

Arthur H. Gardner, *Wrecks around Nantucket* (1915, 1930); *Boston Courier*, July 11, 1838, March 16, 1846; *Annual Report of the . . . Life Saving Service* (1899).

CHAPTER 28: MASS. BAY

The Magnifique: Nathaniel Bradstreet Shurtleff, Boston (1871).

The Elizabeth and Ann: Edward Rowe Snow, *Historical Facts about Winthrop* (1939).

The Vernon: *Salem Gazette*, February 5, 1859; *Boston Globe*, April 24, 1925.

Boston Harbor's Worst Shipwreck: Fitz-Henry Smith, "Storms and Shipwrecks in Boston Bay"; Edward Rowe Snow, *Historic Fort Warren* (1941).

The 1869 Gale: John M. Richardson, *Steamboat Lore of the Penobscot*; information furnished by Captain Sproul.

The 1888 Gale: Edward Rowe Snow, *Story of Minot's Light*; Fitz-Henry Smith, "Storms and Shipwrecks in Boston Bay."

The Norseman: *Boston Post*, March 30, 1899.

The Davis Palmer: *Boston Globe*, December 27, 1909.

The Nancy: *Boston Post*, February 21, 1927.

The Robert E. Lee: *Boston Herald*, March 9, 1928.

The City of Salisbury: Interview with Robert Mackey, October 1943.

The Mary E. O'Hara: Interview with survivor Cecil Crowell one week after the incident.

CHAPTER 29: CAPE COD SHIPWRECKS

The Almira: Sidney Perley, *Storms of New England*.

The Franklin: Thoreau, *Cape Cod*; *Boston Courier*, March 3, 1849; Henry C. Kittredge, *Mooncussers of Cape Cod* (1937).

The Josephus: Henry C. Kittredge, *Cape Cod* (1930); Isaac Morton Small, *Shipwrecks on Cape Cod*.

The Peruvian: Small, *Shipwrecks on Cape Cod*.

The Francis: Small, *Shipwrecks on Cape Cod*.

The Giovanni: J. W. Dalton, *Life Savers of Cape Cod*.

The Trumbull: J. W. Dalton, *Life Savers of Cape Cod*.

The Monte Tabor: Interview with G. H. Bickers.

The Coleraine: Small, *Shipwrecks on Cape Cod*.

The Portland Gale: A. E. Sweetland, "Two Remarkable Snow-Storms," *Blue Hill Meteorological Observatory*, Bulletin No. 2 (1899); *Annual Report of the Operations of the United States Life-Saving Service* (1889); statement of Wesley Pingree.

The Columbia: *Annual Report of the Operations of the United States Life-Saving Service* (1889).

The Calvin F. Baker: Interview with Wesley Pingree; Fitz-Henry Smith, "Storms and Shipwrecks."

The Mertis H. Perry: *Annual Report of the Operations of the United States Life-Saving Service* (1889).

The Albert L. Butler: Interview with the relatives of Michael Hogan; *Annual Report of the Operations of the United States Life-Saving Service* (1889).

The Portland: Talks with waterfront residents of Boston, Provincetown, and Portland; Sweetland, "Two Remarkable Snow-Storms"; testimony at the examination into the loss of the *Portland*; *Boston Herald*, November 27, 1938; Wesley Pingree's signed statement; interview with Thomas Harrison Eames, 1940; letter from Captain A. A. Tarr; Captain William Thomas's testimony at the examination; Thomas Harrison Eames, "The Wreck of the Steamer 'Portland,'" *New England Quarterly*, vol. XIII, no. 2; interview with Captain Pellier, 1936; copies of Weather Bureau charts; Captain Bragg's testimony; Captain Scripture's testimony; Captain Fisher's testimony; letter from Benjamin C. Sparrow; statement of Surfman Johnson; interview with George Henry Bickers; interview with Jot Small; testimony of George W. Bunker; statement of Captain W. W. Cook; *Boston Transcript*, August 31, 1899; *Boston Post*, April 25, 1899.

Index

About the Author

Edward Rowe Snow (1902–1982) was descended from a long line of sea captains. He sailed the high seas, toiled aboard oil tankers, and worked as a Hollywood extra—all before attending college. Later he worked as a teacher and coach, and as a reconnaissance photographer during World War II. His education and work prepared him well for his legendary writing career—which was part maritime history, part show business.

The Islands of Boston Harbor, his first book, was published in 1935. In all, Snow wrote nearly one hundred books and pamphlets, illustrated with many of his own photographs. He also contributed newspaper

columns to the *Quincy Patriot Ledger, the Boston Herald,* and the *Brockton Enterprise*. In the 1950s his radio show *Six Bells* was heard on dozens of stations, and he made many other appearances on radio as well as on television.

Snow is fondly remembered as the "Flying Santa." For forty years he flew in small planes and helicopters over the lighthouses of New England, dropping Christmas parcels for the keepers and their families. His efforts to preserve the islands of Boston Harbor as public lands are less well known. After his death in 1982, the *Boston Globe* lauded his support for conservation: "There are many political leaders and environmentalists who can justly share the credit for the preservation of the harbor islands, but among them Mr. Snow will hold a special place as a link to their past and a guide to their present."

Snow married Anna-Myrle Haegg in 1932. They had one daughter, Dorothy Caroline Snow (Bicknell), two granddaughters, and one great-grandson. The young people who grew up "at his feet," reading and listening to his tales of New England maritime history, are countless.